D0200630

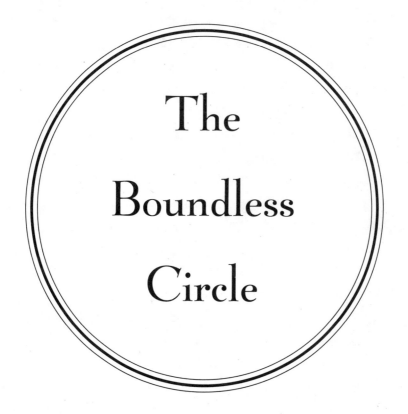

The

Boundless

Circle

The Boundless Circle

Caring for Creatures and Creation

Dr. Michael W. Fox

QUEST BOOKS
The Theosophical Publishing House
Wheaton, IL, U.S.A./Adyar, Madras, India

The Theosophical Publishing House
P.O. Box 270
Wheaton, IL 60189-0270

A publication of the Theosophical Publishing House,
a department of the Theosophical Society in America

Library of Congress Cataloging-in-Publication Data

Fox, Michael W.
    The boundless circle : caring for creatures and creation /
Michael W. Fox.—1st Quest ed.
        p.   cm.
    Includes bibliographical references.
    ISBN 0-8356-0725-9
    1. Animals—Religious aspects. 2. Nature—Religious aspects.
3. Man (Theology) 4. Theosophy.   I. Title.
BP573.A55F68   1996
291.5'691—dc20   95-47409
                                                              CIP

9 8 7 6 5 4 3 2 1 * 96 97 98 99 00 01 02

Printed in the United States of America

FOR ALL OUR RELATIONS

Contents

Acknowledgments

This book has taken several years of research and synthesis, and I am grateful for the support and inspiration of many people and their writings in helping me complete it. I am especially appreciative of the patient and dedicated assistance of Ellen Truong in working on many different versions and revisions. A word of thanks also to my able editor with Quest Books, Brenda Rosen. The last word goes to my wife and kindred spirit Deanna Krantz, whose wisdom and concern for all creatures continues to enrich and affirm my life's work.

Introduction

MANY BOOKS HAVE BEEN WRITten about the need to respect all creatures and to conserve Nature, from many viewpoints, notably, ecology, economics, esthetics and ethics. This book integrates these diverse, yet complementary reasons for respecting and conserving the natural world, taking one necessary and fundamental step further, toward the spiritual. This spiritual perspective goes beyond respecting animals and conserving Nature for our own benefit—be it ecological, economic or esthetic. A reverence for creatures and Creation, linking ethical sensibility with empathetic sensitivity, gives us a sense of wholeness as *part* of Nature and the creative process.

There is a fundamental dichotomy between the two principal ways humans see their place in Nature. Some see themselves as part of Nature, feel a kinship toward animals and regard them as part of the same act or process of Creation. Others see themselves as separate from Nature and superior to animals. They believe in an anthropomorphic God and in their own specialness in God's eyes. For them, the belief that humans have kinship or duties toward animals or that we should give them equal and fair consideration is anathema, since it demeans the human sense of specialness and devalues the sanctity and dignity of human life.

These two worldviews are mutually exclusive. Both claim religious authority, yet only the first is really Christian, or spiritual and ethical, and can give our lives emotional significance and spiritual purpose. Blind faith in the veracity of human dominion over Nature and the Animal Kingdom embraces the assumption that animals, indeed the whole of Creation, has neither independent value nor purpose other than the fulfillment and glorification of humankind. This self-serving worldview is rationalized as being God-given and necessary for the good of society, the advancement of knowledge for knowledge's sake, or scientific and technological progress.

These rationalizations and the worldview that they affirm are wrong, conceptually and ethically, because all living things have a life and a will of their own, independent of our lives, interests, needs and presumed entitlements.

I am not saying that we must never use Nature and other living things to serve human needs. But I am saying that living creatures are simply not ours to exploit. The widely held view that animals and Nature belong to us has its roots in the quasi-religious, moral and philosophical foundations of industrial society. As will be shown, these roots and the worldview that they sustain are ultimately self-destructive.

The intent of this book is twofold. First, to show that respecting other living beings and conserving Nature is enlightened self-interest—a spiritual and survival imperative. And second, to show that without a fundamental change in our attitudes toward the natural world, the deeper significance of our own lives as participants in the creative process will elude us, as we become prisoners of our own egotism, seeing Nature and the rest of Creation as being for our exclusive and selfish gratification. Ultimately an attitude of reverential respect for life and for the environment will benefit humanity since it is the basis for a just and sustainable society.

An Animal Bill of Rights

- Animals have the right to equal and fair consideration and to be treated with humane concern and responsibility.

- Animals have the right to live free from human exploitation, whether in the name of science or sport, exhibition or service, food or fashion.

- Animals have the right to live in harmony with their nature, rather than in accordance with human desires.

- Animals have the right to live on a healthy planet.

- Endangered species have the right to life and habitat preservation.

- Animals have the right to be protected from physical or mental suffering when subject to any form of human exploitation for which there is no alternative; and every effort should be made to develop appropriate alternatives.

- Domestic animals have the right to live in adequate physical and social environments.

- Animals have the right to be regarded as "ours" only in sacred trust.

How Aware Are Animals?

W E DEMEAN ANIMALS IN MANY ways, and as a culture we are shockingly ignorant of how aware, sensitive and intelligent they can be. As Native American leader Dan George advised, "If you talk to the animals they will talk with you and you will know each other. If you do not talk to them you will not know them, and what you do not know you will fear. What one fears one destroys." According to legend, there was once a Golden Age when humans could communicate with animals, and some aboriginal peoples purportedly still have this ability. In contrast to aboriginal peoples' attitude of respect toward animals and deep knowledge of the behavior of species both wild and tame, philosophers, theologians and other academicians of the Western industrial world contend that animals can't think or reason or have emotions. We have become so far removed from other animals that the notion that humans could once "talk" with them seems quite absurd. To talk is to communicate, and we have little chance of communicating with animals if we lack respect and understanding and believe that they cannot feel or think. Such blind prejudice makes for a dumb world.

Invariably, when people discuss or contemplate the behavior of some animal, such as salmon or geese migrating, wolves hunting or zebras protecting their young from lions, the term *instinct* comes up. And very often it is used in either a demeaning way or in a way that dismisses animals' intrinsic abilities by implying that the behavior is mechanical, automatic, unconscious. "Well, after all, it's just instinct," makes my hackles rise instinctively.

The word *instinct* connotes a natural aptitude or hereditary factor in behavior, a natural and unreasoning prompting to action, as the web-building instinct of spiders. Instinctive behavior is demeaned because it is presumably devoid of *reason*, the power of intellectually comprehending and inferring. In other words, instinctive behavior is mechanical, unconscious behavior that needs no intelligence for its occurrence. By definition, intelligence is the power or act of understanding, and of being able to meet any situation, especially a novel one, successfully by proper behavioral adjustments. Another definition is the ability to apprehend the interrelationships of presented facts in such a way as to guide action towards a desired goal. But would it not be remarkable if, in the absence of the ability to apprehend consciously the interrelationships of presented facts, an animal's actions are still guided toward a desired goal? We would call this intrinsic unconscious ability "instinct." Yet is this not another form of intelligence, an inherent wisdom no less remarkable than the homeostatic, rhythmic and self-regulatory physiological functions of our own bodies, which are governed primarily by the largest endocrine gland in the body, the brain? The eighteenth-century British philosopher David Hume contended that animal instinct and human reason are different degrees of the same quality, which was in direct opposition to the widely held view that humans differ in kind and not in degree from animals because the latter cannot reason. Hume concluded that "experimental reasoning was nothing but a species of instinct." Instinctual actions and reactions are inborn or innate capacities, as are our abilities to reason and communicate verbally.

I believe that instinct and animals alike are demeaned, not only because of the Cartesian view that animals are unaware, unfeeling autonomous machines, but because the terms *intelligence* and *intellect* are confused. All behavior, all organic structures and functions, and all body and Earth processes manifest intelligence, be it conscious or unconscious. Intellect, in contrast, is the power or faculty of knowing, especially the power of reasoning, judging and comprehending. But animals are not without intellect, which by definition they must possess, since studies have shown that insects and protozoa have the ability to judge by making simple sensory discriminations on the basis of differences in sound, shape, temperature, taste, etc.

The writings of two eminent scientific authorities, Professor Donald Griffin in his book *The Question of Animal Awareness*, and Dr. Stephen Walker in his book *Animal Thought* show very convincingly that animals are, to varying degrees, consciously aware and capable of reason, insight and intelligent behavior.[1,2] Over a century earlier, Charles Darwin, in his book *The Descent of Man*, concluded: "We have seen that the senses and intuitions, the various emotions and faculties, such as love, memory, attention, curiosity, imitation, reason, etc., of which man boasts may be found in an incipient, and, even sometimes in a well-developed condition in the lower [sic] animals."[3]

Is it correct to conclude, therefore, that more highly evolved animals possess greater intellectual capacities than those that are less evolved? I believe it would be more correct to say that those animals that are more flexible behaviorally, and more social, curious, playful and creative, have greater intellectual capacities than species that are more dependent upon and governed by instinct. It would seem that there are two kinds of intelligence: one unconscious (inborn wisdom), and the other conscious (acquired knowledge), which occur in different proportions and function together in various species. This creates the illusion of a linear evolutionary hierarchy and of superiority and inferiority, while in fact we may be dealing instead with a nonlinear evolutionary heterarchy in which each species has its place not in some great chain of being with human beings at the top, but within interdependent ecospheres of being, or biological niches, the image being closer to wheels within wheels than a ladder leading to some high point or perfection. Is not a butterfly perfect? And if so, why should it be inferior to a human being? Butterfly-beings may be less intellectual and more under the governance of the inborn wisdom of instinct. Considering its short life, lack of maternal protection and vulnerability to avian and reptilian predators, a butterfly could not survive long if it had to learn everything entailed in becoming and being a butterfly, step by step. It would be maladaptive for a butterfly to be even half as intelligent as a human being. In truth, the butterfly is superior biologically and psychologically to any human being, at being a butterfly.

All animals embody some fraction of the intelligence of the Earth as each possesses a will to live. To Albert Schweitzer's observation, "I am life which wills to live in the midst of life which wills to live," we may add the ancient passage from the Indian sacred text, the *Upanishads*: The inorganic is life that sleeps; the plant is life that feels; the animal is life that knows; and man is life that knows that it knows.

Animals' Instincts and Emotional Awareness

Instinct, a term that many ethologists now regard as obsolete, is still commonly used to label much of the behavior of animals. It is defined as "a largely inherited and unalterable tendency by an organism to make a complex and specific response to environmental stimuli . . . and is a behavior that is mediated by reactions below the conscious level."

People say that birds instinctively feed their young, deer instinctively run when they sense the presence of a hunter, and dogs and cats instinctively know how to swim and to take care of their young (at least those that aren't too disturbed by the effects of domestication and domesticity).

Yet we tend to believe that when such animals behave instinctively, following innate or inborn stimulus and response patterns, that they are not aware. Animals are thus "mechanomorphized." Since many instinctive reactions are innate or unlearned, does that mean that the animal does not need to be consciously aware in order to react instinctively? Like a person driving a car, an animal need not be aware of and deliberately controlling its every movement. But it must, like the driver, be aware of what it is doing, of what the goal, purpose or outcome of its behavior will be.

But perhaps not so. Do bees conceive of a hive before they build it? I think not. But their collective social behavior ensures that a hive will be built. An architect builds objectively from plans. A bee builds internally from a similar but subjective plan that is genetically programmed. The immediate environment of the bees slowly changes as they build or repair a broken hive. It is these proximal microenvironmental changes that stimulate, guide and inhibit the animals' reactions. The animal is a receptor to its environment, and one fulfills the other, which ecologists and evolutionary biologists objectify phenomenologically as adaptation and fitness to the environment. Since the environmental stimuli are directing the animal's behavior, and the animal is behaviorally responsive to the environment, the two, in the monadic unity of organism-environment, reflect an intelligently organizing consciousness that does not exist (or rather is not embodied, like the consciousness in our rational minds) either exclusively in the environment or in the animal. It is an intelligence that arises from the interaction or biofeedback between the organism and its environment. Thus, the consciousness of the animal when reacting instinctively is inseparable from its immediate environment and its own internal motivational state, which is affected by neuroendocrine, receptor-threshold, circadian, seasonal, social, genetic and other variables. And so the poet's and mystic's image of the animal and Nature being one, like Einstein's unified field theory and Martin Buber's I-Thou state of nonduality, is probably an accurate description of reality from the point of view of the animal's oneness with its environment.

In his *Duino Elegies*, Rainer Maria Rilke wrote:

Did consciousness such as we have exist in the sure animal that moves towards us upon a different course, the brute would drag us round in its wake. But its own being for it is infinite, inapprehensible, unintrospective, pure, like its outward gaze. Where we see Future, it sees Everything, itself in Everything, for ever healed.

And yet, within the wakefully-warm beast there lies the weight and care of a great sadness. For that which often overwhelms us clings to him as well—a kind of memory that what we're pressing after now was once nearer and truer and attached to us with infinite tenderness. Here all is distance, there it was breath. Compared with

---

How Aware Are Animals?

that first home the second seems ambiguous and draughty. Oh bliss
of *tiny* creatures that *remain* for ever in the womb, that brought
them forth![4]

Human psychologists refer to the almost womblike consciousness
of a human neonate, when the baby is in a state of semiconscious
symbiosis with those aspects of its mother that are essential to its
nurturance and survival. By analogy, as an animal psychologist, I
would agree with Rilke and hypothesize that animals—especially
mollusks and many kinds of insects and parasites—are in a similar
state of semiconscious symbiosis with their "second womb," their
environment. Nature, for some species, is thus little different from
the first "womb" of the egg, hive or chrysalis.

A moth has such at-onement with its environment that it will
self-immolate in a candle's flame. A parakeet will attack or court
its mirror image, seeing its reflection either as a rival or as a lover.
Biological accident or a parody of narcissism or suicidal love, as these
instances may be, they illustrate dramatically the unity that can exist
between an organism and its environment. Such little self-awareness,
where there is virtually no distinction between Self and other, is the
primary narcissism and innocence of the human infant and of many
animal species. Through such analogies, we may better understand
and thus more accurately empathize with the life that is within the
clam, the worm and the fly: they, like we, possess a will-to-be.

Yet surely all creatures, except the most womb-regressed and
unconscious of internal parasites, have some primal, deep and unconscious sense of separation, not of individuation per se, but of
that without which they are incomplete. Hence they are motivated
variously to seek food, water, light, dark, warmth, etc., and to avoid
those conditions that might harm or kill them. Some may be free
from fear and anxiety if they cannot learn to avoid injury, like the
moth before the flame, and cannot learn to be afraid of fear, of
actually being harmed or suffering or dying.

In themselves, animals are thus more complete and "healed"
(whole), as Rilke proposes, than we, because it is primarily we humans whose lives cannot be so simply satisfied. We need assurance,
security, predictability and control over our world so that our anxieties and longings may be assuaged. And perhaps we are the only

Earthlings to be burdened by the awareness and *angst* of our own mortality.

Animal Emotion

A deer, upon hearing another's alarm call, shows an increase in heart rate, pupil dilation and adrenal activity. This is an anticipatory reaction to being harmed, part of the inborn alarm response. If the alarm, fright and flight response in an animal is *physiologically identical* to that of a human, and the animal behaves instinctively by freezing or fleeing just as we do when alarmed and frightened, then can we infer that the animal is also *aware* of experiencing fear, panic or terror? If it can learn to fear being harmed—and Pavlovian conditioning long ago demonstrated this—then the animal is probably experiencing anxiety as well as showing instinctive (unconditioned) and learned (conditioned) reactions to the anxiety or fear-evoking stimulus.

If an animal's behavior and physiological reactions are similar to ours when we experience fear and react instinctively, then surely the subjective experience must be the same for both the animal and the human subject. The only grounds for thinking otherwise are a human-centered and prejudicial Cartesian perception of animals as "unfeeling machines," or a simplistic notion that if they cannot verbalize their emotions, they cannot be aware of their feelings. Since the diencephalic and limbic brain structure of most vertebrates is similar to ours (this portion of the brain mediates our emotional rather than cognitive, rational and analytical states of consciousness), then it is logical to conclude that an animal's subjective limbic experience of pain, fear or anxiety is analogous to ours. This is especially likely since we, like they, usually respond instinctively and nonrationally when we experience intense fear or anxiety. Since all vertebrates down to the bony fish, excluding cartilaginous vertebrates and invertebrates, have been shown to have benzodiazepine receptors in their brains, which can be blocked by anxiolytic drugs like Valium, then it is most likely that they are capable of experiencing anxiety.[5,6]

Instinctive, reflexive and conditioned reactions to harmful stimuli are seen in most living beings. When the reaction can be conditioned and anticipatory fear and avoidance reactions are manifested, then can we say animals are afraid and aware of pain? If their physiological reactions and behavior are similar to ours in response to pain and fear-evoking stimuli, and if all vertebrates, and invertebrates like earthworms, possess natural opiates that in part function to dampen pain and fear reactions, then can we doubt that animals are aware?[7] That, like we, they can be *in* pain and fear?

To conclude that animals cannot experience fear and anxiety, and that they are "unconscious" when executing instinctive behaviors, is biologically and logically inconsistent. While there may be a discontinuity between human and nonhuman animals in terms of rational intelligence, or perhaps more correctly in the capacity to objectify and rationalize, there appears to be a very clear continuity of sentience, the capacity to suffer and experience various subjective emotional states.

Sentience is an adaptive, survival and social attribute of the emotional (limbic) system that is evident in most vertebrate animals. It is not an exclusive property of *Homo sapiens*, nor is sentience necessarily absent when an animal is behaving instinctively rather than rationally. As the eminent British neurophysiologist Lord Brain concluded:

> I personally can see no reason for conceding mind to my fellow men and denying it to animals. . . . Mental functions, rightly viewed, are but servants of the impulses and emotions by which we live, and these, the springs of life, are surely diencephalic in their neurological location. Since the diencephalon is well developed in animals and birds, I at least cannot doubt that the interests and activities of animals are correlated with awareness and feelings in the same way as my own, and which may be, for ought I know, just as vivid.[8]

Our own emotional sensitivity and awareness have become so suppressed that we even doubt the existence of emotional sensitivity and awareness in animals. Psychologists, for example, who perform experiments on animals which are designed to model human depression, fear and anxiety, have claimed that while such experiments may help find ways to alleviate such problems in humans, it is anthropomorphic and sentimentally misguided to infer that their animals could be suffering as we do. But indeed they must, if the animal model is of any relevance to such human problems.

Animal Sounds and Emotion

Behavioral studies of birds and mammals have shown, with sonograph analysis of their vocalizations, that they generally share three basic classes of sounds.[9] These sounds give a very clear indication of their intentions and emotional state. First are high-pitched sounds of varying intensity which are generally associated with pain, distress, care-solicitation, friendly or submissive intent, or excitement (cheeps, mews, whines, yelps, squeals, etc.). Then there are lower-frequency sounds associated with contentment (grunts, purrs), and louder growls, snarls and hisses linked with offensive threat, rivalry, dominance and aggressive intent. Higher intensity, medium to low-pitched sounds of shorter duration (clucks, barks and coughs) are associated with alarm, protest and defensive threats of "self-proclamation." These three classes of sound can also be mixed, either in succession or simultaneously superimposed, such as a whine followed by a growl or a combined yelp-bark. This means that animals can express and therefore experience a range of mixed emotions, as well as discrete emotional states of varying intensity. These basic preverbal vocalizations can also be identified in human speech, in terms of tonal quality and emotional content and intent. Such comparative behavioral research shows that birds and mammals do indeed experience and express emotional states in similar social contexts just as humans do, thus resolving all doubt as to their capacity to experience subjectively the same essential emotions as humans.

Further evidence in support of this contention can be found in the visual displays or body language of animals, which express varying intensities of different emotional states and intentions.[10] Even stronger evidence of animals having comparable subjective emotional states is provided by brain research, in which selected brain regions are stimulated with electrodes. For example, distress calls have been elicited in guinea pigs with electrodes implanted in specific brain regions, more intense calls being given when naloxone, a drug that blocks the brain's natural opiates (which function to dampen pain and elicit pleasurable sensations), is injected into the animal.

How animals and humans express different emotional states via body language and vocalizations is primarily instinctual or innate, but this does not mean that either we or animals are incapable of consciously feeling various emotions such as fear, anxiety or pleasure. The presence of "hard-wired" instinctual actions does not rule out the existence of an inner subjective world of thought and feeling. The human smile, like cats purring and dogs wagging their tails, is instinctive but consciously controlled; otherwise, we would behave inappropriately. Cats purr and dogs wag their tails both instinctively and consciously. If they didn't, their behavior would be meaningless, and they could never communicate with each other.

In expressing a particular sound associated with a particular emotional state, other animals (or empathetic persons) hearing the sound may actually feel and share that emotional state. Either through associating their own feeling-experiences when they emit a similar sound, or from prior learning, animals understand each other's "emotional language." Many signals, visual and olfactory as well as vocal, actually trigger profound physiological reactions in the receiver, which are the basis for understanding, communication and sympathy.

Love and Affection in Animals

Do animals really experience and express love when they display affection to their owners, or is love a quality exclusive to human beings? Is the care and affection "pet" owners give their animal companions misplaced because animals are incapable of appreciating such love? For animal lovers, the answer to these questions is obvious, but for those who do not enjoy or appreciate the deep emotional bond that can be established with an animal and acknowledge that animals have feelings, there is much doubt.

An irate dog trainer and judge expressed her outrage to me that her teenage daughter had been chastised for challenging her biology teacher, a nun, who maintained that "animals do not suffer; they are incapable of having feelings." The girl protested, pointing out that her dog became obviously jealous when they acquired a new puppy and was very depressed when he was put in a kennel before the family went on vacation. No doubt the teacher believed that animals can't suffer because they do not have souls.

We can have communion and share love with our animal companions through the understanding and trusting communication of touch. An animal, in willingly allowing someone to touch it, is show-ing more than innate docility or learned trust: it is consciously making itself vulnerable to another, baring its soul.

Like people, many animals are too shy or fearful to be touched all over, or to be touched in certain places. But like a totally relaxed, ac-cepting and loving person, many animals, when they get used to being petted, groomed and, ideally, massaged, will relax completely. Their muscle tension decreases, along with their heart rate and respiration, often preceded and announced by sighs in dogs and by purring in cats. (See my book *The Healing Touch*, Newmarket Press, 1983.) Similar reactions occur in people when they pet their "pets"; people relax and their blood pressure declines. This state is comparable in many ways to the mental and physiological states of prayer, meditation or contemplation. An animal well socialized to humans will not simply show no fear, it will display affectionate greeting behaviors, just as it would to one of its own species with whom it has an affectionate bond. It may, as an adult, solicit attention and playful interaction with a human and even show sexual or courtship intentions or regard the human as a sexual rival.

These reactions, which demonstrate how closely animals may bond with humans, should not be dismissed as instinctual or dis-counted as unnatural consequences or even evil perversions of do-mestication. Rather, the social bond is a window into the animals' emotional, subjective world, which reveals to us that we are not the only beings capable of enjoying another's affection and of expe-riencing and expressing love.[11] Our animal companions give us a glimpse of divinity and of their angelic innocence in their devotion and unconditional love. In this respect they are superior to many of us. I have never heard of a dog abandoning its master, no matter how abusive or uncaring.

Animal Sympathy and Empathy

Can animals sympathize? This is a tricky question. Husbands sometimes feel sympathetic pains when their wives are in labor, especially if they are attuned to their spouses, as through the Lamaze method of childbirth. And "pet" owners sometimes feel sympathy pains when their "pets" are giving birth. Veterinarians also occasionally experience pain in their bodies in exactly the same place as in the animal they are examining. I call this *sympathetic resonance,* and modern physics tells us that this phenomenon is a universal principle. When it is consciously willed or accessed, it is empathy—the power of nurturing love and the art of the healer.

What evidence of sympathetic resonance do we have in animals? "Pet" owners have often related to me how attentive their animals are when they themselves are sick or depressed. Of course, some dogs, like children, feel neglected or rejected, but others will bring slippers or, like cats, sit close to their owners and quietly lick them in an affectionate and nurturing, rather than a solicitous way. More than one dog has acted with sudden distress and agitation when a loved one—another dog or human companion—has died or had an accident miles away.

Mice about to have blood samples taken show signs of stress as cage mates wait to be handled. Scientists have called this "contagious anxiety." Signals—possibly odor and ultrasonic calls—given by mice being handled affect others emotionally and physiologically.[12] I often wonder how animals waiting to be slaughtered are affected by those ahead of them in the killing line. Pigs especially are easily "upset," according to their handlers at slaughterhouses.

Can animals will themselves consciously into a state of sympathetic resonance? I believe they can—like the dog who comes over and kisses a child who has fallen and is crying. According to some psychologists, this altruistic ability is related to the animal's awareness of self: the greater the self-awareness, the greater the ability to empathize, to willfully extend oneself to nurture another and alleviate another's suffering. Animals that seem to lack empathy and altruism still show sympathetic resonance. What is more, they can become empathetic. Mice willfully tend their young due to the influence of sensitizing hormones and the physical presence of their offspring.

Without some awareness of its own subjective states of pain, hunger, fear and other emotions, an animal could not understand or communicate with others expressing similar motivations and intentions. Cognition and emotion (sapience and sentience) are interwoven, together comprising what we experience as awareness of inner subjective states. While our own self-awareness and understanding of others is often limited and our interpretations sometimes wrong, this does not mean that we can never know what another animal or human is feeling. The more aware we are of our own motivations and subjective states, the more likely we are to understand others.

I am not sure by what process it occurs, but it is a fact that cats, and especially dogs, often "take after" the emotions and temperaments of their human companions. This may be due to sheer coincidence, to careful choice or unconscious identification and selection by the owner and, of course, to developmental and socialization factors: namely, how animals are raised and thus affected by the owner's emotionality and temperament. I have known companion animals that were emotionally affected by their owners' rage and depression, becoming fearful and aggressive, or withdrawn and depressed themselves. The more sympathetically attuned animals are to the emotionality of their human companions, the more they can be harmed or benefited, as the case may be. This is easily demonstrated by a person scolding or playfully soliciting an animal who is emotionally attached to him, or to people in general. The closer or more symbiotic the attachment, the more vulnerable and responsive the animal will be.

Considering, therefore, that our emotional states can harm or benefit animals, more attention needs to be given to two aspects of the human-animal bond. One is the bond of stewardship, as with laboratory- and farm-animal husbandry. If there is no empathetic bond and the steward's attitude toward the animals is negative (demeaning, exploitative, controlling, superior), rather than positive (nurturing, compassionate, patient, understanding), then the animals may suffer.[13]

The other aspect is the bond of companionship, as with a dog or cat. Sympathetic resonance may be emotionally exploitative, as when a person is overcontrolling, or it may be beneficial, as with a playful and attentive owner. A person who is depressed, angry, paranoid, overdependent, hypochondriac or otherwise emotionally disturbed and insecure will have a negative impact on an animal. The animal may feel rejected, depressed, afraid and perpetually anxious and uncertain. Worse yet, it may become a fear-biter or develop psychosomatic disorders and other diseases, ranging from epilepsy and heart disease to cancer and colitis; in turn, the owner may also experience such illnesses, even in the same organ systems. This correlation should cause little surprise since it is known that emotions and temperament affect the body—its physiology, metabolism, disease resistance and organ-system diathesis or susceptibility. Genetic and other environmental factors, such as nutrition, also play a significant role in such problems, but they do not mitigate the significance of the emotions in the etiology of health and disease. Our emotions, temperament and attitude do affect the physiology, behavior, emotional state and well-being of others, be they other humans or animals under our care. An important aspect of empathy is knowing how we affect others through sympathetic resonance and how others perceive us. This is, I believe, a long-neglected, yet fundamental, area of veterinary medicine and animal husbandry that warrants far more recognition and objective study.

Perhaps we are losing our sense of awe, wonder and reverence for all life because our lives are connected more than ever with machines of our own creation, and less and less with animals that are not "man-made" or domesticated. Machines behave and function; so do animals. Animal science has supplanted animism with mechanism: we know how animals behave and function. The distinction between animals and machines becomes blurred, and we become blind to the numinosity of living beings, making profane the eternal mystery that animates all beings and from which all life arises.

And now with our new-found power over the gene, scientists have begun to put human growth-stimulating genes into mice, sheep and pig embryos to create giant animals. The genetic engineering of animals to make them more "useful" to us is the new frontier of biotechnology. And as we redesign for our own ends, so the nature of reality is being restructured and the sanctity and dignity of life are demeaned, subordinated and perverted in the name of material progress toward some future utopia. Profanely turning animals into biological machines is surely the final act of separation and alienation from the wonder and mystery of Creation, as all of life becomes subverted to serve the insatiable needs of humanity. We have yet to learn the wisdom of creative participation and the folly of abusive dominion for selfish ends.

The following statement by Albert Schweitzer, reminiscent of Buber's I-Thou relationship, makes this point clearly: "If you want to know what the will-to-live of another creature is like, you must love and serve it. In such service, it will be revealed. Your will-to-live will become one with its will-to-live. Science cannot tell you anything except where the will-to-live has been."[14]

Do Animals Commit Suicide?

Before I answer this common yet profound question, it should be remembered that animals, like many humans, kill for food, sometimes kill each other and even engage in infanticide, geronticide and the equivalent of tribal war.

Animals that are extremely depressed, as after the loss of a mate or human companion, often refuse to eat and lose all interest in life. Some have died as a consequence of this intense emotional reaction to loss. Because their immune defenses are weakened by this reaction, death from infections, such as pneumonia, is not uncommon. Similar reactions occur in wild animals placed in captivity.

The loss of the will-to-live in these grieving and suffering animals is often regarded as suicide. However, there is no evidence that such animals have any deliberate intent to take their lives. There are no accounts, to my knowledge, of animals deliberately killing themselves by throwing themselves over cliffs or into water to drown. Folktales of Norwegian lemmings doing this have been scientifically investigated. Biologists find no evidence that these little rodents, stressed by overpopulation pressures, deliberately kill themselves. Like a locust swarm, many die on the way to finding greener pastures. Captive animals that drop dead after throwing themselves around their cages may seem to have committed suicide. But most likely they were terrified and wanted to escape, not kill themselves.

In sum, humans are the only animals on Earth who deliberately kill themselves, exterminate whole populations of their own kind, animal kind, and experiment on and torture other creatures. And it is only humans who have ever sacrificed animals to graven images, and to the gods of prosperity, progress and scientific knowledge. Suicide may be a biologically aberrant and exclusively human behavior linked with our capacity to separate mind (or spirit) from body, to objectify self and world and to split self from being.

How Aware Are Animals?

Having now detailed some aspects of the subjective realm of animals, we are in a better position to discuss the question of whether animals have souls. This controversial subject is explored in the next chapter.

Do Animals
Have Souls?

T HE VIEW THAT ANIMALS HAVE
souls has been regarded as pagan and unchristian for centuries. It
was widely held that only humans have immortal souls and can
live for eternity in heaven as a reward for being good; that is, for
living lives of social and political conformity. While the populace
might envy the freedom of wild animals, they were comforted by the
belief that animals were unworthy of immortal life. Furthermore, the
"unsoulment" of animals, or at least the belief in them as spiritually
inferior, gave religious sanction to the wholesale exploitation and
destruction of the Animal Kingdom for the good of society.

In posing the question, Do animals have souls?, I do not wish to
perpetuate or endorse the dualistic view that animated beings *possess*
souls, which implies that body and soul are separate. My own belief
is that all life forms are inspirited. They do not *have* souls but rather
are living souls by virtue of the creative union of body and spirit. The
idea that animals are inferior, soulless automatons governed purely by
machinelike drives and instincts arrived with the Greek rationalists.
Aristotelian philosophy was embraced by the early Roman Church to

form the Greco-Roman basis of modern Christianity. As theosophists rightly emphasize, the teachings of Aristotle started the West on a path that culminated in the crass materialism and mechanism of the nineteenth century. Aristotle, in proposing that animals have only sensitive souls and humans, rational souls, laid the groundwork for the unsoulment of animals because, the Church argued, only rational souls have the ability to make moral choices. It was also held that only rational souls can contemplate their existence, be aware of or conceptualize God and thus, through union with God, become immortal.

It was St. Thomas Aquinas who implanted into Christianity Aristotle's belief that only humans have immortal souls, while animals have only sensitive mortal souls. Aristotle's idea of a great chain of being, with humans superior to animals since animals don't have immortal souls, is widely embraced even today.

The French philosopher and theologian René Descartes, with his mechanistic philosophy, later accomplished the total unsoulment of animals by convincing academicians and society that animals were unfeeling machines. As historian Keith Thomas notes, Descartes's followers took one step further, declaring that animals do not feel pain: "The cry of a beaten dog has no more evidence of the brute's suffering than the sound of an organ, proof that the instrument felt no pain when struck."[1]

The screams and struggles of animals being vivisected were discussed as external reflexes divorced from any inner awareness or sensation and were regarded as analogous to the sounds that machinery makes when breaking down. This mechanomorphic attitude toward animals, no doubt stimulated by the emphasis upon the mechanistic sciences and inventions of the times, served to separate humans from animals, giving us the security of knowing that only we, after all, have immortal souls and are special in God's eyes.

Thomas emphasizes how Cartesianism safeguarded religion:

Its opponents, by contrast, could be made to seem theologically suspect, for when they conceded to beasts the powers of perception, memory, and reflection, they were implicitly attributing to animals all the ingredients of an immortal soul, which was absurd: and if they denied that they have an immortal soul even though they had such powers, they were by implication questioning whether man had an immortal soul either. Cartesianism was a way of escaping both of these unequally acceptable alternatives. It denied that animals had souls and it maintained that men were something more than machines. It was, thought Leibniz, an opinion which its supporters had foolishly pushed "because it seemed necessary either to ascribe immortal souls to beasts or admit the soul of man could be mortal." Little wonder that Cartesianism is alive and well today.[2]

Descartes, in his *Discourse on Method*, wrote that of all theological errors, "there is none more powerful in leading feeble minds astray from the straight path of virtue than the supposition that the soul of brutes is of the same nature as our own."[3] One can but wonder about Descartes's motives. Other than mechanomorphizing animals to permit a conscience-free pillage of the natural world, it may well have been politically expedient to promise the proletariat eternal life (immortality of their souls) as a reward for conforming to church and state orthodoxy, while maintaining that animals, free from such constraints, were said to have inferior souls that perish upon death.

In the thirteenth century, St. Thomas Aquinas, also, like Descartes, a member of the Paris Faculty of Theology, was more charitable toward animals in terms of their having mental capacities and an afterlife. He embraced the Aristotelian concept of a great chain of being, which Darwin's theory of evolution also reflects. He also gave credence to Plato's belief that souls are present in inanimate objects and that humans and animals have souls, the former being intellective and sensitive, the latter sensitive but less intellective. It was difficult, therefore, for Aquinas to reject the possibility that animals have immortal souls, a position which was demolished by Descartes in the seventeenth century, in consonance with the rise of industrialism. And now, three centuries later, we can begin to appreciate the political significance of this change in attitude toward Nature and animals, and its devastating ethical, spiritual and ecological ramifications.

Not all of the intelligentsia of the times followed Descartes. English philosopher John Locke said that all who accepted the animal-as-a-machine belief did so "only because their hypotheses required it." After over a century of such controversy, Julien Offrey de la

Do Animals Have Souls?

Mettrie, a French physician and religious skeptic, satirized Cartesian philosophy in his book *L'homme Machine* (1748), arguing that if animals were machines, then so were humans. But by the time of the Enlightenment, we find two streams of thought, representing the split between humanism and the humanities, and mechanism and the sciences; and between a return to holism, cultural value and ethics on the one hand, and a perseverance of Cartesianism and pursuit of technological and economic expansion on the other.

Nineteenth-century German philosopher Immanuel Kant also contributed to the human alienation from animals. He argued that reason is the guide of all action and that only rational beings can be worthy of moral concern. He regarded animals as being irrational, governed by instinctive impulses and desires and incapable of being moral agents. Thus, they are not worthy of moral concern. Like Thomas Aquinas, however, he opposed cruelty towards animals because it was a sign of bad character and could lead to cruelty toward humans. In contrast, nineteenth-century British philosopher Jeremy Bentham spoke out on behalf of animals, saying that we should not ask if they can think or reason in order to be worthy of moral concern, but if they can suffer.

According to Keith Thomas, in the 1770s, the British Calvinist Augustus Toplady, " . . . declared that beasts had souls in the true sense, adding that he had never heard an argument against the immortality of animals which could not be equally urged against the immortality of man. 'I firmly believe that beasts have souls; souls truly and properly so called.' "[4] Thomas, from his extensive study of peoples' attitudes towards animals and Nature between 1500 and 1800, concluded that the "idea of animal immortality seems to have made more headway in England than anywhere else at this period; and it was undoubtedly to 'pet' lovers that it made its greatest appeal." Furthermore, "acceptance of evolution posed the dilemma more sharply, for if men had evolved from animals, then animals had immortal souls or men did not."[5] Thomas cites theologian Henry More, who, in 1655, said that the best of philosophers were not averse to conceding that animals have immortal souls. That St. Paul (Epistle to the Romans, 8:21) promised "the creation itself also should be delivered from the bondage of corruption into the glorious liberty of the children of God" gave support to the idea that animals have an afterlife. Animals as well as humans were cursed with the corruptibility of the body and death after the Fall, from which Christ would deliver them on the Judgment Day of his Second Coming.

The reasoning of Descartes and adherents to his philosophy goes like this: Since consciousness cannot have its origin in matter, it must arise from or be associated with the soul. Consequently, since only humans possess souls, animals cannot possess consciousness! Animals are machines. Philosopher Robert M. Young, in his critique of Descartes's doctrine that animals are machines without minds, writes:

> To attribute minds to animals would threaten traditional religious beliefs, since the psychological concept of mind was conflated with the theological concept of soul. Descartes argued that it would be impious to imagine that animals have souls of the same order as men and that man has nothing more to hope for in the afterlife than flies and ants have. Similarly, God could not allow sinless creatures to suffer without souls, animals would not suffer, and man would be absolved from guilt for exploiting, killing, and eating them. But he considered the most important reason for denying souls to animals to be their failure "to indicate either by voice or signs that which could be accounted for solely by thought and not by natural impulse." (Letter to Henry More, Feb., 1649)[6]

This view became incorporated into mainstream Roman Catholicism and is exemplified by the statement of Jesuit Joseph Rickaby who maintained that "we have no duties of charity, nor duties of any kind, to the lower animals, neither to sticks nor stones." Little wonder that Pope Pius IX, in the middle of the nineteenth century, refused to allow an animal protection society to be established in Rome because it would imply that humans have duties toward animals.

The following letter from the *Toronto Star* (June 3, 1980) to the Reverend Dr. Graham Cotter entitled "Bereft Teen Is Agonizing Over a Dead Dog's Soul," illustrates the irony of this demeaning and alienating attitude toward nonhuman beings:

> Dear Dr. Cotter: My dog has just died and I can't stop worrying about her soul. Yes, I believe she had one because she showed to me more intelligence and love than many people. My family

tends to reject religion, so I asked some of my religious friends and teachers at school if they thought animals went to heaven. They all said animals have no spirits and that only humans go to heaven. It doesn't seem fair that brainless, destructive people could get to heaven if someone as lovely as my dog couldn't.

Dr. Cotter's answer was perfect. He replied:

Traditional Christianity does not say all people go to heaven; it says also that some may go to hell—for example, the destructive ones that you talk about. Do you think "bad" animals should go to hell? Is there any such thing as a "bad" animal in the moral sense?

The reason why traditional Christian theology has excluded animals from enjoying heaven is that they are not considered to have "rational souls." It's a bit of a joke to suggest that human beings have rational souls, given the way they behave most of the time. The distinction is supposed to be, however, that animals do not have the habit of self-conscious reflection which can make them aware of both themselves and of God. The ability to enter God's presence (i.e., in "heaven") thus seems to depend on the awareness of God's being.

The funny thing is that animals and plants seem to be very much aware of God. The real issue is probably that they do not need to be saved from sin if they are incapable of sin. They may well be able to enter God's presence with awareness but they do not need Christ's cross and resurrection to bring them back to God.

You have raised an important point. I think theologians should take some sharp looks at the boundaries of consciousness in human and other beings from a theological point of view. St. Paul says the whole of creation has been moving towards the salvation brought by Christ. I think our understanding of these matters may be in for revision, and that your instinctive feeling about your dog should be attended to by believers.

In his 1892 book *Animals' Rights*, Henry S. Salt observed:

If we are ever going to do justice to the lower races, we must get rid of the antiquated notion of a "great gulf" fixed between them and mankind, and must recognize the common bond of humanity that unites all living beings in one universal brotherhood.

As far as any excuses can be alleged, in explanation of the insensibility or humanity of the western nations in their treatment of animals, these excuses may be mostly traced back to one or the other of two theoretical contentions, wholly different in origin, yet alike in this—that both postulate an absolute difference of nature between men and the lower kinds.

The first is the so-called "religious" notion, which awards immortality to man, but to man alone, thereby furnishing (especially in Catholic countries) a quibbling justification for acts of cruelty to animals, on the plea that they "have no souls." "It should seem," says a modern writer, "as if the primitive Christians, by laying so much stress upon a future life, in contradistinction to *this* life, and placing the lower creatures out of the pale of hope, placed them at the same time out of the pale of sympathy, and thus laid the foundation for this utter disregard of animals in the light of our fellow-creatures."[7]

It is worthy to note that other religious and philosophical traditions have long recognized that animals are ensouled beings. Professor James E. White writes:

According to Jainist metaphysics, the locus of all value is not human beings, but souls (*jivas*) which are eternal, blissful, and omniscient. These souls are not found only in human beings, but also in the bodies of animals and plants. All of these souls have the same properties and the same moral status; there is no important difference between the souls found in humans and those found in non-human creatures and living things. The reason for not killing an animal, then, is that it is an "ensouled" person just like a human being.

In Hinduism, the locus of value is again the soul, but this soul or *Atman* (according to the *Upanishads*) is identical with the all-pervasive, ultimate reality called the *Brahman*. Animals have the same moral status as humans because they have souls too, and that is the main reason why it is wrong to kill them and eat them. In fact, insofar as everything participates in *Brahman*, everything is "ensouled" and should be treated with respect. Surely this is not anthropocentrism as it is usually understood. Certainly it is not the sort of anthropocentrism that one finds in Christianity where only humans have immortal souls and animals do not. . . .[8]

Do Animals Have Souls?

In Hinduism, the soul is higher than intelligence, being that immortal spark of divinity, the *Atman*, in all beings. Swami Prabhupada, in the *Bhagavad Gita As It Is*, states, "The symptom of the soul's presence is perceived as individual consciousness. . . . The soul is conscious and conscious." It is eternally unchangeable and remains stoic (as *Atman*) in relation to the infinite Supreme Soul (or *Brahman*, God). The *Bhagavad Gita* states, "one who sees the Supersoul (Brahman) in every living being and equally everywhere does not degrade himself by his mind." In essence, the soul is therefore the Self, the divinity within, the witness-consciousness of consciousness. It is not one's mind, thoughts, sensations or emotions, but that which apprehends all that is thought, felt, and sensed, that is the soul, Self or witness-consciousness. Selfhood is thus synonymous with being ensouled. Thus to deny that animals have souls is to deny their selfhood. That they have mental processes and can sense and feel is clear evidence to negate all such denial and skepticism.

Crow Indian Chief Plenty Coups had this to say about whether animals have souls:

> My horse fights with me and fasts with me, because if he is to carry me in battle he must know my heart and I must know his or we shall never become brothers. I have been told that the white man, who is almost a god, and yet a great fool, does not believe that the horse has a spirit [soul]. This cannot be true. I have many times seen my horse's soul in his eyes. And on this day on that knoll I knew my horse understood. I saw his soul in his eyes.[9]

Belief in the soul or Self as being part of or an atomistic (*Atman*) spark of omnipresent divinity (*Brahman*) is the basis of Eastern pantheism. This in turn leads to panpsychism when the soul or Self is regarded as the center of conscious awareness. Sioux Indian Lame Deer called this the "power" in all natural entities: "You have to listen to all these creatures [stones, grasshoppers, eagles, deer, elk, bear, etc.] . . . listen with your mind. They have secrets to tell."[10] In the Arcane School (as outlined by Alice Bailey and the Tibetan Master Djwhal Khul in *The Soul: The Quality of Life*), the soul is regarded as the quality which form manifests. "[Consciousness] which is the result of the union of the two poles of spirit and matter, is the soul of all things—it underlies all forms, whether it be the form of an atom, or the form of a man, a planet or a solar system. The soul of matter, the *anima mundi*, is the sentient factor in substance itself."[11] From this perspective, "what is called one's own soul" is an infinitesimal part of the world soul. We are a sentient part of a sentient whole, for, according to Bailey, "the soul is a Being, a Being that is responsible for all that appears upon the phenomenal plane."

The Arcane School regards the soul as omnipresent, macrocosmic and microcosmic, brought into being by the interfusion of spirit ("Father") and matter ("Mother"), and the mediator between this fundamental duality, whether in Nature or in the human being. In sum, the soul may be defined "as that significant aspect in every form (made through the union of spirit and matter) which feels, registers awareness, attracts and repels, responds or denies response, and keeps all form in a constant condition of vibratory activity."[12]

The physical, sensory, emotional and intellectual dimensions of the mineral, plant, animal and human kingdoms can be conceived of respectively as one-, two-, three- and four-dimensional soul-fields. The soul may thus evolve through developmental and transformational stages or dimensions of being-in-awareness under the will of the Holy Spirit, which is fractionated, individuated and expressed in the will-to-be of all living things, and in the intelligent harmony of Nature. The fifth dimension of the evolving human soul may well include intuition, empathy, humane ethics and "ecocentric consciousness," a broader ethical and spiritual dimension, compared to the characteristically "egocentric" consciousness of the times. This developmental-evolutionary view of the soul implies reincarnation.

As Albert Schweitzer recognized the will-to-live of all creatures as their soul or essence, so Hubert Benoit calls this animating vital principle the soul, "while nature, the universal 'will-to-live,' of which the soul is the individual representation, can be called the *spirit*."[13] Benoit sees the soul as the articulation between the universal and the individual, part immortal and part mortal. The soul "shares in the death of the body if one looks at it from the point of view of the body, and in the eternity of the spirit if one looks at it from the point of view of the spirit."[14]

The belief that the immortal aspect of the soul of each living thing returns to the All or source of all being is too depersonalized for most people. Yet we can intuit this same impersonal, or rather

---

Do Animals Have Souls?

transpersonal sense of unity as pure, intelligent being and potential in nature. Benoit calls this sense the cosmic mind, Self or spirit. And in this intuitive knowing, which is like a "coming home," a kind of return to one's origin, the sense of Self as a separate, autonomous ego is lost. There is no distinction between that which is one's Self and that which is other or not Self. This experience is like a kind of death. With the loss of duality between Self and other, spectator and spectacle, persona and Nature, the absolute world of nonduality explodes like a warm light within and without. Such illumination reveals that there is fundamentally no separation; that beyond the relative dualistic world of our distorted and blind perceptions is a unified field of which we and all things are an integral part, now and forever; that there is no personal "self" that is lost or retained upon death, for there is only one Self, immanent in being and in all things, and transcendent also. In the *Bhagavad Gita* it is written: "He who sees that the self in himself is the same in all that is, he becomes selfless . . . it is the highest of mysteries. And in the desiring, one can see the manifestations."[15]

Today the idea of soul is regarded as unscientific and mystical nonsense. I respect healthy skepticism, but I find irksome the belief that only things which can be weighed and measured actually exist. We can make a preliminary definition of soul as an essence, a substance or animating principle which expresses itself in the thinking, feeling and willing of all living things. Professor J. Hick, in *Biology and the Soul*, states:

> The soul can be identified with certain fundamental dispositional characteristics—presumably our basic moral and religious attitudes . . . the soul remains the core of the individual's being, his essential nature, consisting in a structure of personal and ethical characteristics. . . .[16]

Animals likewise possess an "essential nature." Do we not have proof over and over again that animals have emotions, wills of their own, and can even reason and demonstrate a sense of right and wrong?

Some people say that only humans are aware of death, and that this proves our souls are immortal. But several species of animals seem to be aware of death and will mourn the loss of a close companion. Cats, dogs, wolves, foxes, elephants, chimpanzees and many other species often show great distress and obvious mourning at the loss of companions. One "pet" owner wrote to me that when her parakeet died, its long-time companion, a dog, stopped eating and eventually died of depression. A woman phoned for help with her dog who would not respond to anything since her husband's death. Another correspondent was heartbroken as her dog lay depressed for weeks beside the bed of her dead child.

All religions teach that love is the highest expression of the soul. "He that loveth not, knoweth not God. For God is love." If love is an expression of the soul, then certainly the devotion our animals show us is evidence of our spiritual kinship. In Greyfriar's Square in Edinburgh, a bronze statue is erected in memory of a terrier dog, Bobbie, who for fourteen years kept a daily vigil at his master's grave in a churchyard close-by. There can surely be no greater love. Some people, of course, demean an animal's love as mere instinct, obedience and dependence, but many species of wild animals disprove that put-down, showing great affection towards each other.

Several instances of loving tenderness among wild animals have been recorded by scientists. Elephants act as midwives, assisting herd-mates when giving birth. Whales and dolphins keep sick or injured companions above the water to breathe, often, in shallow water, at the risk of their own lives. Wolves bring food daily to injured pack-mates. Chimpanzees clean each other's teeth with twigs and even remove one another's loose and infected teeth. Adult zebras and baboons turn and face predators, such as lions and wild dogs, to drive them off and give pregnant and infant companions a chance to escape. In a small village in India, I saw a male dog tenderly licking the sores on the face of a sick female dog and snapping at the flies around her. When I gave them some bread because I could see they were starving, the male sat by and let his companion eat first. Such altruism involves empathy—the ability to put oneself in another's place.

Many "pet" owners express to me how surprised and impressed they are at their "pets'" ministrations when they are themselves sick. "My cat knows when I'm ailing," a woman wrote. "She becomes super-quiet and nondemanding. It's touching." Another "pet" owner wrote to me stating:

Do Animals Have Souls?

My dog lies down in bed beside me, as though to comfort me. And indeed, he does. . . . Once as I was slowly getting out of bed, he searched for and found my slippers, delivering them tenderly to me. He had never done this before.

Play is another spontaneous, creative activity in which animals express their souls. To a feline, a fleck on the wall is an insect to jump at, a flashlight beam is the show of shows and a ball of wool is a mouse to hunt. These behaviors express imagination—another aspect of the soul. And when different species play together, be it a child and a puppy or a dog and a kitten, a spark of recognition leaps across the species barrier, and there is a feeling of oneness, kinship and love.

When an animal consciously and deliberately makes itself vulnerable to another animal or to us by soliciting attention and affection and wanting to be groomed, stroked or played with, it is "baring its soul." While animals may not be able to reflect objectively upon such soul-baring behavior, we can. We call it communion. As I described in my book, *The Soul of the Wolf*, wolves express their souls in their howls. They have communion with each other through ritualized howl-singing ceremonies preceded by friendly tail-wagging, face-licking and submissive whining toward the leader and other high-rankers.[17] The complex songs of humpback whales may be a similar soul-expressing phenomenon.

Spirit, derived from the Latin word *spiritus*, meaning breath, refers to the force or principle of life that animates the bodies of living things. The word *animal*, from the Latin adjective *animalis*, means that which is living and breathing, while *anima*, the female complement of *animus*, meaning mind, refers also to breath or spirit. In Taoism, the soul (Tao) is regarded as a composite of yin (anima) and yang (animus). Soul is regarded as the seat of human personality, intellect, will and emotion, qualities also evident in animals whose bodies are likewise inspirited, animated, willed consciously and unconsciously by minds possessing varying degrees of intelligence and physical and emotional sensitivity. The Hebrew term *nefesh chaya*—meaning living being or living soul—was applied in Genesis 1:21 and 1:24 to animals as well as people, implying that humans and animals do not *have* souls but rather *are* living souls.

THE BOUNDLESS CIRCLE

Such esoteric thinking is regarded by many today as unscientific, mystical nonsense because the presence of a soul cannot be proven, empirically verified, or objectively quantified, weighed, measured, manipulated and controlled.

Yet the existence of an immaterial ego or "I" is empirically self-evident, thus providing axiomatic proof of the existence of an immaterial soul or conscious Self in human beings. Soul is comprised of two immaterial qualities: sapience and sentience—intelligence and sensibility. Since these two qualities are also evident to varying degrees in all living beings (along with the third, quality of will), it is illogical to conceive of soul as being an exclusively human attribute, even though it finds its most highly evolved form right now in most members of the human species.

In the twentieth century, we still find Cartesianism alive and well and academicians still arguing that animals, if they do have souls, have souls inferior to ours. For instance, psychologist and Jesuit James E. Royce adopts St. Thomas Aquinas's definition of the soul as the substantial form of a living thing. According to Royce, the human is neither a body nor a soul, matter nor spirit, but rather, as Aristotle and St. Thomas proposed, one being composed of two principles, prime matter and substantial form. Since plants and animals are similarly composed, Royce concludes, they, too, possess souls:

> Since any living being must have a substantial form which makes it essentially different from the nonliving, it is clear that in this sense every live plant and animal has a soul. . . . There are as many kinds of soul as there are kinds of living beings, for soul is what makes the being live in this way. The empirically observable difference between a living being and a corpse is real and essential, providing inescapable logic to support the existence of soul as the substantial form of a living thing.(18)

Royce writes that the soul is the principle of actual unity while matter is the principle of potential multiplicity. The soul therefore cannot be divided: it is simple and indivisible. It may be regarded as that coinhering and unifying aspect of all living things that actualizes the potential multiplicity of matter into substance, form and being. Likewise the world soul, or *anima mundi*, denotes a universal spirit or soul that functions as an organizing principle, Plato being the first to state that this concept held the same relationship to the world as the human soul did to the body. (In Hinduism, this world soul is called *Brahman*).

However, Royce believes that the human soul differs because it can engage in "the spiritual operations of intellection and volition," while plants and animals cannot. Recent studies in animal behavior would dispute this conclusion, which Royce uses to argue that only humans have immortal souls. By *immortal*, he means a being that has a beginning but no end, as distinct from an *eternal* being, which has neither beginning nor end; immortal also means immune from corruption or dissolution. Royce does accept that humans possess the inherent soul-qualities of plants and animals, such as vegetative and sensory capacities, but the rational, intellectual aspects of human nature, along with self-awareness, make human souls immortal, or capable of union with God. Yet these qualities develop with maturity, so a counter-argument could be made that very young infants (and brain-damaged adults), lacking these qualities, also lack immortal souls. Royce proposes that the "evidence all points to the soul being a coexisting form when united with matter, but an existing thing when man dies. It is both a being and a principle of being, but not at the same time." But is it not illogical "speciesism" to propose that humans have immortal souls and animals only mortal souls because they are intellectually less developed than mature, normal humans?

Royce is correct, I believe, in proposing the teleological rather than theological argument that the ultimate goal of the human soul is "a state where its two highest basic capacities are satisfied by an adequate object: infinite knowledge and love."[19] These two ends—*logos* and *agape*—are reflected in the biological and spiritual evolution of increasing sapience and sentience in the various phyla of plants and animals. These two qualities can be objectively measured and quantified, providing empirically verifiable evidence of what may be interpreted as a biospiritual gradient of increasing complexity—consciousness in the development of the substantial form or soul of living beings.

The human spirit, the essence of our being, is most intensely expressed and experienced through music, poetry, art and dance. These things, as well as things of great natural beauty—a vista of mountains, a sunset, an eagle soaring in the sky—touch our souls. So do the songs of birds, a fawn in dappled shade, a dolphin cresting the waves. Do we perhaps experience a divine presence during such moments of inspiration? Animals may or may not have similar experiences, but that is more a question of how self-aware they are, than whether or not they possess souls.

Some believe that only humans have a spiritual connection with God, which enables us alone to have God-consciousness and to know right from wrong. Some animals do have "rational" souls because they have a sense of right and wrong. I believe this sense of right and wrong is an aspect of God-consciousness, which is further enhanced by our greater sense of self-awareness, ethical sensibility, emotional sensitivity, intellectual creativity, and linguistic and esthetic abilities. But the lack of apparent reason and moral-ethical sensibility in "lower" animals does not mean that animals are inferior to us in the eyes of God, for as Jesus said, "What you do unto the least of my children, you do unto me." That animals are less aware, like innocent children, does not give us the right to treat them inhumanely or to exploit them wantonly. That animals seem to be unable to conceive of God as Creator, or of Jesus as personal Savior, does not mean that they are not part of God and thus not worthy of our respect and reverence. How do Christians who believe in heaven and doubt that animals go there, account for the white horse of the apocalypse in the Book of Revelation?

The more we come to know the unique individual personalities of animals and look into their eyes, the mirror of their souls, the less doubt we will have that there is spiritual quality in all life. In *The Unexpected Universe*, Loren Eiseley wrote: "One does not meet oneself until one catches the reflection from an eye other than human."[20] We are all one in the eyes of the Creator, according to the Bible. The book of Job (12:7–10) states:

> Ask now the beasts and they shall teach thee; and the fowls of the air, and they shall teach thee. Or speak to the earth, and it shall teach thee, and the fishes of the earth shall declare unto thee. Who knoweth not that in all these that the hand of the Lord hath wrought this? In whose hand is the soul of every living thing, and the breath of all mankind?

Do Animals Have Souls?

Theologian Paul Tillich has done much to foster the change in Christian thinking that is occurring today. He contrasts the accepted Christian view of nature as being under unconditional human dominion with the Pauline concept of God being All in all (Rom. 15), a concept elaborated also by Teilhard de Chardin. The Buddhist view of Nature, as Tillich points out, is one of sympathy.[21] This is evident in the Buddhist idea of *ahimsa* or nonviolence toward the animal world, a view which New Age Creation-centered Christian spirituality is now embracing. Buddhism, like Christianity, teaches compassion or empathetic "suffering with," so identifying with another that the other's suffering becomes one's own. It is also inconsistent with Christian theology not to show compassion and charity to all of God's Creation for their own sakes, or to selfishly discount the suffering, welfare, or rights of others, be they human or nonhuman. We do not need to believe that animals are ensouled beings in order to treat them with respect and reverence. But it is the belief that they are not like us, that distances us from them. And this distance, created by our chauvinism or speciesism, impairs our ability to identify with animals empathetically.

Do Animals Have Immortal Souls?

It is a common assumption that the soul is in the body, but some say that the body is in the soul. If both views are true, perhaps the living body *is* the soul. There is no duality if the body is ensouled and the soul is embodied. Curiously in our culture, the soul is often regarded as being separate from the body and in some way connected with divinity, or the breath of Creation. The soul is therefore held in reverence, while the body is not accorded the same respect. Body and soul are somehow separate, the one imperfect, the other immortal (at least for humans). In a dualistic, reductionistic and materialistic culture that objectifies other beings (as in sexism, racism and speciesism) generally in the process of exploiting them, such an attitude and perception is understandable. But the tragic consequences of this demeaning attitude toward the body are all too evident in the world today.

The trinity of the Father (God), Mother (goddess) and Child is also broken by patriarchal religious tradition into Father, Son and Holy Ghost. With this separation and subordination of the female (Mother-Creatrix, Nature) and the separation and supremacy of the male, the divine union, coequality and coinherence of the male and female cosmic principles are no longer acknowledged. One consequence of this male-centered worldview is its separation of body (Mother-Nature) and spirit (Father-God) and the consequent inability to recognize that every living soul is the product of this creative union (body + spirit = soul). In Taoist philosophy this is recognized as (yin + yang = Tao).

Some theologians adhere to the so-called Cartesian duality of mind and body as separate. Reasoning from this viewpoint, to quote Basil Hume, Archbishop of Westminster, animals "do not have an immortal soul because they are not endowed with intellect and will as in humans." However, intellect and will are psychophysical attributes of mind that are well developed in many animal species. It is indeed curious, if not illogical, to use these biological aspects of the mind-body *gestalt* as spiritual criteria for the immortality of the soul and the promise of eternal life after death.

It is a common fundamentalist belief that the human body, like the Earth, is only our temporary home—and "fallen", too—and that the real home of the human soul, once it has been "saved," is in some heavenly afterlife. This materialistic corruption and dualistic perversion of the Creation-centered mystical teachings of the Christian, Judaic and Islamic traditions (that speak of a triunity of Creation, Creator and being; of body, spirit and living soul) is ultimately self- and world-negating. While it may promise salvation in some paradise hereafter, it can never give self- or world-affirmation and fulfillment in the here and now, notably in the forms associated with world peace, justice and the integrity and glorification of Creation. Rather this attitude is escapist, nihilistic and soulless, for in demeaning the inherent divinity of all ensouled beings, it negates its own. This attitude is manifested by the historical and continuing denial of equal and fair consideration for others, including women, minorities, and the Animal Kingdom.

These attitudes that distance us from fellow creatures and the numinous, spiritual dimensions of the phenomenal world may have been a necessary prerequisite to the wholesale commoditization of animals and the industrial rape of Nature. The pathological consequences of this alienating, dominating and destructive attitude toward creatures, Creation and Creator are now self-evident. These consequences cannot be rationalized as God's will or as a natural evolution of the species unless we embrace a god that cares nothing for the creatures and Nature we have vanquished, or we adhere to the pseudo-scientific anthropocentric notion that the human is the highest expression and ultimate purpose of the entire evolutionary process. Both views are absurd. The tragic consequences of the attitude of mind and heart that believes that only the human soul, separate and apart from the body, has any divine or higher purpose cannot be lightly dismissed, least of all by the leaders of the world's monotheistic traditions.

Perhaps the whole question of animals having souls, and also rights, intellect, feelings and will, should be reframed. Instead we should ask, What are our duties and obligations toward animals? Unfortunately, this question turns the focus away from animals and encourages a moralistic human-centered response, rather than a empathetic, animal-centered one.

From the former perspective, a Christian theologian might well respond by saying we have a moral responsibility to treat animals humanely because they are God's Creation, "given" to us in the sacred trust of dominion. But dominion has come to mean domination with the caveat of "humane exploitation." From a more animal-centered perspective, this is a contradiction in terms. But oxymorons and polarizations aside, the animal rights and protection movements will not countenance the utilitarian, self-serving and patronizing chauvinism of accepting animal exploitation if it is done humanely. Does a "humane" explosive harpoon device make the killing of whales morally acceptable, like the padded offset trap for killing wild creatures to make fur coats?

And so it is prudent, in these times of intensifying destruction of the natural world which is God's Creation, as we witness the annihilation of wildlife habitats and the holocaust of the Animal Kingdom to ask, as the Archbishop of Westminster wisely suggests, Do animals have intellect, will and therefore immortal souls? If the answer is, from a deeply theological and therefore animal- and

Creation-centered perspective, to the affirmative, then the consequences would be profound; indeed, revolutionary, but destructive
only of the attitude that still condones the desecration of Earth's
Creation and the exploitation of God's creatures.

While it can be argued that a person doesn't need to believe
that animals have souls in order for that person to respect them as
beings worthy of moral concern, there is a vast difference between
respect, based upon some legal or moral code, and love and reverence,
founded upon empathy and understanding. Animals, when respected
and loved in the spiritual way, cease to be mere "things" or objects
of property. One's relationship changes fundamentally from one of
ownership and superiority to kinship and humane stewardship. This
does not necessarily rule out our right to use animals to fulfill human
needs, but places such needs and rights in a more egalitarian framework, a framework which will help ensure that the greater good
will be served rather than some purely self-serving or trivial good to
society at the animals' expense.

Soul is not something supernatural. Rather it is an essential natural
and universal aspect of all living things. Our own immortal souls are
part of the continuity of our essence in the life process itself, which as
it evolves within and around us, is expressed as reason, compassion,
harmony and beauty. I have argued that because animals are part of
the same creative process as we, they are living souls: thus we should
respect the sanctity and dignity of their lives. Not to have reverence
for all life is not to have reverence for God. Animals have no sin, but
humans sin when they fail to use the gifts of reason and compassion to
serve, preserve and enhance the beauty and harmony that is implicit
and explicit in the life processes that comprise the Earth's creative
unfoldment. As we come to resonate empathetically with all life and
experience the joy of our connectedness with the creative process,
our task of planetary stewardship is more clearly defined: personal
fulfillment and the well-being of others are one and the same.

Possibly the considerable public interest in animals having souls
reflects the unconscious awakening in our hearts and minds to the
realization that we and all life are one, and that our disconnectedness
and alienation from the rest of Creation may be the emotional and
ethical-spiritual problem that underlies our contemporary economic,
political and environmental crises. These in turn lead us to question

contemporary values and explore new directions for solutions, meaning and truth.

A therapist friend offered another intriguing explanation for why people are so interested in the possibility that animals have souls. If animals have souls, it would mean that human beings are not so special after all; that we are not the ultimate purpose of Creation or of the evolutionary process. Moreover, if we are not the chosen Creation of God, uniquely favored with a soul, God is not likely to help us cope with our problems.

We, like the rest of the Animal Kingdom, are responsible for our own destiny. If we do annihilate ourselves, there will still be life—insects, bacteria and other microorganisms, or at least some organic molecules will survive a nuclear holocaust or other mega-ecological catastrophe. These molecules will be the substrate for the continued evolution or creation of new life. Egalitarianism and humility spring from such awareness.

Another psychotherapist and former minister felt that a positive public interest in the possibility of animals having souls was an expression of a need for connectedness. He felt that our alienation from the rest of Creation, and the destructive consequences of this alienation upon society and our own personal lives, along with the anxiety that such disconnectedness evokes, are leading people to seek a sense of belonging and significance. This self-healing—physical, emotional and social—is contingent upon Earth-healing. The re-ensoulment of animals and resacralization of Nature are part of becoming whole, at one with all of Earth's Creation.

A question people often raise when considering whether animals have souls is: "Where does one draw the line—what about pests, cockroaches, rats, harmful bacteria and parasites, and animals that we eat?" The answer should by now be apparent. Drawing a line reflects linear, hierarchical thinking. We must instead think holistically and draw a circle, embracing all life with equal respect and reverence. After all, the fly's life is as valuable to the fly, as the whale's life is to the whale. Only from this position can we act ethically and with enlightened self-interest, destroying or harming what we must only when there is no alternative and only when such destruction is justifiable ecologically, or necessary to prevent greater harm and suffering to other living beings. To destroy life or to cause it to suffer primarily for profit or pleasure, or for reasons of custom, convenience or sheer expedience, is a violation of the sanctity and dignity of life and an abuse of our power of God-given dominion.

The Human Soul of Compassion

Poet Robert Bly speaks of the ancient tradition that teaches that the proper recipe for soul-making is spirit (masculine principle) plus body (feminine principle); only the marriage of the two will yield a soul. Psychotherapist R. D. Lang regards soul as experience, while Bly suggests that it is unlikely that such a marriage between body and spirit can happen before the age of forty because of the overdominance of the male element and the devaluing of the body through materialism and dualism. The essential quality of the mature soul is compassion.

Compassion is a central tenet of all faiths. Gautama Buddha observed, "All things are born of the unborn, and from this unity of life flows brotherhood and compassion for all creatures." St. John Chrysostom (A.D. 347–407) likewise concluded that we ought to show animals "great kindness and gentleness for many reasons, but above all because they are of the same origin as ourselves."

Our loss of compassion may be related to the overemphasis on the male principle in modern society. It is a startling fact that the Hebrew words *compassion* and *womb* are from the same root, while the Greek word for *womb* is derived from and related to the word *hysteria*. Matthew Fox concludes, "The suppression of compassion in the West is related to the suppression of the female aspect of human nature."[22]

Charles M. Fair, in *The Dying Self*, has suggested that not only compassion but soul itself is dying in our civilization. He defines soul as potentiality:

It corresponds to something potential in all of us—which is to say potential ultimately in the structure and working principles of the human brain. It owes its hold, as a new idea, to the fact that it releases new energies in us: not fancy powers, but real ones, even though, in fact, only a few ever came into full possession of them.[23]

Do Animals Have Souls?

Echoing C. G. Jung's book, *Modern Man in Search of a Soul,*
Matthew Fox observes:

> A soul that is truly human, i.e., compassionate, is something
> that needs to be carved, discovered, given birth to.
> We are invited from a preoccupation with redemption of an
> introverted and caged soul to the redemption of the world which
> *is itself a soul.* The world soul. The cosmic egg. The universe. It is
> *our* soul and not merely my soul nor the soul of any isolated object
> whatsoever. Therefore, though vast it is truly personable and a truly
> relational soul.
> Compassion is a law of our universe. The new world soul will
> come about when we believe this law deeply enough to start acting
> on it and doing it.[24]

Following Meister Eckhart's intuition that "The soul is not in the
body, but the body is in the soul," Matthew Fox goes on to observe:

> Our new search for soul will refuse to succumb to the era of
> sublimation and sexual repression; it will not look for ascents of the
> soul any longer. Instead we will look for extensions of the soul—
> to become a "world Soul"—and even a cosmic-souled people once
> again. Compassion has always been the first victim of ascent-of-
> soul spiritualisms. . . . The exile of soul is ended. And the exile of
> compassion. Humanity finds a home in the universe once again.
> The home is a verb, not a noun. Its name is compassion.
> The word *re-ligare* means to bind back or to bind again . . . by
> re-connecting and re-binding the rift between God and humanity.

Fox concludes:

> The healing must come in mending the broken distance be-
> tween God, humanity, and nature. It should be emphasized that
> the Platonic view of soul is to make it into a noun while in fact it is a
> verb of being, especially of being connected and compassionate.[25]

As Meister Eckhart said, "You may call God love; you may call
God goodness: but the best name for God is compassion." The hall-
mark of the human being is not simply a rational soul, but a compassionate one.

A position of compassion also requires that animals are worthy of an afterlife. Roman Catholic Dom Agius, in *God's Animals*, presents several arguments supporting the notion that animals can go to heaven. He notes that *The Priest*, a publication directed to Catholic clergy, declared in March 1965, " . . . animals (or at any rate those that have at least developed their nature in a moral direction) have a life after death proportional to their faculties here."[26]

Moreover, the eminent Christian thinker C. S. Lewis, in *The Problem of Pain*, suggests that a tame animal owes its selfhood or personality to its master and may attain immortality, not in itself, but in its master's immortality. While such a human-centered view may be praised for implying that if we do not treat animals kindly, they will not go to heaven, Lewis's argument ignores the plight of wild animals that have no "masters."

Looked at from the following perspective, Lewis's notion does seem to make sense. An animal, wild or domesticated, raised from early life with humans, usually develops a distinct personality. A hand-raised crow or dog appears to have more character than a wild dog or crow. But is this actually true? When colonies of crows and wild-dog and wolf packs are closely observed, very distinct individual personalities can be identified. In sum, therefore, I would conclude that all animals, wild and tame alike, have distinctive personalities and possess a selfhood or soul quite independent of any contribution to their evolution from human beings.

Clearly, Lewis's idea is inadequate and may embody the notion that as human redemption is in our subordination and conformity to theocratic authority, so the redemption of animals is in their subordination and conformity to their master's authority. Respect and devotion aside, this human-centered view is simply an extension of the sophisticated anthropocentrism of modern Christian thinking.

In conclusion, an excellent essay entitled "Do Animals Have Souls?" by philosopher Helmut F. Kaplan quotes two renowned European ethologists who support the contention that they obviously do. First, Professor Konrad Lorenz:

> The fact that our fellow humans are similar, and feel similarly, to us, is evident in exactly the same sense as mathematical axioms are evident. We are *not* able *not* to believe in them. Karl Buhler,

who to my knowledge was the first to call attention to these facts spoke of "you-evidence."

We have the same axiomatic certainty for animals' souls, as we have for supposing in our fellow humans the existence of a soul (which means the ability to experience subjectively). A human who truly knows a higher mammal, perhaps a dog or a monkey, and will not be satisfied that these beings experience similarly to himself, is psychologically abnormal and belongs in a psychiatric clinic, as an impaired capacity for "you-evidence" makes him a public enemy.

Second, Professor Adolph Portmann:

May one truly ask in earnest, whether animals have a soul—is the answer not obvious—is it not self-evident for everyone whose heart is open to animals, that these creatures are ensouled, that they perceive and experience similarly as we do, that they are subject to moods as we are, that they exhibit attachment and rejection among themselves, as in intimacy with us humans?[27]

3

Changing Christian and Other Attitudes Toward Animals

Historian Keith Thomas con-
cludes that in England "in the seventeenth century it became increasingly common to maintain that nature existed for God's glory and
that He cared as much for the welfare of plants and animals as for
men." Thomas cites John Ray who, in 1691, expressed this change in
the traditional Church position on animals:

> It is a generally received opinion, that all this visible world was
> created for Man [and] that Man is the end of the Creation, as if
> there were no other end of any creature but some way or other
> to be serviceable to Man. . . . But though this be vulgarly received,
> yet wise men nowadays think otherwise.[1]

Thomas identifies urbanization as one factor contributing to the
movement toward greater benevolence for nonhuman animals. City
people began keeping "pets," discovering natural history, and they

45

were not involved in the utilitarian exploitation of animals like their country cousins. Another factor was the replacement of draft animals with machines.

In the United States today, there is, according to Stephen Kellert, a clear division in people's attitudes toward animals which correlates with where they live and how educated they are. Rural people and those who regularly attend church have predominantly utilitarian and dominionistic attitudes, while urban people and those not affiliated with organized religion have predominantly esthetic, humanistic and moralistic attitudes. Kellert suggests that:

> the most common attitudes toward animals in contemporary American society, by a large margin, are the *humanistic, moralistic, utilitarian* and *negativistic* attitudes. In many respects, these attitudes can be subsumed under two broad and conflicting dimensional perceptions of animals. The *moralistic* and *utilitarian* attitudes clash around the theme of human exploitation of animals. The former opposes many exploitative uses of animals involving death and presumed suffering (e.g., hunting, trapping, whaling and laboratory experimentation), while the latter endorses such utilization, or other human activities which might adversely affect animals, if significant human material benefits result.[2]

In a pilot study in Connecticut of children's attitudes towards animals, Professor Kellert found, as in adults, the most common attitude was a humanistic one; that is, a strong affection for individual animals, mainly "pets." The naturalistic appreciation for wildlife was much more common in children than in adults, especially in eleventh graders. The study revealed distinct stages through which children's attitudes toward animals evolve. Between second and fifth grades, children showed a dramatic increase in their concern, sympathy and affection for animals. Interests in animals became less narrow, and early childhood fears began to disappear. Between fifth and eighth grades, factual knowledge about animals showed its greatest increase. From eighth to eleventh grades, children gained a deepening concern for wildlife protection, a greater understanding of ecological concepts and a relatively high moral concern for animal rights and cruelty issues.

Of particular concern and significance are Kellert's findings that regular churchgoers have predominantly negativistic, utilitarian and dominionistic attitudes toward animals compared to nonchurch-goers, who have a more humanistic and moralistic regard for animals. He writes:

> One of the more interesting demographic results was the impor-tance of participation in formal religious activities as a differentia-tor of basic attitudes and knowledge of animals. . . . These results suggested this aspect of American life has a substantive and possibly profound impact on sympathy, concern and affection for animals and the natural world.

> Major differences among religious participation groups in knowledge, interest and affection for animals were indicated by sig-nificant naturalistic, humanistic, negativistic and knowledge scale results. For example, respondents who rarely or never attended religious services had among the highest knowledge scores of any demographic group, in contrast to those who participated once a week or more who had very low knowledge scores.

> Large and significant differences also occurred on the natural-istic and humanistic scales with respondents who rarely or never attended religious services being among the highest scoring demo-graphic groups on these dimensions. Apparently, basic differences in affection and affinity for wildlife, the outdoors, and pets dis-tinguished the varying religious participation groups. Respondents minimally involved in religious activities were characterized by considerably greater affective interest and cognitive understanding of animals.

> Strong differences also existed in concern for the ethical treat-ment and exploitation of animals and their natural habitats. Specifi-cally, those rarely or never participating in formal religious activities scored far higher on the moralistic and lower on the utilitarian scales than respondents who attended services at least once a week or more. Nonparticipants, in fact, had among the highest moralistic source of any demographic group; an empathetic concern for the rights of animals also reflected in extremely low dominionistic scores. These protectionist differences were also reflected in sig-nificant ecologistic scale results.[3]

Changing Christian and Other Attitudes Toward Animals

Moreover, a report by the Presbyterian Animal Welfare Task Force in South Dakota created and authorized by five Presbyterian congregations serving the northwestern quarter of South Dakota in 1982 concluded that animals' welfare is, from a scriptural perspective, adequately met if they are provided with food, water and shelter, and veterinary care when economically feasible. The Task Force urged that a reduction in "necessary" stress now experienced by farm animals as a result of the environment, economic requirements, general care, transportation and slaughter should be sought. Significantly, the Task Force concluded, "As the handiwork of God, the Creator, all animals are our fellow creatures of which we have been made stewards. While we are responsible for all animals, God has graciously given us domestic animals for our benefit." There was no reference in this report to animals' interests, to their emotional, behavioral and social needs. Believing that animals' welfare is adequately met if their physical needs are provided for is a wholly mechanistic and utilitarian attitude toward animals, lacking in any understanding of and empathy for their psychological needs and emotional well-being.

This exploitative and dominionistic worldview, while claiming religious authority, is a self-serving perversion of the Christian doctrine of reverence for all Creation. These disturbing findings warrant a closer look at Christian attitudes toward animals.

Animal Sacrifice

While some twenty million vertebrate animals are sacrificed in laboratories each year in the United States alone, most people are not aware that thousands of animals are also sacrificed in the name of religion every week. Santeria, a mixture of African spirituality and Catholicism, has come to Miami, New York and Chicago with Cuban immigrants. Other cults involving a blend of animal sacrifices and Catholicism are widespread in Caribbean and Latin American countries, especially Brazil. Pope John Paul II has taken a surprisingly moderate stand on these African-based spirit cults, reportedly stating that purified of negative values, superstition and magic, these groups can help spread the Gospel of Christ. It is surely a "double-think" rationalization to accept unethical means, such as animal sacrifice, in order to achieve some justified end, like the spreading of the Gospel of Christ.

Rather than oppose these superstitious and barbaric practices for fear of turning practitioners of animal sacrifice away from Catholicism, they are accepted. Regardless of the crude psychological value of such animal exploitation, it is ironic that the Catholic Church should, like the scientific priesthood that sanctions the vivisection of laboratory animals, condone unethical means for salvific ends. Without a reverence for all life, can we ever be well in body and soul? Pope John Paul II recognized this in his address before forty thousand people in St. Peter's Square on October 3, 1983, at a celebration of the 800th anniversary of the birth of St. Francis of Assisi:

> By learning to love and respect inferior creatures, man will also learn to be more human with his equals. . . . I am happy to encourage and bless all those who work so that animals, plants, and minerals may be considered and treated, in a Franciscan way, as brothers and sisters.

In speaking out in relation to other animal-related abuses, the Pope said: "It is necessary and urgent that, following the example of the poor little man of Assisi, it be decided to abandon ill-considered forms of dominating custody of all creatures." It is unclear, however, if the "Franciscan way" of treating animals, plants and minerals as brothers and sisters is to help us "learn to be more human with [our] equals" or is motivated by the perception of inherent divinity in all of God's Creation. That the Pope refers to *other humans* rather than *all living beings* as our equals casts doubt on the spiritual motivation to treat animals in a Franciscan way. In his view, the humane treatment of animals is motivated not by any spiritual perception of animals, but upon their utility in helping us learn to be more human with our equals. This view can be traced back to St. Thomas Aquinas, and not to St. Francis, who taught that all creatures are God's Creation and thus should be treated as our brothers and sisters.

Christianity and Humaneness

C. W. Hume traces the mechanistic and utilitarian attitude toward animals back to Greek rationalism, which seriously impaired early

Christian teachings, the development of science and the treatment of animals.[4] He also points out that early Roman jurisprudence held that only a person who was a citizen and family head was legally entitled to rights. Wives, sons and daughters, like slaves and prisoners, were not regarded as legal persons and thus had no rights. However, this view is contrary to the Christian principle that it is more virtuous to give than to receive, and thus our obligation or duties toward others are more important than our own rights. Hume further argues that since anticruelty statutes and other laws obligate us to treat animals humanely, animals now have rights under the laws of the land as have all family members, prisoners and workers.

It was St. Thomas Aquinas who promoted the idea that we should treat animals humanely because cruelty toward animals could lead to cruelty toward people. In the thirteenth century, he wrote:

> If in Holy Scripture there are found some injunctions forbidding the infliction of some cruelty towards brute animals . . . this is either for removing a man's mind from exercising cruelty towards other men, lest anyone, from exercising cruelty upon brutes, should go on hence to human beings; or because the injury inflicted on animals turns to a temporal loss for some man, either the person who inflicts the injury or some other; or for some other meaning, as the Apostle expounds, Deut. 25.[5]

Aquinas, whose writings were accepted around 1800 by Pope Leo XIII as official doctrine of the Roman Church, also wrote:

> God's purpose in recommending kind treatment of the brute creation is to dispose men to pity and tenderness towards one another.[6]

But not all early theologians held such views. St. Basil, Bishop of Caesarea (circa A.D. 400) wrote the following liturgy:

> The earth is the Lord's and the fullness thereof. O God enlarge within us the sense of fellowship with all living things, our brothers the animals to whom thou hast given the earth as their home in common with us. We remember with shame that in the past we have exercised the high dominion of man with ruthless cruelty, so that the voice of the earth, which should have gone up to Thee in

song, has been a groan of travail. May we realize that they live, not for us alone, but for themselves and for Thee, and that they love the sweetness of life.[7]

However, this compassionate position did not prevail in Church doctrine. The *Catholic Dictionary* proclaimed in 1897:

They (animals) have no rights. The brutes are made for man, who has the same right over them which he has over plants and stones. He may kill them for his food; and if it is lawful to destroy them for food, and this without strict necessity, it must also be lawful to put them to death, or to inflict pain upon them, for any good or reasonable ends, such as the promotion of man's knowledge, health, etc., or even for the purpose of recreation.[8]

In a scholarly essay on Eastern and Western views of reverence for life in religion, Reverend Gerald E. Jones sums up Church teachings:

In the thirteenth century Aquinas advocated kindness with a caution. The important thing is not the rights or feeling of the animals, but the attitude of man that needs training. This became the standard rationale for mainline Christianity. What usually only theologians realize is that Francis of Assisi became a saint in spite of his love for animals—not because of it. As a modern Catholic editorial points out, there is a danger in showing much concern for animals. The "empathetic fallacy" of humane societies and a reverence for life of a lower nature than man is actually a sin. When old ladies leave a thousand dollars to care for their pets while there are suffering people, it is a sin. Our attention should be towards God, and efforts less than this may go towards our fellow humans— but never to a lesser form of life. Since animals do not have souls nor will they be resurrected, we should not be attracted to the lower material but to things spiritual.[9] Except for rare individuals such as John Wesley (the Methodist), who believed otherwise, there were very few Christians who stood against the vast majority who had no reverence for animal life. There were some important individuals, such as the philosopher Pierre Bayle,[10] who spoke for animal rights independent of the church of the time and argued that animals had an eternal soul.[11]

Thus, except for a few individuals, most Christian theologians have used Church doctrine to argue against animal rights. Augustine essentially canonized Aristotle's concept of the hierarchical chain of life in which nonrational animals were seen to exist for the benefit of rational (human) beings: "Man . . . is a rational animal, and consequently more excellent than all other animals on earth."[12]

St. Thomas Aquinas supported kindness to animals so that "they may not bear witness against us in the Day of Judgement." This position reflects the salvation-oriented ideology that places greater emphasis upon redemption and the life hereafter than the significance of life here and now, and the spiritual and practical virtues of humane stewardship.

Aquinas also reasoned that "both their life and their death [of animals] are subject to our use."[13] Aquinas affirmed this view, later incorporated into mainstream Roman Catholicism, in stating that, "According to the divine ordinance the life of animals and plants is preserved not for themselves but for man." He also insisted, "Charity does not extend to irrational creatures [because] they have no fellowship with man in the rational life."[14] This dominionistic attitude toward the rest of Creation was also supported by John Calvin, who insisted that man is the "lord of the world" and that "what was the end for which all things were created, namely, that none of the conveniences and necessaries of life might be wanting to men."[15]

However, Martin Luther did not accept these views towards animals and the Creation, reasoning that Adam "would not have used the creatures as we do today."[16] Adam and his descendants would have used their power of dominion over animals "for the admiration of God and a holy joy which is unknown to us in this corrupt state of nature."[17] Since the Fall and the Flood, according to Luther, "animals are subjected to man as to a tyrant who has absolute power over life and death."[18]

The situation is little better today. Attorney and former Jesuit priest Peter J. Riga has supported the use of animals in research for human benefit. He rejects the idea that animals should be given equal and fair consideration because humans are superior. This superiority, in his mind, is not based upon intelligence, but upon what he calls "human dignity." He holds that:

human dignity resides in each person's capacity—real or potential —to make moral choices, to choose to hate or to love, to grow with others or to reject them—the freedom to love or hate lies at the heart of being human. It has never been shown that animals have this freedom in any capacity. What ever is in other animals, is there through instinct or learned manipulation. While we can love them, they can only *respond* to love.[19]

He goes on to reason that animals are "innocent" because they are "free" of moral choices. If Riga's argument is valid, why don't we also permit experiments upon innocent human babies and children and the mentally handicapped who cannot make moral choices? All the arguments fabricated to prove human superiority over animals in the final analysis demonstrate our inferiority in terms of feeling for and understanding of animals. The love and gentleness of companion animals toward human infants and their devotion and loyalty to their human companions is surely more than "instinct and learned manipulation."

For Riga and others of like mind, animals are denied emotion; they cannot love but "can only *respond* to love." Since, in his thinking, "human dignity" is based upon the capacity to make moral choices, he implies that emotion lies at the root of moral or socially appropriate human behavior. Clearly then, since animals cannot love, they cannot make moral choices. This kind of thinking surely demeans human dignity; for if, as Riga argues, human dignity is based ultimately upon the capacity to have feeling for others and to make moral decisions based upon such feeling, to deny animals the capacity to love as well as the ability to make moral choices, is to have no feeling for them.

Another contemporary theologian, Reverend Andrew Linzey, makes a similar argument:

Theological reflections upon man's superiority over animals, particularly with regard to their intelligence and rationality, led some of the earlier Christian thinkers, such as St. Thomas Aquinas, to regard animals as incapable of possessing an immortal soul—a tradition, incidentally, which still widely characterizes Catholic theology to this present day. . . . The concept of man's dominion over animals has in consequence led to the formulation of another idea which has widely influenced secular moral judgements, namely that animals hold an instrumental value to human beings. One Roman Catholic theologian, Karl Horrman, argues in this way: "It is evident to natural reason that among the things which exist, the less perfect are there for the sake of the more perfect, that plant life should serve for the maintenance of animals and both serve man."[20]

In terms of human superiority over animals, Reverend Linzey continues:

Let us begin by agreeing that humans are supremely moral beings. Alone and unique in the universe we do appear to be the only species capable of those capacities for morality and rationality, no matter how infrequently we may use them. This observation is supported by recent Biblical exegesis of Genesis where it is suggested that the concept of man's dominion over animals, far from meaning the human tyranny the Christian tradition has often supposed it to be, actually finds its meaning within the theology of Kinship and the exercise of responsible authority under God. We are, according to the Biblical writers, responsible to God for our treatment of the natural world. We hold in stewardship and like all stewardship it involves accountability. We need to hold in tension therefore our understanding of ourselves as superior with the Biblical insight that we are morally accountable.[21]

Linzey emphasizes, however, that behavioral and psychological studies of animals have shown them to be rational as well as sentient, and that this evidence makes them "prime candidates for immortal souls," because earlier arguments that animals do not have souls were based in part upon the unfounded belief that they are irrational beings.

While it is a matter of historical record that organized religion has had little regard for the plight of animals, to be fair we must note that several saints, popes and other Church officials have expressed deep concern over inhumanity to God's creatures. Pope Pius V regarded bullfights as "a spectacle for demons rather than men," and excommunicated all who took part in them (*Encyclical de Salute Gregis*, 1567).

Dom Agius agrees:

Since cruelty is a sin and sin wounds or destroys the supernatural
life of the soul, anything or anybody that helps us fight against sin
is to be welcomed from any quarter. . . . The animals in all their
variety speak to us of God, and all we do for them we do for
Him. . . . The Holier we are, then the more our sympathy with
animals increases, as the Saints showed, the better Christian we
prove ourselves to be.[22]

Indeed, as Dom Agius has emphasized:

This love of animals in the Saints had the element of *respect* and
reverence for God's handiwork. At the same time it fed their own
spiritual life and their love of God and its daily expression. So
doing, it *integrated* all their diverse powers and energies, physical
and spiritual: recognizing, as we have forgotten to do, the *unity of
Nature* under the hand of God.[23]

Cruelty toward animals is disrespectful of God since they are
God's creations; it is a sin, a sacrilege and a crime against the laws
of Nature. St. John of the Cross urged us to "cultivate the vivid
contemplation and knowledge of creatures with heart and faculties
of a mystic."[24] Agius provides further evidence that Catholics have
spoken out eloquently on behalf of animals. Cardinal Rafael Santos,
Archbishop of Manila, wrote in 1963: "Whatever treatment we give
to lesser creatures is a reflection of the state of our soul in relation to
their Creator."[25] And he cites Monsignor Hawes:

An animal has not got a rational soul, but it has an animal soul,
and of such a sort that those most beautiful of God's gifts of love
and loyalty (virtues not found in cabbages) shine out in prominent
degree in the said animal soul. Love is not a perishable thing,
whatever tinpot theologians (whom the Church never endorsed)
might say to the contrary.[26]

The Fall and "Original Sin"

I have difficulty accepting the notion from St. Paul, reflected in
the Maryknoll Missal, that "every created thing shared in the fall and

punishment of the first man and woman, and, with mankind, awaits the eternal restoration of peace and order." Pope Paul VI, speaking to veterinarians in Rome in 1969, agreed: "Creatures, in their mute suffering, are nevertheless a sign of the universal stigma of sin and of universal expectation of the final redemption, according to the mysterious words of St. Paul."

That suffering, bodily corruption and death are equated with sin is surely a denial of reality. To suggest that animals are stigmatized with sin—a vitiated state of human nature in which the self is estranged from God, or a transgression of the law of God—is absurd, no matter in what good faith and intent this concept is offered. Matthew Fox concludes:

> The destruction of our ecosystem proves that we have trivialized sin. Environmental exploitation is a sin of our time, yet the churches . . . seem unaware of it. We trivialize sin by saying it is usually on a personal level. We must get in touch with the beauty, law and justice of the universe if we are to survive.[27]

Professor Jean Guitton of the Academie Francaise also disagrees with the idea that animals are sinful. He emphasizes that since an animal is innocent, it resembles an angel.[28] This view, which I fully endorse, was evident in the teachings of St. Clement of Alexandria (circa A.D. 300) who equated the beauty of animals with that of angels by whom animals are guided when not interfered with by humankind. Father Thomas Merton also recognized the angelic quality of animals, saying that every non-two-legged creature is a saint.

Other advocates of the idea that animals are "fallen" include Creationist fundamentalists who have long opposed the Darwinian view of humankind's kinship with the Animal Kingdom, because they believe that only humans were made in God's image. However, evolutionary theory actually supports the Christian notion of our kinship with all life, because it shows that we are part of the same Creation as other animals. Evolutionary theory also holds that life and Creation are not static but dynamic, constantly active and ongoing processes. This accords with the new Christian movement that is emerging today called Creation Spirituality, which advocates a reverential and creative participation with Nature and thus with God and Jesus Christ. It is through "good works" that help these processes that we are "saved" and redeemed.

The redemption doctrine of Christianity, which judges Creation as flawed (even though it is clearly stated in the Old Testament that all God created "was Good"), provides a basis for the denigration of Creation. Yet we could interpret St. Paul's letter to the Romans (8:19–23), in which he states that all Creation "groaneth and travaileth until now" and waits with eager longing for the revealing of the children of God, not as a promise of salvation and escape from the world, but as an observation that moves us to empathize with the world's suffering and to help in its alleviation.

Monsignor Knox's interpretation of St. Paul's statement that "all creation groans and travails in pain until now" clearly rejects the view that animals and Nature, like humans, are "fallen." Knox concludes:

> Nature was innocent: it was man that sinned. Nature nevertheless hopes for and groans for delivery from the effects of man's sin and from the frustration of its present life. Its hope is for: a setting free from corruption due to man's sin, a share in the subsequent transfiguration of man and his ensuing freedom.[29]

Another theological argument often cited to justify contempt for animals is that only human beings are created in the "image of God." This belief needs closer scrutiny. Dr. Roger Timm says this about the phrase "image of God":

> This phrase has been interpreted in a variety of ways, but most frequently it has been taken to mean that humans share some characteristic of God that no other creatures have, such as rationality. This interpretation has supported the view that humans are qualitatively distinct from and superior to other creatures. Such a dichotomy between humans and other creatures can serve to legitimize the use or abuse of animals for human purposes with little regard for how the animals are affected. It turns out, however, that the "image of God" probably does not imply that humans possess some divine characteristic, but rather that they have been assigned a special function by God. That is, just as kings in Biblical times would place their statue ("image") in distant parts of their realm to remind their subjects of who was king, so humans are to represent

God in all parts of the earth. The phrase "image of God," then implies that humans have the responsibility to represent God on earth and to treat and care for the earth in ways that are consistent with the Creator's will for the earth.[30]

Rabbi Harold S. Kushner points out that human beings are not the only ones created in God's image, for after the fifth day when the animals had been created, God said, "Let us create a new creature in *our* image," as distinct from in *my* image (Gen. 1:26). Rabbi Kushner proposes that God was talking to the animals, the "us" referring not to the Holy Trinity but to God and the creatures that had already been created.[31] Genesis thus recognizes the dual nature of the human, part animal, part God, a being possessing animal instincts and an ethical consciousness.

Keith Thomas notes that in early modern England the belief that humans were not essentially different from the rest of Nature was a rising sentiment. He states:

"If man be fallen," wrote Richard Overton in his *Man's Mortality* (1644), "and the beasts be cursed for his sake, man must (be) equally mortal with them." It was this which made the heresy so offensive. By rejecting the Christian dualism of body and soul, and denying that the spirit could exist independent of the body, the mortalists were not just weakening the belief in rewards and punishments on which the good behavior of the lower classes was thought to depend: they were also removing the essential prop by which man's right to rule the lower species was usually supported. When Overton argued that men and beasts were equally mortal he was accused of treason to the human race. "This dangerous traitor," said an opponent, was "trying to rob man of his superiority." To predicate mortality in the soul, agreed Sir Kenelm Digby, "taketh away all morality and changeth men into beasts." "Atheists" and "epicures" were thus associated with the view that animals and humans were equal to the extent that they shared a common mortality. For mortalists, man's pre-eminence over the beast was something which only became evident at the Resurrection.[32]

Indeed, the Fall is in part a biologically correct concept in that when we acquired the power of dominion and used this power selfishly, we lost the innocence that we once shared with animals. Thomas Merton writes of original sin as abject human selfishness:

> Buddhism and Biblical Christianity agree in their view of man's present condition . . . that man is somehow not in his right relation to the world and the things in it. . . . Avidya, usually translated as "ignorance," is the root of all evil and suffering because it places man in an equivocal, in fact impossible position. . . . It is a disposition to treat the ego as an absolute and central reality and to refer all things to it as objects of desire or of repulsion. Christianity attributes this view of man and reality to "original sin."[33]

Eco-theologist Thomas Berry agrees:

> In the modern western world the strange thing is the silence of Christian tradition on this basic issue of human relationship with the earth. Although this is essentially a religious, a spiritual and an ethical issue, our religious traditions, our spiritualities, and our moral codes do not function in this order of magnitude. We can identify the moral evil of suicide, homicide and genocide, yet we have no principles on which to deal with biocide and geocide, evils that are infinitely greater in their consequences and their absolute range of moral acts.
>
> What we do have is a complex of traditions that must all be turned toward a creative functional relationship with the dynamics of the earth. The one thing necessary is to appreciate that the earth itself and all its living and non-living components is a community, that the human is a member of this integral community and finds its proper role in advancing the well-being of this community. There can be no sustained well-being of any part of the community that does not relate effectively to the well-being of the total community. We might note particularly that we cannot have a healthy human community on a sickened, disintegrated, toxic planet.
>
> The glory of the human has become the desolation of the earth. This I would consider an appropriate way to summarize the twentieth century. A further statement that might be made is that the desolation of the earth is becoming the destiny of the human. Indeed, the total fabric of living beings is so closely woven that none of its components can be damaged without harming the others.[34]

A rising chorus of Christian and other voices is supporting this new holistic consciousness. In a personal communication, Reverend Loren Horst, a Mennonite minister in Fairfax, Virginia, has written:

Continuing to rape and denude the land is a *violation* of the Biblical concept that "the earth is the Lord's." Biblically speaking, man does not own the land, he is only a steward of it. An early settler may carve out of the forest a plot of land, shoot wild game with no thought of endangered species, and in such a way "have dominion" over his surroundings. Yet the same activity today, when nature itself is endangered to the point that neither man nor animals may be able to survive in certain areas of the earth, is neither right nor Biblical. The Bible can be used about anything people like. Yet the appropriate way to read it is with an ear turned toward listening, understanding, following. Applying the Bible toward our own ends is really an attempt to "have dominion" over God.

Scientists like René Dubos have warned of the consequences of ignoring our connection to the Earth and its creatures:

A relationship to the earth based only on its use for economic enrichment is bound to result not only in its degradation, but also in the devaluation of human life. This is a perversion, which, if not corrected, will become a fatal disease of the technological societies.[35]

Likewise, the late Secretary of the United Nations U-Thant maintained that either we develop the first global civilization, provide for its conscious, direct growth, or we shall perish, if not with the "big bang" of a nuclear holocaust, then with the whimper of a species that has run out of air, water, resources and food. Subsequently, the General Assembly of the United Nations adopted a World Charter for Nature which states:

The moral code of action entails defining and adopting those ethical, legal, and other parameters . . . especially economic and technological . . . that will not only ensure that the lives of endangered species are protected, but also that their natural habitats are preserved. This is the great task that now challenges our civilization.[36]

This statement is almost identical to the proclamation of the six nations of American Indians (Haudenosaunee) in their circulated letter entitled *A Basic Call to Consciousness:*

> The people who are now living on this planet need to break with the narrow concept of human liberation, and begin to see liberation as something which needs to be extended to the whole of the Natural World. What is needed is the liberation of all the things that support life . . . the air, the water, the trees . . . all the things which support the sacred web of life.[37]

And, according to Dr. Charles Birch, at a meeting of the World Council of Churches in Nairobi in 1975:

> It is a cockeyed view that regards ecological liberation as a distraction from the task of liberation of the poor. One cannot be done without the other. It is time to recognize that the liberation movement is finally one movement. All creatures are fellow creatures and human responsibility extends infinitely to the whole of creation. . . . If we are to continue to inhabit the earth, there has to be a revolution in the relationship of human beings to the earth and . . . to each other.

This empathetic and sacramental worldview compels us to treat the Earth, the animals, each other and all Creation with equal and fair consideration: with reverence. Thomas Merton, in his final talk delivered two hours before his death, said: "The whole idea of compassion is based on a keen awareness of the interdependence of all these living beings which are part of one another and all involved in one another." The Very Reverend James Parks Morton, Dean of the Cathedral of St. John the Divine, has echoed this view:

> This bringing together of all creation into the New Age of the Christ is precisely the mystery celebrated in the Holy Communion: earth rises to heaven, the joys of heaven permeate earth, the future bursts into the present and the past is recovered, forgiven and transfigured. All is made new. In the Holy Communion God transformed the stuff of everyday reality into the Body of Christ, the Corpus Christi, in such a miraculous way that literally . . . everything, every rock, every atom, every galaxy, every man, woman,

child, every flower, every wolf, every whale become linked, connected, bound together as kin, mutually transparent to the divine radiance. Therefore the vision of Saint Francis is indeed the vision of this Holy Communion, in which the sun becomes our brother and even death our sister.[38]

Domestication: A Broken Covenant

There is considerable public readiness, if not eagerness, to accept the solipsistic and self-serving notion that the domestication of animals is a natural evolutionary phenomenon. This anthropocentric, pseudoscientific view has been touted as scientific fact in *The Covenant of the Wild: Why Animals Chose Domestication* by Stephen Budiansky. Since we find purported examples of this phenomenon in the Animal Kingdom, like ants who herd and milk aphids, then it is reasoned that domestication is natural. But in reality, these relationships in Nature are co-evolved examples of commensalism and of symbiotic mutual interdependence. One must conclude from this line of thinking that the wolf has domesticated the deer, and the great whales the krill. Budiansky's claim that "life with man was a better evolutionary bargain for domestic animals than life in the wild"[39] echoes a paternalistic attitude that thinly veils and abdicates responsibility for the reality of domination and exploitation.

Such anthropomorphic reasoning ignores the fact that the selective domestication of plants and animals has caused great harm to the Earth's ecology, especially through deforestation, dam building for irrigation and the draining of swamps to create more agricultural land to raise primarily monoculture crops, some forty percent of which—worldwide—are fed to four billion livestock and eight billion poultry.

This is a *scolex*-brained worldview. A *scolex* is a tapeworm's sucker and hook-covered head, evolved to secure the parasite to its host's intestines. Such a view fails to see that we do *not* have a relatively healthy, symbiotic and commensal relationship with the majority of domesticated animals; it is more one of parasitism, on an industrialized scale. Our relationship is parasitic because it is harmful to the host—which includes not only those animals whom we exploit on "factory" meat, milk, egg and fur farms, and in biomedical and industrial research laboratories—but also the planet Earth itself. The sickening condition of the entire planetary ecology, its atmosphere, and the loss of natural biodiversity as humans and domesticated plants and animals proliferate, is indicative of a sickened state of mind that sees domestication as natural evolution. Parasitism for the human species means devolution; and global parasitism will mean extinction, if not of *Homo sapiens* per se, then of countless plant and animal species.

Our gatherer-hunter ancestors—those of our own kind who once held all of Creation in awe and reverence—were of such heart-mindedness for some fifty thousand years, but their worldview was gradually supplanted by the advent and spread of agriculture and the wholesale domestication and propagation of selected plant and animal species of high utility. Occurring over the past four to six thousand years, this change of worldview was as insidious as it was profound. The covenant of the wild was broken when pastoralists, such as livestock herders, systematically destroyed predators and when crop farmers eliminated large wild herbivores along with their forest and savanna habitats, and when their own numbers and fields increased. As agriculture spread, the ecology changed along with the human mind.

Commensal and symbiotic relationships with Nature and with animals, wild and tame, became increasingly commercial and parasitic. During the last thirty to forty years, we have seen the sudden industrialization of agriculture, and as the ecology has been transformed, so have our minds in our acceptance of this intensified process of domestication as normative. One cardinal symptom of this pathological state of mind is the acceptance of creating "transgenic" animals with human genes ("humanimals") as a natural and logical evolutionary step for *Homo sapiens*. In the very act of creating humanimals, the biotechnocrat fails to see that his is a highly invasive act, analogous to parasitism. It is as far removed from earlier, if not gentler, forms of animal exploitation as the urban industrial populace is from its gatherer-hunter roots.

We cannot all return to a traditional way of life, for our roots have been severed. But can we sensibly continue on our present destructive and parasitic path? The best that we can aim for, through acquiring humility and empathic knowledge of how natural systems and life processes function, is a more symbiotic, compassionate and co-creative relationship with the life community of this planet. We might then experience a deeper sense of communion, and enjoy the fruits of being well in body, mind and spirit, by living more in harmony with this sentient world. Theologian John B. Cobb warns that we must not minimize the effects of past cruelties:

> From the beginnings of domestication of animals, interest in their freedom from suffering has been subordinated to economic considerations. One should not minimize the suffering that has been inflicted on these creatures throughout the centuries. But with the advent of factory farming, the evil has been terribly accentuated. Animals are treated as machines for meat production. The personal relation with animals characteristic of traditional small-scale farming is gone. Quantitatively the suffering of these creatures is vastly increased. It is difficult to justify participating in a system of food production and consumption, as meat eaters do, that involves such suffering.(40)

As consumers, we can all help restore a moral balance by supporting farmers and ranchers who follow humane and sustainable animal-husbandry practices, and by opposing intensive animal-husbandry practices that deny farm animals their basic freedoms—freedom to execute normal physical activities, such as grooming and wallowing or dust bathing. The deprivation of such basic behavioral needs is surely a violation of animals' rights and of any "covenant" that we might have made with them when, in innocence and not as opportunists, they became domesticated. That they have contributed so much to society and to the economy over several millennia incurs in us an enormous indebtedness. It is now time to settle that debt by restoring the Covenant of the Wild. This will entail more concerted efforts to protect and restore wildlife and wildlands, the adoption of humane husbandry practices and of alternatives to using animals for various purposes, as in biomedical research, that lead to a more compassionate, egalitarian and symbiotic relationship with all creatures wild and tame.

The Christian theocracy of our industrial technocracy still endorses and advances a chauvinistic attitude toward fellow creatures. It is evidently prejudiced against those millions of people who support the humane animal and environmental rights movements, and who oppose all injustices against any and all life. Liam Brophy, writing in *The A/V Magazine*, cites one such Christian patriarch, Cardinal Ratzinger (who, in 1989, had Creation-concerned Dominican priest Matthew Fox silenced for one year; note that Fox has since left the Roman Catholic Church), who sees these movements as being based on "somewhat anti-technical, somewhat anti-rational concepts of man as united to nature, and have an anti-humanist element."

"Man as united to nature" is what the theocracy and technocracy of these times reject and regard as pagan, heretical and antisocial, thus evil. From Cardinal Ratzinger's perspective, Creation-centered spirituality is wrong. His prejudice is based upon the erroneous belief of human superiority over and separateness from Nature, whom pagans call the Earth Mother of us all. Prejudice is based upon fear, as Liam Brophy states:

> It is indeed a negative attitude rather than a thought out judgement, a hasty or premature appraisal of individuals and groups, an emotional and rigid view of those who feel their prestige or positions threatened, an antipathy based upon faulty and inflexible generalizations.

Christian attitudes toward animals are beginning to change, however, as more theologians question our responsibilities toward them. Theology professor John B. Cobb concludes:

> Human beings do have the right to kill many other animals. But, like all rights, this one is limited in many ways. Human beings have the right to use creatures of other species for human ends, but they should not use them as if they existed for human purposes alone. They have value in and of themselves apart from their value to humanity. The human use of these animals always involves some element of loss, and the suffering they experience is an intrinsic evil. Further, that suffering is shared by God. When Christians forget that, as most of them have forgotten through most of Christian history, legitimate use becomes illegitimate exploitation.[41]

There is a significant difference in animals' capacity to suffer, which is often overlooked in simplistic discussions of species' degrees of sentience. For example, while fear and pain may be subjectively the same for a chicken or a dog, these species react very differently when they witness the death or injury of one of their own kind. We should be mindful, therefore, that highly social, empathic species like dogs, pigs, whales, elephants and wolves, to name a few, suffer when one of their group is harmed or dies. In determining a species' degree of sentience or capacity to suffer, we should therefore consider both the individual's reactions and the group's response to individual suffering and death.

It is appropriate, at this point, to look at the life and teachings of St. Francis of Assisi, the patron saint of ecology, whose kinship with animals and all of Creation will be familiar to many readers. The life and teachings of St. Francis are even more relevant today than in his time because of the magnitude and urgency of the problems we face and the need to find effective solutions for all life on Earth.

The Life and
Teachings of
St. Francis of Assisi

THE LIFE AND TEACHINGS OF St. Francis of Assisi have great relevance to the many problems that we face today, especially in terms of our perception and treatment of fellow creatures and the natural world. The first part of the chapter reviews historical accounts of St. Francis' relationships with animals and his perception of Nature as revealed by his life and teachings. The second part explores the nature of divinity and the divinity of Nature, which is the apotheosis of Franciscan sacramentalism.

In his time, St. Francis was an antidote to the profane and dualistic beliefs of human superiority and separateness from the rest of Nature, a view of the world that is still widely held. Today, as we confront the secular materialism that was just emerging in his time, St. Francis is an inspiration and guide for the human relationship with and responsibility for the life and beauty of this planet.

Born in 1182 into an expanding mercantile class as the feudal epoch was drawing to a close, St. Francis, surrounded by poverty and inequality, was moved to "live simply so that others might simply live." St. Francis spent much of his short life in his hometown of Assisi, Italy, in the once wild and beautiful hills and pastoral vales and plains of the region called Umbria. This *poverello* (poor man) of Assisi died on October 3, 1226. Though never ordained as a Catholic priest, he was canonized in Assisi on July 16, 1228, by Pope Gregory IX. The relevance of St. Francis' life and teachings could not be more acute today as science, on the one hand, affirms the sacred unity and interdependence of all life, and on the other, serves those industries and ideologies that are destroying this unity and interdependence.

For millions of people, St. Francis of Assisi, patron saint of ecology and Catholic action, is the embodiment of compassion and concern for all creatures. Yet his life and teachings have not yet had a significant influence on Western civilization, or on religious thought and tradition. If they had, the industrial revolution might have been very different, and its consequences far less harmful to humanity and the rest of Earth's Creation. As we face the coming new millennium and a world in chaos, we might in our personal lives and in our national and international policies and priorities benefit from a little hindsight. Those who forget their history inevitably repeat it.

The spirit of St. Francis arose in a time of transition and social upheaval in Europe. But even though his spirit lives on in myth and legend, it endures in isolation from our own personal lives and from the affairs of the world. It is now time to integrate his spirit—his teachings, the principles of his way of life—into the mainstream, not simply of the Christian tradition, but into the secular realms of our own lives and of the worlds of commerce, science, industry, politics and economics.

Environmental philosopher and historian Susan Power Bratton writes that "to consider St. Francis' attitude towards nature to be an anomaly is to misunderstand his place in history. Far from being the first or only nature-loving monastic, Francis was the ultimate expression of traditions that had been growing and interweaving for centuries."[1] She draws this conclusion from historical records of the late sixth- and seventh-century Celtic monks, and the earlier fourth- and fifth-century Desert Fathers who began the Christian monastic tradition in the Middle East. Compassion toward hungry, thirsty and injured wild animals, including lions and wolves, and a relationship based upon friendship rather than exploitation are consistently recorded aspects in the lives of the earliest Christian saints. Since this tradition—if it might be so called—was continued, if not culminated, in the life and teachings of St. Francis of Assisi, we might wonder why it reached its ultimate expression in St. Francis and then abruptly ended.

St. Francis, from this historical perspective, can be seen as the end of a Christian tradition that began in the harsh North African desert, where, to paraphrase the desert monastic Anthony, who died in A.D. 356, when asked by a philosopher how he could live in the desert without books, replied, "My book, philosopher, is the nature of created things, and as often as I have a mind to read the words of God, it is at my hand."[2]

This tradition was effectively expunged from Christianity by the Church of Rome that initially saw Francis as a heretic but later canonized him for political reasons. Under the Church of Rome, the Christian tradition of compassion and kinship with God's creatures and Creation was broken by the influence of Aristotelian philosophy that St. Thomas Aquinas assimilated into Christianity to rationalize patriarchy and the subordination of animals and Nature to human need, industry and greed. This new theology provided the ethical and moral framework of the bioindustrial revolution—the Age of Reason, whose founders, like Francis Bacon and René Descartes, were enabled to fabricate a new theology for a materialistic and industrial civilization that condoned the rape and desecration of the natural world and the subjugation and exploitation of animals.

But as Bratton concludes, "when we put aside our self-interest and look to the good of the entire cosmos [like St. Francis and the earlier saints], we will live at peace with all Creation. Then we, too, will sleep with lions."[3]

St. Francis of Assisi, Animals and Nature

There are several accounts of St. Francis' encounters with Nature and with animals both wild and tame. Some have been clearly distorted by inaccuracies of translation from earlier documents. These were no doubt compiled from his followers' oral testimonies, which were often magnified by a sense of the miraculous. Other accounts, which have become legend, reflect a naiveté about the ways of animals and a lack of objectivity concerning the actions and feelings of St. Francis himself toward nonhuman creatures. However, many of these accounts clearly demonstrate his empathy and compassion toward fellow animals and the joy that he experienced when contemplating the beauty and wonder of Earth's Creation—the flowers of the fields and the birds of the sky.

What is remarkable, if not disturbing, is that his followers and later chroniclers found his actions and feelings toward nonhuman Creation so extraordinary. St. Francis once liberated two lambs, tied up across the shoulders of a farmer, who were bleating pitifully on their way to market where they would be slaughtered. St. Francis removed worms from a busy road and put them at the roadside so that they might not be crushed under the feet of passersby. He would become ecstatic over the sight of a field full of flowers or a grove of trees filled with bird song. Such actions reveal much about St. Francis and about those who regarded such behavior as extraordinary; others neither felt nor acted in these ways.

Thomas of Celano wrote:

When he found an abundance of flowers he preached to them and invited them to praise the Lord as though they were endowed with reason. In the same way he exhorted with the sincerest purity cornfields and vineyards, stones and forests and all the beautiful things of the fields, fountains of water and the green things of the gardens, earth and fire, air and wind, to love God and serve Him willingly. Finally he called all creatures *brother*, and in a most extraordinary manner, a manner never experienced by others, he discerned the hidden things of nature with his sensitive heart.[4]

Edward Armstrong has emphasized that St. Francis was a Nature mystic, a devoted sacramentalist:

For him, nature spoke of God. All Created things pointed beyond themselves to their Creator. . . . It was because nature revealed in sight, sound and fragrance the handiwork and glory of God that he admired and rejoiced in things of beauty. He envisaged all Creation, man supremely, as worshipping the Creator.[5]

St. Bonaventura tells us that St. Francis taught the brethren "to praise God in all things and through all His creatures." As W. R. Inge in his book *Christian Mysticism* concludes, "All Nature (and there are few more pernicious errors than that which separates man from Nature) is the language in which God expresses His thought."

Panentheism and pantheism are often confused. In *pantheism*, God is *in* the tree, the animal; in *panentheism*, the tree, the animal and all, are *in* God as God is in all. Thus, panentheism is synonymous with Franciscan sacramentalism. It also corresponds with the non-dualistic Hindu/Vedanta realization, *Tat-tvam-asi:* Thou art That. (As Jesus said, "I and the Father are One.") This view is judged to be heretical by monotheistic fundamentalists who believe in a purely transcendent God.

Armstrong captures the panentheistic worldview of St. Francis by emphasizing that:

The Incarnation sanctified all life. As the Saviour had come mani-festing God in human form, so God could and did represent Him-self or symbolize His Nature to mankind in the creatures of His Creation—whether worms or birds, trees or flowers, fragrance or fire, water or rocks, sun or moon. They were all outward signs of divine grace. Francis, overwhelmed by God's goodness in mani-festing Himself in innumerable ways to man, not only appreciated and gave thanks for the beauty, interest, and wonder of all the earth affords but felt that such beauty must naturally call forth tenderness and reverence. In the midst of natural beauty, he was on holiday with God. Only those who in some measure are nature mystics and know the ineffable delight of being surrounded by loveliness far beyond their capacity to appreciate can understand the joyousness of the saint's spirit. Every living thing shone with Divine radiance. God was revealing Himself, and man had but to look, listen, and worship to be carried to high heaven.[6]

In his beautiful treatise, Armstrong shows how St. Francis' in-fluence occurred at a time in the history of Western Christianity when many were reaffirming their spiritual kinship with Nature and

Creation, "enlarg[ing] their outlook by revealing the lark and the wildflower as sacramental and all nature singing out to man to join in adoration to the Creator."[7] However, many of the accounts of St. Francis' interactions with animals were distorted by his biographers' attempts to prove his magical powers of control over animals, and to match certain anecdotes about St. Francis with biblical parables and the life of Jesus Christ. In some instances, it seemed as though God was responding directly to St. Francis by making the animals behave in certain ways toward him, and that the obedience supposedly shown by the animals to holy authority was something that all people should emulate.

As Armstrong suggests, St. Francis' biographers reflected "the medieval tendency to discover esoteric significance in the behavior of birds and beasts. Piety and superstition alike were nourished by such thinking."[8] Their thinking was further influenced by the belief that animals were bound by, and subject to, the principles of Christian morality, and also that, as St. Thomas Aquinas insisted, they could be possessed by the devil and used for evil purposes. In all fairness, even though Aquinas helped close the door on the belief that animals have souls, he did write that since God is the true object of human charity, charity should be extended to all of God's Creation, including "the creatures without reason . . . fish and birds, the beasts and plants." Armstrong concludes, "The ambivalent medieval attitude toward animals arose from the belief that they could be used by, or be manifestations of, supremely good or utterly evil powers. This preconception stood in the way of any objective evaluation of the behavior of animals."[9]

Even so, some Franciscans, such as St. Bernardino, seemed more aware than others of the behavior of animals. He drew a moral from his own knowledge of animals when he said, "Look at the pigs who have so much compassion for each other that when one of them squeals, the others will run to help. . . . And you children who steal the baby swallows. What do other swallows do? They all gather together and try to help the fledglings. . . . Man is more evil than the birds."[10]

St. Francis was seen as possessing miraculous power over animals —an ability to control them. He was once given a wild pheasant to eat but instead kept him as a companion. The bird, when separated from him, purportedly pined and refused to eat until the two were reunited. On another occasion, St. Francis was given a fish and, at another time, a waterfowl to eat, but he was so moved by the life and beauty of these creatures that he set them free. Upon release, the fish stayed by the water's edge close to him for some time, and the bird remained in his lap, both appearing to be attached to him.[11]

This behavior can, however, be interpreted differently: the waterfowl was terrified and in a state of catatonia, and the fish was semiconscious from oxygen deprivation. What appeared to be a sign of some powerful or mystical influence upon the animals by the saint could, instead, have been a reflection of the observers' and chroniclers' lack of knowledge of animal behavior. The best-known example of St. Francis' supposed control and power over animals is the legend of the taming of the old, wild, man-eating wolf of Gubbio. Armstrong, however, doubts this legend and questions whether the wolf and his ostensible relationship with the saint ever existed. He also notes that medieval outlaws were treated like wolves—they were killed on sight. In Italy, such a malefactor was called a *capo lupino*, or wolf's head. According to some historians, therefore, the wolf of Gubbio could actually have been a human outlaw, not an animal at all. Armstrong concludes, "the story has its own truth as a glimpse of the Earthly Paradise." He writes:

The story of the Wolf is a parable relying on traditional associations and natural emotional responsiveness to conventional imagery, an offshoot of that ideal and myth which has been embodied in different guises throughout history, depicting man, no longer at strife with nor subject to nature, establishing harmony with it, an ideal that in this its religious form differs profoundly from the magical concept in which man as sorcerer or magician, or in league with unnatural powers, subordinates nature and its processes to his will and wishes. The magician is the instrument of crude power, the saint, the vehicle of moral and spiritual power, whose influence resides in his approximation to the state of the Blessed who are able to say "In his will is our peace" (*Paradiso*, iii.85). The parable of the Wolf portrays the consummation of man's dreams: reconciliation by virtue of holy power between nature and himself.[12]

Having spent some years studying captive and human-raised wolves, I do not completely agree with Armstrong. That an aged and hungry wolf could develop an attachment to a fearless and caring human is not beyond the realm of possibility. But I would agree with him when he concludes:

> The animal stories in the Legend can be understood . . . as teaching patience, tolerance, sympathy, and outgoingness. In telling them, the biographers were writing better than they knew, although they were manifestly portraying the saint as the personification of holy love, able to elicit affection and establish concord among all the creatures of God. Animal instincts are shown overcome by virtue, not only as a power exercised by man in the person of Francis, dominating and subduing them, but as a divine, benignant influence, pacifying, appeasing, redeeming, and converting. . . .[13]

Miraculous, prophetic and legendary as these various anecdotes may seem, the single thread that connects them all is St. Francis' compassionate sense of kinship with the life and suffering of fellow creatures. Many skeptics and critics of St. Francis, however, have used one horrendous incident involving the butchering of a pig to discredit his entire image as an exemplar of compassion toward all living things. It has been said that one of his followers once cut off one leg of a pig to give to a sick man, leaving the pig bleeding and crippled. There is no evidence that the saint rebuked his brother monk for treating the animal so cruelly. Such treatment may not have been uncommon in St. Francis' day. Animals' limbs were sometimes removed for human consumption, and hot oil or pitch was poured over the wounds to cauterize them. Nor is there evidence that St. Francis espoused or practiced vegetarianism. His attitude toward animals was, in part, a product of the times. However, his deep identification with the suffering of all living things, and the active compassion that he often demonstrated, set him apart from his fellows. The story of the pig serves to remind us how widespread the lack of compassion toward fellow creatures must have been during the saint's lifetime.

It is clear that St. Francis was not unaware of the widespread cruel treatment of animals. In his *Admonitions* he says, "Be conscious, O man, of the wondrous state in which the Lord God has placed you, for He created you and formed you to the image of his beloved Son—and (yet) all the creatures under heaven, each according to its nature, serve, know, and obey their Creator better than you."[14]

St. Francis' forbearance with a plague of mice is also documented.[15] While he was sick and almost blind, mice ran over his table at mealtimes and over him as he slept. He used no miraculous powers to banish or still them but instead regarded their irritation as a "diabolical temptation," which he apparently met with patience and restraint, again demonstrating his compassion toward all creatures.

In his *Salutation of the Virtues*, St. Francis writes that one who upholds the virtue of holy obedience "is subject and submissive to all persons in the world and not to man only but even to all beasts and wild animals so that they may do whatever they want with him inasmuch as it has been given to them from above by the Lord."[16] In other words, humans should subordinate themselves to the animals insofar as it is believed that animals are the instruments of God's will. Being subordinate implies letting creatures be.

It is quite apparent that many of the recorded accounts of St. Francis' loving and compassionate interactions with animals have been distorted by those seeking the miraculous in his behavior. For instance, he once greeted a flock of sheep and, as tame and curious sheep sometimes do, they ran toward him. Observers who saw this concluded that St. Francis was truly "a great man whom the brutes venerate as their father and, though they lack reason, recognize as the friend of the Creator."[17]

Presumed divine or magical power over animals has long been an attribute of the shaman. This "power" may be derived, in part, from a deep sense of empathetic identification coupled with great trust and a lack of fear. Unlike Native American and other shamans, however, St. Francis "solicitously admonished all birds, all animals and reptiles, and even creatures that have no feeling, to praise and love their Creator, for daily, when the name of the Savior had been invoked, he saw their obedience by personal experience."[18]

Biographers of St. Francis have recorded that he spoke to the birds, acting "as if they shared human understanding." If the creatures even momentarily seemed to respond to St. Francis as though they comprehended what he was saying, then it might appear to be miraculous. But miracle or no, was it saintly, eccentric or naive for St. Francis to address the birds in such a way? Today, countless people talk to their dogs, cats and other animal companions "as if they shared human understanding." Indeed, it is more normal than not. How else could St. Francis, or any of us, talk to animals except in words? To do so does not necessarily imply that we believe animals "share human understanding." But they probably understand far more than we think they might.

It is worth reflecting on the fact that wild and domestic animals, socialized by humans at an early age, are extremely responsive and affectionate toward their human foster parents. People ignorant about animal behavior might interpret such reactions as resulting not from the expression of human love but from some magical power or wizard's spell. This, coupled with the belief that animals could be possessed by evil spirits, surely contributed to the demise of many animal lovers and their animals during the witch hunts of the late Middle Ages. As is stated in Leviticus (20:27), "A man also or a woman that hath a familiar spirit, or that is a wizard, shall surely be put to death." The animal companions of witches were referred to as familiars, one definition of *familiar* being "a supernatural spirit often embodied in an animal at the service of a person." A socialized deer or raven, or affectionate black cat, then, could be seen as a possessed familiar and his or her human companion as a witch or wizard. St. Francis certainly did much to dispel such superstition and prejudice toward nonhuman animals. Perhaps his greatest "miracle" was to teach others how to live in reverence with Creation so that by love's communion, God is praised through—by way of—all of God's creatures and other manifestations that comprise "the language in which God expresses his thought."

St. Francis apparently regularly began to preach the word of God to animals after the following incident. One day he left his companions in the road and ran eagerly toward a large flock of doves, crows and jackdaws who had gathered together, possibly to feed. When he was close enough to them, "seeing that they were waiting expectantly for him, he greeted them in his usual way. But, not a little surprised that the birds did not rise in flight, as they usually do, he was filled with great joy and humbly begged them to listen to the word of God."[19] However, Armstrong notes:

A later tale may indicate some scepticism concerning the Sermon. It begins: "Brother Masseo has said that he was present when the Blessed Francis preached to the birds." This story describes how, rapt in devotion, the saint noticed a flock of birds by the roadside and turned aside to preach to them as he had done on the previous occasion. They all flew away and he reproached himself bitterly: "What effrontery you have, you impertinent son of Pietra Bernardone!" He did so, it is explained, because he realized that he was expecting them to obey him as if he, and not God, were their Creator. . . . Perhaps, while Francis' humility is thus emphasized, Brother Masseo's veracity is gently questioned. We may detect a tendency to correct some of the exaggerations of Celano and Bonaventura which stress Francis' miraculous power over nature rather than his compassion and obscure his nature mysticism with stories of prodigies.[20]

Celano's biography of St. Francis implies that wherever Francis went from this time on, "even irrational creatures recognized his affection for them and felt his tender love for them."[21] It is not clear, however, if his "power" was so great that animals were always "obedient" toward him and lost their conditioned fear of humans when in his presence. A more reasonable explanation could well lie not in St. Francis' possession of some magical power over animals, but in the quiet joy and gentle reverence he exuded when he came upon the birds. The birds acknowledged this by not flying away, and by so doing, filled him "with great joy" and thus changed his behavior toward them from that time on.

Canticle of the Creatures

Purported miraculous powers aside, St. Francis is to be remembered for his compassion toward all creatures and joyous reverence for Earth's Creation, a view which set him apart from his contemporaries. It is especially through his *Canticle of the Creatures*, written in 1225, that he is best remembered by many today who acknowledge him as the one outstanding voice for animals and the rest of nonhuman Creation during the early history of Christianity.

The *Canticle* reveals the sensitivity and vision of its author and is a
key to his inner self. According to one early chronicler, St. Francis
said, "For his [God's] praise, I wish to compose a new hymn about
the Lord's creatures, of which we make daily use, without which
we cannot live, and with which the human race greatly offends its
Creator."(22) This last phrase—"with which the human race greatly
offends its Creator"—is as pertinent today as it was in St. Francis'
time. St. Francis' *Canticle*, composed in the garden of San Damiano
shortly before his death, was also known as *The Canticle of Brother
Sun*. He referred to such natural creations as the Earth, Sun, Moon,
and the elements of wind, fire and water, as Brothers and Sisters.
By so doing, he affirmed our kinship with the whole of Creation. In
1980, he was proclaimed the patron saint of ecology by Pope John
Paul II.

Inspired by all of Creation, St. Francis felt the presence of divinity
in the natural world and sang praises to the Creator. It was *through*
Nature that he praised the Creator and not simply *for* the gifts of
Nature that sustained humanity in body and spirit. Thus in one
translated scholarly version of the *Canticle* he says, "Praise be You,
my Lord, *through* our Sister Mother Earth, who sustains and governs
us. . . ."(23) And in another version we find, "Praise be Thou, my
Lord, *for* Mother Earth who sustains and rules us. . . ."(24) While this
translation is the most common one, yet another version reads, "Praise
be my Lord, *by means of* our Sister Mother Earth, which sustains and
keeps us. . . ."(25) Franciscan scholars Armstrong and Brady note that
this difference in translation may be due to the corruption of the
Latin *per*, or the Italian *par*. Thus they state, "It may be translated
'*for*,' suggesting an attitude of thanksgiving; '*by*,' expressing a sense
of instrumentality; or '*through*,' indicating instrumentality as well
as a deeper sense of mysticism in perceiving God's presence in all
creation."(26) This latter view is preferred by these two Franciscans,
though they avoid making any reference to the panentheistic (as
distinct from pantheistic) quality of the *Canticle*.

Matthew Fox links panentheism with sacramentalism, noting:

. . . panentheism is not pantheism. Pantheism, which is a declared
heresy because it robs God of transcendence, states that "everything
is God and God is everything." Panentheism, on the other hand, is

altogether orthodox and very fit for orthopraxis as well, for it slips in the little Greek word *en* and thus means, "God is in everything and everything is in God. . . ." Panentheism is desperately needed by individuals and religious institutions today. It is the way the creation-centered tradition of spirituality experiences God. It is not theistic because it does not relate to God as subject or object, but neither is it pantheistic. Panentheism is a way of seeing the world sacramentally . . . the primary sacrament is creation itself—which includes every person and being who lives. . . . The sacramental consciousness of panentheism develops into a transparent and diaphanous consciousness wherein we can see events and beings as divine. . . .[27]

In praising the Creator *through* or *by means of* the Creation, St. Francis expressed, in the purest and most profound way, that his awareness and appreciation of divinity lay in his perception and feeling for animals and Nature. He did not simply praise the Creator for these things, which, from a human-centered point of view, were made by God for our own exclusive use. Rather, it was *through* or *by means of* the manifestation of God's Creation that his God-centered, sacramental perception of the cosmos arose. As Father Lanfranco Serrini writes:

Since God can express his will through all of his works, Francis was submissive to all creatures and scanned creation attentively, listening to its mysterious voices. In his *Canticle of Brother Sun*, the Saint calls all creatures his brothers and sisters because they are God's gifts and signs of his providential and reconciling love. To God alone do they belong, to him they bear a likeness, and in his name Mother Earth, our sister, feeds us. In his personal relationship with all creatures, St. Francis recognized his duty to reciprocate divine love with love and praise, not only in the name of creatures, *but in, with, and through them* (italics mine).[28]

The gifts Serrini refers to are not gifts in a utilitarian sense; rather, they are gifts of revelation in a spiritual sense that moved St. Francis to praise and glorify all of Earth's Creation. H. Felder, in his detailed treatise on the ideals of St. Francis, concludes, "His entire relation to nature is essentially religious. It begins and ends with nature's God.

It may be condensed into the two words: from *Creator to creature* and from *creature to Creator*."[29]

This panentheistic view is evident in Celano's statement: "He called all animals by the name *brother*. . . . For that original goodness that will be one day *all things in all* already shown forth in this saint *all things in all*";[30] and in I Cor. 12:6: "It is the same God which worketh all in all." St. Bonaventure affirms this by stating, "When he considered the primordial source of all things, he was filled with even more abundant piety, calling creatures no matter how small by the name of brother or sister because he knew they had the same source as himself."[31]

The God and Creation-centered spirituality of St. Francis is as relevant and ecumenical today as it was in his own time, almost eight hundred years ago. Its simplicity and purity shine across the centuries like an illuminating ray of hope for all of humankind. In our times of global industrialism, as in his own mercantile times, St. Francis' life and teachings make a radical and affirmative political and ecological statement that is as fundamentally antiestablishment today as it was theocratically heretical then. War, poverty, inequitable distribution of wealth, destruction of Nature, cruelty and indifference to the suffering of human and nonhuman beings alike were as prevalent in his lifetime as they are today. However, the scope and scale of the suffering is surely much greater now. Certainly, by virtue of increased numbers, the suffering of humanity has intensified, as has the desecration and destruction of the created order and the exploitation and suffering of animals under the socially sanctioned and sanctified institutions of medical research, agribusiness food production and wildlife management for the hunting and trapping industries. The way of life adopted by St. Francis, as he endeavored to live according to the Scriptures, may seem too ascetic for most people to fully comprehend. However, his kind and gentle way of living simply and treating all of Earth's Creation with respect and love is relevant to the emerging philosophy and ethics of a wiser and more sensitive humanity.

It would be an injustice to St. Francis' life and teachings, however, for him to become only a sentimental figure of conservation and animal protection. Indeed, as Paul Weigand emphasizes, the vision of St. Francis, the example of his life, "beckons us to change, by means of poverty and simplicity, avoiding all pretense, want and desire to power. It is a plan perfectly suited to an ecological recovery for a world scarred by insatiable 'wants.' Its value lies not in romantic notions of birds and nature, but of a steeled reverence for life, of taking only what is needed and letting go of all the rest."[32]

A point that is not missed by his more sensitive biographers is that St. Francis opposed any kind of hierarchical structure, be it within his order of Brothers, which he insisted must be egalitarian, or within relationships between people, or between humans, other animals, and the whole of Creation. Even though this view was contrary to the established theocracy of his time, its spiritual verity was recognized by the Roman Catholic Church and was not opposed because it was in accord with the Scriptures. Hence, the Franciscan order was recognized by the Vatican. Still today, St. Francis' view remains contrary to the Judeo-Christian tradition, which sees relationships in a hierarchial and therefore dualistic way. Nature and animals are seen as being inferior to humanity; and divinity is not coinherent but something separate and transcendent only, rather than being immanent as well as transcendent.

St. Francis experienced the immanence of divinity not as a pantheist but as a sacramentalist-panentheist. He was receptively open and aware of the wonder and beauty of the manifest world—God's Creation and divine presence—through which, or by means of which, the mystery and love of divinity can be seen and felt. Some fear this view, believing it has pagan, pantheistic implications. However, it is not pagan to revere or even experience divinity *through,* or *by means of,* Nature and the beauty, harmony and *mysterium tremendum* of Creation. This was the way of St. Francis.

But what natural religion and reverence for divinity can there be when Nature has become so unnaturally transformed and desecrated, and the sacred order and harmony defiled? To cite G. K. Chesterton, "It was no good to preach natural religion to people to whom nature had grown as unnatural as any religion." Today, the sacred order and harmony of Creation are being defiled by a perverted reverence for Nature as a source of power and wealth. Perceived primarily as a resource, Nature has become an end in itself, not a means whereby divinity can be revered, praised and celebrated through our creative participation in preserving the beauty, order and harmony of Creation. Today it is not the old, degenerate form of paganism that is so destructive of the beauty, order and harmony of Creation and which blinds us to the realization of "one God who is Father of all, over all, through all, and within all" (Eph. 4:6). It is the new and widespread "neo-paganism" of secular materialism, with its technological enchantment, doctrines and destructive impulses of rationalism, industrialism and scientific imperialism that make the teachings and example of St. Francis more relevant and urgent now than ever before. Chesterton writes, "The whole philosophy of St. Francis revolved around the idea of a new supernatural light on natural things, which meant the ultimate recovery, not the ultimate refusal, of natural things."[33] And that light, that numinous quality of divine immanence, is a beacon for all humanity in this darkening, profane age of materialism.

Shining through the biographies and legends of St. Francis is his intense sense of wonder regarding Nature. It is especially this sense of wonder that leads the Nature mystic to worship—but not in a pagan or pantheistic sense—the Creator through the whole of Creation, each aspect of which is a source of inspiration and divine revelation. As Armstrong writes:

> Enthralled by the beauty and mystery of Creation, he believed and showed that love of God, love of man, and love of nature were not only compatible with one another but the natural, divinely purposed state of humanity. He did not separate the interests of God, man and nature, as we do, to our detriment spiritually and the earth's impoverishment.[34]

To make such separations is, in my mind, the essence of "original sin." To be separate from Nature, to place one's own interests outside and above those of Nature and other living souls, is to separate oneself from God. As all Christians were enjoined "to dress and to keep" the Garden of Eden (Gen. 2:15), so it is incumbent upon all of humanity to restore the planet to a semblance of her original beauty and vitality for the benefit of all and for the glory of the Creator.

The possibility still remains for humanity to be redeemed, to be "new-created in a new-created world," as Armstrong proposes, by experiencing the wonder, glory, mystery, beauty and harmony of the natural world, and so of God. But this possibility becomes ever more remote as the natural world is desacralized and perverted to satisfy the gods of greed, industrialism and materialism, and as we as a species become increasingly separated and alienated from the Creation and Creator alike. That many people can still partake of the wonder, glory, mystery and beauty of the world and strive to preserve and protect that beauty by endeavoring to live in some degree of harmony—if not in total reverence and peace—is surely grounds for hope.

By sensing the Universal in the particular, and the particular in the Universal (like William Blake's vision of the Whole Universe in a grain of sand) and *acting accordingly* by living in reverence with all of Creation, St. Francis of Assisi became a living symbol to the world of illimitable love and universal compassion—the essence of democracy and the foundation of world peace. It is not a coincidence, therefore, that in 1986, Assisi, Italy, was chosen for an interfaith conference on world peace, an international conference on the conservation of Nature and the protection of endangered wildlife, and the focus for the establishment of an international interfaith center for religion and animals.

The following excerpts from a sermon given by the Very Reverend James Morton in the Cathedral of St. John the Divine, New York City, on the Feast Day of St. Francis, 1986, shed further light on a significant aspect of St. Francis' life, which has not been covered in this brief review.

> For Francis, poverty is, in a sense, the flip side of the richness of creation. *Poverty is simply not possessing—not owning*—in order that one's openness can welcome God's richness. If we are competing with God with our possessions, we miss the whole point.
>
> We don't own animals, any more than we own trees or own mountains or seas or, indeed, each other. We don't own our wives or our husbands or our friends or our lovers. We respect and behold and we celebrate trees and mountains and seas and husbands and wives and lovers and children and friends and animals.
>
> Our souls must be poor—must be open—in order to be able to receive, to behold, to enter into communion with, but not to possess. Our poverty of soul allows animals to thrive and to shine and be free and radiate God's glory.

The Life and Teachings of St. Francis of Assisi

For St. Francis, love and compassion is the medium, the means through which one learns to become open—through which one is enabled to embrace poverty in order to commune in the diverse richness of God's glory and creation.

In sum, the teachings and symbolic significance of St. Francis of Assisi are being recognized increasingly by the leaders of the world's major religions, the political and social influence and relevance of which are being questioned today. It is a matter of planetary survival for all peoples to awaken to St. Francis' call to conscience—that we at last begin to recognize our common origin—our kinship with all life—and live accordingly.

The Apotheosis of Nature, Human and Animal

St. Francis of Assisi's sacramentalist attitude toward animals, Nature and the Creation is comparable in many ways to what contemporary thinkers call *panentheism*. As St. Francis endeavored in his teachings to unify concern for humanity, the Animal Kingdom and the whole of Creation, so we find the ethical and spiritual principles of contemporary panentheism unifying two complementary yet historically long-separated movements: conservation, or "deep" ecology, and animal protection, or animal rights.

The apotheosis of Nature, human and animal, is one and the same. *Apotheosis* means raising a person or thing to divine status or to its highest development. While the Creation is "unfinished," at every moment it is perfect in its totality. Thus, it can be reasoned that our perception of the coinherence of divinity in Nature and all existence is not idolatry but rather the apotheosis of the Higher Self or divinity within. For the Christian apotheosisis is the realization of the Christ within. This is accomplished through love and empathy with the suffering of the world.

The essence of Jewish mysticism is in the perception that God is not in the world, but rather the world is in God. Kabbalists accept absolute unity as the basis of their system—a God who is at one and the same time the cause, the substance and the form of all that is, as well as of all that can be. To experience oneself as part of one life in God is the apotheosis of the Self. It is an experience devoid of any self-aggrandizement because it is imbued with the suffering of the world caused in part by our own selfishness and ignorance. This insight gives rise to humility.

As the Buddhists say, when there is enlightenment—purity of perception—everything is Buddha. One of the fundamental teachings of the Koran, as espoused by Islamic Sufis, is that all things are in God and God is in all things. Apotheosis for the Buddhist and the Hindu is analogous to the realization that the Atman (the Higher Self) and Brahman (God and Creation) are one and the same. When a Christian is "born again" in this way, everything is in Christ as the Christ within. Realization of the unity of being in God through love's communion is the apotheosis of the observer and the observed. Part of the Christian apotheosis is to love and suffer empathetically with the body of Christ that is now being crucified—the Earth and all of Creation under humankind's selfish and destructive dominion.

This apotheosis—this change in perception and feeling for the world—ultimately leads to a radical change in behavior. This change is marked by a very different relationship with the Creation and by a shift in consumer habits and lifestyle toward voluntary simplicity, nonviolence (*ahimsa*) and conscientious consumerism, as exemplified by vegetarianism and not wearing furs, in order to minimize adverse environmental consequences and harm to other sentient beings.

This same apotheosis will revolutionize such institutions as health and education and various industrial corporate activities, notably agriculture and the power and energy industries. These institutions and industries, and the economies of the developed and developing nations alike, will ultimately fail if we, as a species, fail to recognize our dependence upon the unity of all life and continue to treat the environment and its inhabitants without reverence or equal and fair consideration.

Fundamentally there is but one crisis—and it is a spiritual one. It has arisen because our collective state of mind is still human-centered and not—as St. Francis of Assisi realized—Creation- or God-centered. If we fail to make the next evolutionary step, the suffering and destructive turmoil in the world will intensify, and our extinction may well be inevitable. We are not superior to the animal

Creation. As Ecclesiastes 3:19 states, "Man hath no preeminence over the beast." We are equals as co-evolved and co-inhabitants of this beautiful planet in which we, abusing our power of dominion over animals and Nature, cause much unnecessary suffering and destruction. Let us all seek the will and inspiration to put an end to the holocaust of the Animal Kingdom, to the desacralization of Nature and to the poisoning of the environment that is fast becoming an uninhabitable wasteland.

It is not natural evolution or God's will to see all of Creation exploited and perverted to satisfy purely human ends and for animals to suffer in the process—on factory farms, or in research laboratories, roadside zoos, rodeos and in steel-jaw traps. Animals are ends in themselves, not a means to satisfy our own selfish ends, be it through genetic engineering or other manipulative exploitation. We violate the sacred trust of dominion when we fail to recognize our kinship with fellow creatures. As the Koran proclaims, "There is not an animal on earth, nor a flying creature on two wings, but they are like unto you." Let us also reflect upon the book of Isaiah (66:3) where it is said, "He who kills an ox is like he who kills a person." As Gautama Buddha advised, "The key to a new civilization is the spirit of *maitri*, compassionate kinship with all creatures"; and, "Friendship toward all creatures is the true religion."

The Right Reverend John Austin Baker, Anglican Bishop of Salisbury, said:

> To shut your mind, heart, imagination to the sufferings of others is to begin slowly but inexorably to die. It is to cease by inches from being human, to become in the end capable of nothing generous or unselfish—or sometimes capable of anything, however terrible. You in the animal welfare movement are among those who may yet save our society from becoming spiritually deaf, blind and dead, and so from the doom that will justly follow.
>
> As we know, Christians, like others, are apt to justify leaving animal welfare aside on the grounds that human needs are more urgent. We must hammer home that love is indivisible. It is not "either-or"; it is "both-and," because a society that cannot find the moral energy to care and act about gross animal suffering and exploitation will do little better about human need. And looking

at the world today, is that an unfair comment on our western culture?

Rights, whether animal or human, have only one sure foundation: that God loves us all and rejoices in us all. We humans are called to share with God in fulfilling the work of love toward all creatures . . . the true glory of the strong is to give themselves for the cherishing of the weak.[35]

Reverend Gary Kowalski concludes that "Animal liberation, which at its heart is a call for a shift from an ego-centered to an eco-centered spirituality, also implies human liberation, for it frees us from an idolatrous concept of God."[36]

Theologian Thomas Berry has observed:

The industrial age, as we have known it, can be described as a period of technological entrancement, an altered state of consciousness, a mental fixation that alone can explain how we came to ruin our air and water and soil and to severely damage all our basic life systems under the illusion that this was progress.[37]

But now the trance is passing, and we have before us the task of "reinventing the human." This "reinvention" entails a virtual restructuring of industrial civilization and thus the way in which we perceive the world and construct the reality in which we live. Our intellectual development and technological abilities have far outstripped, if not actually inhibited, the maturation of other human qualities, especially feeling, empathy and intuitive wisdom. Indeed our emotional awareness and ability to empathize are so limited that it is now considered almost heretical to attribute feelings to animals, and the living Earth is seen simply as a resource of inert matter.

As a culture, have we not come to value intellect and instrumental knowledge over emotion and feeling? This explains in part, I believe, why we have become emotionally and empathetically disconnected to varying degrees from the rest of Creation. If this were not so, then we could not bear the pain of seeing and feeling the rape and destruction of the natural world and the cruel exploitation and suffering of animals around us. The majority of the populace would rise up in protest and actively oppose such needless suffering and destruction. This inability to empathize and the associated avoidance of others' distress is being more widely recognized as a serious and prevalent disorder. The sickness of being unable to suffer may be compounded by the apathy of despair. In avoiding the realities of death and suffering, our sensitivities of love and empathy are impaired. In the absence of love and empathy, we seek security through power while exchanging spiritual faith for scientific knowledge and technological control over life.

Philosopher Marti Kheel has proposed that since animal rights philosophy is intellectually framed, it is limited because it lacks the dimension of emotion, which in itself is cognitively significant, influencing how we think and perceive. Our worldview, ethically and empathetically, becomes holistic when Nature as a whole, along with every living and nonliving natural entity, is given the same respect and consideration as we are morally bound to give our own species. Kheel and other feminist philosophers conclude that *holism* will remain an "ism" (like pacifism and vegetarianism) until it is lived and experienced both intellectually and emotionally.[38] Philosopher Robin Morgan terms the fusion of feeling and thought "unified sensibility."[39] Being humane entails not only empathetic caring but also awareness of the consequences of one's actions, beliefs and perceptions. When there is "unified sensibility," one feels good because one's actions do not cause harm to others or to oneself.

How, then, can we attain such a sensibility? Kheel answers:

This sensitivity—the "unified sensibility"—cannot, however, be developed on only an abstract, rational plane any more than I can learn to love someone that I have never seen. It is a sensitivity that must flow from our direct involvement with the natural world and the actions and reactions that we bring about in it. If such direct involvement is often not a possibility for many of us, this does not mean that we should abandon the attempt to achieve the sensitivity described. Although in our complex, modern society we may never be able to fully experience the impact of our moral decisions (we cannot, for example, directly experience the impact that eating meat has on world hunger), we can, nonetheless, attempt as far as possible to experience emotionally the knowledge of this fact. . . . The problem of unifying our own nature is compounded further when we, ourselves, are removed from the rest of nature. Emotion

easily divides from reason when we are divorced from the immediate impact of our moral decisions. A possible step, therefore, in
striving to fuse these divisions is to experience directly the full
impact of our moral decisions.[40]

Take a person who *thinks*, for example, that there is nothing
morally wrong with wearing the furs of murdered animals. A visit
to a factory-fur ranch or seeing wild animals struggling to escape
from a snares or steel-jaw traps might profoundly affect that person's
position. If those who wear furs don't want to become aware of the
brutal killing of fur-bearing animals, let alone participate directly in
their suffering, then, as Marti Kheel concludes:

> We ought, perhaps, to question the morality of indirectly paying
> someone else to do this on our behalf. When we are physically
> removed from the direct impact of our moral decisions—i.e., when
> we cannot see, smell, or hear their results—we deprive ourselves
> of important sensory stimuli which may be important in guiding
> us in our ethical choices.[41]

The importance of feeling is exemplified by the fact that how we
feel influences how we perceive, think and respond. Our attitudes
and beliefs are not purely rational and objective; many are based quite
subjectively upon how we feel about things. How we view the world
and value other living things is therefore influenced by our feelings
or lack of them, a fact we often have difficulty acknowledging.

It has been said, "Where there is no vision, the people shall perish"
(Prov. 29:18). When there is holism and nonduality, the vision of the
sacred unity of all life and the sanctity of being is recognized and
respected. Without this visionary feeling and realization, there can
be no reverence for life and no justice or lasting peace. There can
be no enduring sense of security if we do not feel part of something infinitely more vast, wondrous and mysterious than our own
predictable and frail mortal existence and the shallow values of a
secular, materialistic society.

The German philosopher Schopenhauer asks, in his celebrated
essay, *On The Basis of Morality:*

> How is it possible that suffering that is neither my own nor of my
> concern should immediately affect me as though it were my own,

and with such force that it moves me to action? This is something really mysterious, something for which Reason can provide no explanation, and for which no basis can be found in practical experience. It is nevertheless of common occurrence, and everyone has had the experience. It is not unknown even to the most hard-hearted and self-interested.(42)

His answer to this question is that the empathetic response represents a breakthrough of a metaphysical realization—namely (as he states in Sanskrit), *tat tvam asi*—"thou art that." He continues:

This presupposes that I have to some extent identified myself with the other and therewith removed for the moment the barrier between the "I" and the "Not-I." Only then can the other's situation, his want, his need, become mine. I then no longer see him in the way of an empirical perception, as one strange to me, indifferent to me, completely other than myself; but in him I suffer, in spite of the fact that his skin does not enfold my nerves.(43)

The concept of individualization is but one of many possible perceptions of the state of being. Hence the seeming multiplicity of differences that distinguish individuals are likewise mere perceptions. They exist, but only in one's mental representation. One's own true inner being actually exists in every living creature as truly and immediately as one's consciousness exists in oneself. This realization is the basis of compassion and unselfishness and is expressed in every good deed.

Jewish philosopher Martin Buber termed this empathetic relationship "I-Thou."(44) The coinherence of the Self that makes two into one is the Atman and Brahman of Hinduism, and is expressed in the "God in all/all in God" of panentheism. When there is vision of the sacred unity and sanctity of all being, duality and dualistic perception—in which separateness of the self from the rest of Creation is seen as the true and only nature of reality—are recognized as illusory, or at least a half-truth.

Anthropocentrism, like rationalism, racism and speciesism, is a consequence of dualistic perception which influences, if not determines, how we feel and act. This perception and the resultant worldview is responsible for the existential terror of life's uncertainties—

the possibility of suffering, loss of control and the inevitability of death. As is stated in the *Upanishads*, "He who fears only sees duality."

We try to avoid death, or the fear of it, by killing people in the name of peace, and animals in the name of medical necessity. We avoid suffering by failing to empathize with the suffering of people, whom we allow governments to threaten, incarcerate, torture and kill. We also avoid suffering by failing to empathize with the suffering of animals, whom we permit scientists to experiment upon, and slaughterers and trappers to kill and skin. There is no difference, fundamentally, in the ways in which human and nonhuman beings are mistreated and suffer. But where there is acceptance of life's sacred unity and sanctity, there is also no difference in the way we treat our own kind and other living beings. There is no difference because there is no duality between self and other. Thus, other living beings are treated, as St. Francis of Assisi urged, as our brothers and sisters, with the same respect and concern as we would hope for ourselves and wish for our kin.

This is not conditional love; it is unlimited love. Conditional love is a false construct of dualism, blind to the kinship of suffering and the will-to-be that we share with all creatures. Real love is limitless, boundless, and it is from such love that the Golden Rule is extended to all living things and not just to those who belong to one's own family, tribe, class, race, nation, religion or species.

What destroys the vision and defiles the sacred unity and sanctity of life is the antithesis of love—not hatred, but ignorance and fear.[45] Ignorance of the nondualistic or holistic nature of reality, as it is manifested politically, theologically and technologically today, is destroying the created order of the world as we endeavor to control and remake it in our own image for our profit, security and gratification. The final barrier to wholeness is fear—fear of life and death.

The allegory of Adam and Eve, with their loss of innocence and fall from grace, provides every generation with the answer to its existential crises. The allegory begins when Adam and Eve pick fruit from the tree of the knowledge of good and evil. The fruit does not simply represent power and freedom of choice, or freedom without moral responsibility. The fruit also contains the essence of dualistic perception and objectivity (Adam and Eve became aware of their own nakedness and, thus, their differences), and of moralistic thinking (right and wrong). Its flavor is tart with the fear of death that comes with the self-awareness of a finite existence.

The story of Adam and Eve represents the history of the evolution of human consciousness—from the "Golden Age" of innocence in the Garden of Eden before the Fall, to the dualistic, egocentric worldview that all the descendants of Adam and Eve up to today have experienced. Joseph Campbell said that "When man ate of the fruit of the first tree, the tree of knowledge of good and evil, he was expelled from the Garden. The Garden is the place of unity, of nonduality of male and female, good and evil, God and human beings. You eat the duality and you are on the way out. The tree of coming back to the Garden is the tree of immortal life, where you know that I and the Father are one."[46]

Our materialistic civilization, now in a critical condition in which industrialism is disrupting the global climate, reacts in fear and anger as the Tree of Life withers before its eyes. But it is not with the power of knowledge alone that we will ever heal the Tree of Life, the Earth, and ourselves. We need the higher power of love and nondualistic perception that reveals the kingdom of Heaven within ourselves and all of Creation.

One of the most poignant illustrations of the importance of feeling a profound connectedness with Nature comes from Australian aborigine Bill Neidjie: "You can look, but feeling . . . that make you . . . if you feel sore . . . headache, sore body, that mean somebody killing tree or grass. You feel because your body (is) in that tree or earth. Nobody can tell you, you got to feel it yourself."[47]

When we are not open to the world, there can be no wisdom, for wisdom comes not simply from what we learn in books, but from what we feel and learn from open experience. When we are not open to the world, there is no bridge of empathy to others to heal and make us whole. Without this empathetic understanding, all our actions, our instrumental knowledge and our power of dominion over the rest of Creation inevitably cause more harm than good. We then become prisoners of our own bad karma that arises from ignorance and insecurity; when we harm others, or the environment, we ultimately harm ourselves.

It is through empathy that we become connected with the world. Psychologist Rollo May wrote:

The capacity for consciousness of ourselves gives us the ability to see ourselves as others see us and to have empathy with others. It underlies our remarkable capacity to transport ourselves into someone else's parlor, where we will be, in reality, next week, and in imagination, to think and plan how we will act. And it enables us to imagine ourselves in someone else's place, and to ask how we would feel and what we would do if we were this other person. No matter how poorly we use or fail to use or even abuse these capacities, they are rudiments of our ability to begin to love our neighbor, to have ethical sensitivity, to see truth, to create beauty, to devote ourselves to ideals, and to die for them if need be. To fulfill these potentialities is to be a person.[48]

The final barrier that we must all overcome before we can connect and become one with the world of being is fear—fear of being open and therefore vulnerable; and fear of suffering, be it our own, or, when we are open and empathetically connected, of others.

The essence of reverence for life is expressed as compassionate love, respect and humility toward all of Creation. This essence needs to be part of religious practice. Its expression is accompanied by a participatory sense of celebration and joyous revelation in the beauty, innocence and transience of life and of each living moment. And it is through this state of ecstatic participation that the spiritual significance of Nature and reality is revealed. This participatory sense of being within Being brings with it such an openness to the world that it constrains one from harming another because one is so connected that there is no distinction between self and other. To harm another is to harm oneself. To kill another is to kill part of oneself. In this state of being-in-the-world, a person is incapable of deliberately harming any other living creature. It is not a state built upon faith or dogma or laws or reason, but upon that state of fellow-feeling called empathy. The beauty, vitality and wonder of the world are realized, preserved and enhanced when Nature is not desacralized and exploited merely as a resource; when animals are not demeaned and treated merely as commodities; and when the creative process is not controlled and directed to satisfy purely selfish ends—all of which result in much suffering.

The greatest challenge that we face today is to learn to live nonviolently and in harmony; to find and define the work, lifestyles and

consumer habits that do not contribute either directly or indirectly to
the destruction of humanity and the environment, and the holocaust
of the Animal Kingdom. When we lack empathy, we lack security,
and we seek the destructive path of power. When we lack empathy,
we lack the sensitivity and wisdom to use knowledge creatively.
Jeremy Rifkin has said:

> The great challenge that lies before our generation is to recognize
> the path to our own freedom. We will need to understand that
> to renounce power is not to give up. . . . It is to let go. . . . Some
> will wonder loud as to whether an empathetic consciousness can
> succeed in a world still largely dominated by a power-seeking
> mind. They fail to see that the very act of repudiating the old
> consciousness and embracing the new is the victory, the most
> impressive victory one could ever hope to claim. . . . If one believes
> in their heart and soul that their own security resides not in control
> but in vulnerability, not in domination but in participation, then
> by what possible threat could they be made a victim?[49]

This radical shift from power to empathy is as relevant to society and
industry as it is to our own personal lives. Rifkin goes on to tell us
that:

> Controlling technologies and empathetic technologies manifest
> two very different ideas about the nature of security. With con-
> trolling technologies, the emphasis is on maximizing present op-
> portunities. With empathetic technologies the emphasis is on
> maximizing future possibilities. With controlling technologies, a
> high premium is placed on optimizing efficiency for the present
> generation. With empathetic technologies, a high premium is
> placed on maintaining an endowment for future generations.[50]

Without empathy, the Golden Rule of treating other sentient
beings as we would like to be treated is simply an unattainable
intellectual ideal that has no meaning in the "real" world of "fallen"
humanity.

The Golden Rule embodies the Christian ideal of pure altruism or
self-giving love (*agape*). In Buddhism and Hinduism it is expressed
as Loving Kindness (*maitri*) and nonviolence (*ahimsa*) toward all

sentient beings. In Taoism, it is recognized as an all-embracing impartiality toward all of Creation. The Golden Rule is the essence of democracy and of limitless rather than conditional love, since it is not conditional upon others to treat us as we would like them to. Indeed, the two related Christian doctrines, love thine enemy and nonviolence as exemplified by the injunction "resist not evil" from the Sermon on the Mount, affirm the unconditional nature of the Golden Rule. Many believe that it is impossible to live by the supreme ethic of this Golden Rule because we have enemies, for example, or because animals cannot reciprocate. Others regard attempting to live by the Golden Rule as too idealistic, unrealistic, irresponsible and even masochistically ascetic. But is extending loving kindness to those sentient beings who are in need, and acting responsibly to help reduce the waste and destruction of natural and beautiful things, harmful to ourselves? It is a mistake to feel that something is lost through such actions; rather, to be able to give of oneself to others is rewarding in itself. Pure altruism, devoid of self interest, is perhaps the only enduring foundation for a community of hope. It necessitates a disengagement from those industries and the economic status quo associated with the desecration of Nature and the cruel exploitation of animals. In sum, the Golden Rule recognizes the right of all living things to freedom and dignity. It is the supreme task for humanity to fulfill itself without denying fulfillment to others, be they human or nonhuman beings.

Attorney-humanitarian Robert F. Welborn writes, "The issue for humankind is not one of selfishness but rather what one includes in oneself. Selfishness is inherent in life. . . . We, the human species, have the power and the potential wisdom and sensitivity to encompass within self all of Nature, all of the elements of this world, animate and inanimate. . . . This means that we become consciously involved with Nature in the story of creation." Welborn sees compassion and reason as vital faculties for this "mutual encompassing: Compassion means passion with. . . . Compassion is the means for spiritual oneness, for the unity of all life and beauty. . . . Reason gives us the understanding that we achieve happiness only with the life and beauty of Nature. It gives us that capacity to preserve and enhance that life and beauty."

The Life and Teachings of St. Francis of Assisi

Reason without feeling and especially without compassion leads to cold, "objective" rationalism. The emotional detachment or disconnectedness of intellectual rationalism is a disease of the times. Consciousness entails more than being rational; it involves feeling and that deeper intuitive wisdom for which instrumental knowledge is no substitute. Without compassion and wisdom, such knowledge becomes linked with power. Its consequences, as history has documented, have been detrimental to humanity both spiritually and ecologically.

To "have communion," or "experience oneness" with another entity, such as a tree or a rock, are terms often used by Nature lovers and Nature mystics. This experiential state is not something out of this world nor is it simply pagan idolatry. Rather it is a feeling of kinship in which the observer and the observed come together. The observer might say, "I am part of the tree or rock and the tree or rock is part of me." This feeling-state may be termed panempathy, which leads to a sacramental attitude toward the natural Creation. It affirms the coinherent nature of reality and divinity that we have termed panentheism. Joseph Campbell writes, "The manifestation of the sacred in a stone or a tree is neither less mysterious nor less noble than its manifestation as a 'god.' The process of sacralizing reality is the same; the *forms* taken by the processes in man's religious consciousness differ."[51]

Religion historian Mircea Eliade concludes: "The sacred tree, the sacred stone are not adored as stone or tree; they are worshipped precisely because they are hierophanies, because they show something that is no longer stone or tree but *sacred*, the *ganz andere* or 'wholly other.' "[52] Hierophanies may be defined as natural entities that reveal more in their being or presence than is evident to the objective eye of the secular humanist.

Joseph Campbell observed, "When the center of the heart is touched, and a sense of compassion awakens with another person or creature, and you realize that you and that other are in some sense creatures of the one life in being, a whole new stage of life in the spirit opens up."[53] In a Christian sense, this awakening, or what Teilhard de Chardin called "Christogenesis," is the heart of compassionate love, expressed in terms of respect and reverence for all life.[54] Humanity is now entering this new stage of life in the spirit. And like birth itself, it is a transition filled with both apprehension and joyful expectations. But unlike birth it also entails death—death of the notion of an autonomous mortal self or ego. As Joseph Campbell concludes, "This opening of the heart to the world is what is symbolized mythologically as the virgin birth."[55] Its existential representation is Christ crucified. In the image of Christ's gift of redemption, we receive the stigmata of the Earth crucified, in joy and pain, binding heaven and Earth with the sweet tears of Creation, through birth, death and eternal transformation.

As each creature is a manifestation of Creation, each creature is a mask of God, a *hierophany* and a spirit power to those who, on the journey of self-discovery, recognize the kinship of alien eyes and the great mystery behind, within and beyond them. That is why St. Francis loved his "little brethren," the wolf, the lamb, and Brother Sun and Sister Moon, and by way of them, felt and praised the Creator. Joseph Campbell concludes, "To experience this sense of compassion, accord, or even identity with another, or with some ego-transcending principle that has become lodged in your mind as a good to be revered and served, is the beginning, once and for all, of the properly religious way of life and experience."[56]

Such was the vision of St. Francis of Assisi. From his way of perceiving the world as sacred, the unity of all life is realized. This is the key to world peace and to a planetary democracy which assures the integrity of Creation for future generations of humankind and animalkind alike.

In closing, I quote the Reverend Basil Wrighton who emphasizes that the attitude of St. Francis toward creatures and Creation "was a breath of fresh air even for the thirteenth century, and it does not seem to have been duly appreciated by Christians even yet. Theologians in particular have been wary of taking the animals to their hearts, preferring like mere peripatetics to stress the total superiority of *homo sapiens*. Perhaps it has been reserved to this age of apocalyptic terrors to find the solution of its crisis in a return to what has been aptly called the 'cosmic piety' of the *poverello* of Assisi."[57]

Panentheism: Animals, Nature and the God Within

Wakan Tanka breathed life and motion
into all things, both visible and invisible.
He was over all, through all, and in all,
and great as was the sun, and good as was
the earth, the greatness and goodness
of the Big Holy were not surpassed.
The Lakota could look at nothing without
at the same time looking at Wakan Tanka,
and he could not, if he wished, evade His presence,
for it pervaded all things and filled all space.
—Luther Standing Bear

T HE CIRCLE IS A SACRED SYMBOL
to many cultures, representing the unity of Creation and the absence
or "voidness" of independent origination. The sacred circle to the

Sioux is called the Medicine Wheel; it is the wheel of change and eternal life to the Tibetan Buddhists, and the Tao of Taoism. The cross of Christianity, like the star of Judaism and yantra mandala of Tantra, centers us, symbolizing our place in the sacred circle. It is central for all existences because there is no hierarchy; all existences are of the same origin and essence—"all return unto one place."

This idea is analogous to St. Francis of Assisi's sacramentalist view that through Nature one can realize God, for all is in the One. This perception is properly called *panentheism—pan* (all) *en-theos* (in God). It is the synthesis of pantheism (a God or gods in all) and transcendental monotheism (one God outside and above all). Panentheism recognizes the transcendent and coinherent (immanent and all-containing) qualities of the Universal Absolute. Theologian Chris Chapple in his book *Nonviolence to Animals, Earth and Self in Asian Traditions* notes that the term panenthesism "was first used by K. F. C. Krause in the nineteenth century, and has recently been reintroduced by process theologians. It emphasizes the presence of deity within each of its manifestations. Panentheism suggests that the world is a dynamic expression of God's creation."[1]

Panentheism is the intuitive and visionary construct arising from what philosophers refer to as "process theology," a biospiritual and bioethical school of thought very much in vogue today. This interest, I believe, reflects a search for unity and deeper meaning that many people feel is now vital for our planetary well-being, for the integrity of Creation, and future of all life on Earth.

Secular-Scientific Materialism

Aside from transcendental monotheism's dismissal of panentheism as a pagan idolatry of natural "objects," we have the reaction of scientific materialism to consider too. Scientific materialism, as Professor Haught has written, is a philosophy that resolves the animate into the inanimate.[2] To this philosophy of the technocracy, any form of theism is dismissed as unverifiable, unquantifiable and thus nonexistent: sheer mysticism. Panentheism is obviously the least palatable of these: a transcendent God is much easier to deal with for those who desacralize and exploit the Creation. To praise and glorify God through or by way of Nature, as St. Francis of Assisi taught, is to have a reverence for Creation that is not even dreamed of in the philosophy of secular materialism. There is reverence only for intellectualism, scientific facts and material inventions. As a consequence of the extreme anthropocentrism of scientific materialism and secular humanism, humans become increasingly separated from both Nature and divinity. In this profane world, only that which is scientifically quantifiable and verifiable is judged and valued as truth. The value of ethical sensibility and empathetic sensitivity is discounted by the overriding will-to-power and control through instrumental knowledge and technological invention.

This state of mind results in life out of balance with Nature, a condition the Hopi call *Koyaanisqatsi*, the antithesis of *Lomakatsi*, life in balance. Sioux Buck Ghost Horse has written: "Humankind seeks Utopia, but strives for it through destruction of the Balance of the Earth. When the spiritual level of humankind reaches the level of balance held by nature then we will have the balance needed to regain Utopia which we once called Eden and Earth People call the Earth Mother."[3]

The Broken Circle

The Circle of Life, its wholeness, beauty and integrity, have been broken since the Fall of humankind. This is due to a kind of mental aberration that leads us to see ourselves and our own individual egos as separate from the whole. To feel outside the Circle of Life and to act egotistically in creating our own circle are to destroy the Circle, its wholeness, beauty and integrity. This is the deeper meaning of the Christian concept of Original Sin, which in Buddhism and Hinduism is ignorance of the true nature of the Self and of the fundamental unity and nonduality of existence.

From the Hindu and Tantric perspectives, desire, hatred and ignorance arise from the illusion in our minds that, as Professor David Lorimer puts it:

each ego is separate and different from all other egos; the apparent isolation of the self is taken as an absolute. This view has emotional, ethical and intellectual consequences. Emotionally the self feels alienated, unconnected, perhaps even insignificant and meaningless; this alienation is expressed in atheism. . . . The ethical and spiritual result of this ego-isolation is fragmentation, violence, and destructiveness: a failure to enter into harmony with the universe.[4]

Once outside this circle, Nature and animals are seen as inferior; hence, ours to exploit. Scientific materialism, secular humanism and transcendental monotheism all affirm this view that ultimately desacralizes or "disgods" the biosphere and cosmos by placing divinity above and humanity outside the Sacred Hoop or Circle of Life. And as traditional peoples insist, this is the cause of much disease, suffering and destruction.

It is ironic that in making God transcendent rather than coinherent, this perversion of the Judeo-Christian tradition has also made humans transcendent. It is then believed that Nature and animals are inferior and are intended primarily for our use. The notion of human superiority may be one way of coping with the fear of death and sense of separation from the Circle of Life that this perception of reality and our place in the world engenders.

Panentheism, like process theology, offers to reconcile these illusory dualities of self and other, God and Nature, spirit and matter. But a major obstacle to its acceptance is that it is often confused with various forms of pantheism and more primitive pagan polytheistic and animistic traditions. It is surely Aristotelian and Cartesian dualistic thinking, specifically the separation of body and soul and matter and spirit so evident in some Christian and other theologies and philosophies, that underlies the rejection of panentheism. The nondualistic philosophy of panentheism, which is eminently Christian, recognizes the unity of body and soul and matter and spirit, because God is omnipresent and coinherent—not simply transcendent.

When divinity is transcendent only, another duality is created between the Creator and all that is created. This serves the secular humanist well, since it allows for the establishment of a hierarchy with the human as the superior being on Earth, made in the "image of God." And in banishing divinity from the world, Nature and the rest of Creation become material resources for humans

---

to exploit for their own exclusive ends without a twinge of conscience. This anthropocentric rather than Creation-centered or theocentric worldview is part of mainstream Christianity today. However, as we have noted, more and more philosophers and theologians are beginning to question this view, since it does not accord with the basic scriptures of Christianity—or of any other major world religion.

Philosopher Michael E. Zimmerman, for example, observes that "A Christian panentheism offers a different interpretation of the meaning of Jesus Christ than do more traditional anthropocentric views. For example, the doctrine of Christ's Incarnation can be interpreted as meaning that the divine is present in creation, not removed from it, and that God is present in *all* creation, not just in human beings."[5]

Panentheism, Animal Rights and Deep Ecology

A spiritual connection between "deep" ecology (ecosophy) and animal rights philosophy is slowly emerging. This is evident, on the one hand, in the interest shown by deep ecologists in Spinoza's philosophy, which is a form of panentheism.[6] The Dutch philosopher Baruch Spinoza held that God is Being, from which all being arises and into which it subsides. Yet while he saw the unity of Nature and God, Nature and Substance, he felt that animals had no rights and that we can treat them as we choose. And on the other hand, we have Albert Schweitzer's philosophy of reverence for the life of the individual, which entails recognition of the inherent divinity of all living things. Contemporary animal rights philosophers speak of respect for the inherent interests or value of animals, only a small step away from Schweitzer's reverence for their inherent nature, which he called their will-to-be or soul.

"Deep" ecology and animal rights philosophy may thus rise and converge to embrace a panentheistic spirituality, the one fostering reverence for the whole—Spinoza's view of God in Nature and Nature in God—and the other a reverence for all living beings, which, as God's Creations, contain a spark of divinity as living souls. (The word *animal* is derived from the root word *anima*, meaning soul.)

Theologically and spiritually, panentheism and monotheism are not mutually exclusive but rather represent complementary aspects of religious life. The pantheism that regards the totality of Nature as being God—that God is swallowed up in the unity of all—is quite distinct from monistic panentheism as expounded by Spinoza, in which God is conceptualized as the all-inclusive essence or substance, the First Cause of the universe, with many attributes, including intelligence, that can be perceived in Nature's lawful harmony. This form of panentheism is based on "the doctrine that God includes the world as a part, though not the whole, of his being."[7] The *Encyclopaedia Britannica* emphasizes the personal and political significance of panentheism:

> Panentheism is then a middle way between the denial of individual freedom and creativity characterizing many of the varieties of pantheism and the remoteness of the divine characterizing Classical Theism. Its support for the ideal of human freedom provides grounds for a positive appreciation of temporal process, while removing some of the ethical paradoxes confronting deterministic views. *It supports the sacramental value of reverence for life.* At the same time the theme of participation with the divine leads naturally to self-fulfillment as the goal of life. Many pantheistic and theistic alternatives claim the same advantages, but their natural tendency toward absoluteness may make justification of these claims in some cases difficult and, in others, some argue, quite impossible. It is for this reason that a significant number of contemporary philosophers of religion have turned to panentheism as a corrective to the partiality of the other competing views (italics mine).[8]

Panentheism as reverence for the sacredness of Earth and for the inherent divinity of animals and all living beings is not pagan, animistic idolatry. It is a view shared by many religions: in Hinduism in the proclamation, "We bow to all beings with great reverence in the thought and knowledge that God enters into them through fractioning Himself as living creatures" (*Bhagavad Gita*); and in Christianity when St. Paul speaks of "one God who is Father of all, over all, through all and within all" (Eph. 4:6). Jesus said, "Believe me that I am in the Father and the Father in me." (John 14:10) Gregory of

Nazianzus proclaimed that "Christ exists in all things that are," and Hildegard of Bingen wrote, "It is God whom human beings know in every creature." The humane and "deep" ecology movements, along with animal rights philosophy, are transformed into a religion when there is devotion or reverence. The devotional inspiration of recognizing the sacredness of the world, of Nature and all living things leads us to virtue and to a morality of compassion that gives equal and fair consideration to all of Creation, as philosopher Michael Zimmerman observes:

> Certain versions of mystical Christianity, for example, hold that nondualistic experience reveals the truth of the doctrine of *panentheism*. Panentheism, seeking to reconcile divine transcendence with divine immanence, maintains that God is present in but not identical with creation. Divine awareness gives rise to creatures and in some measure participates in the life of those creatures, but is not wholly identical with them. Evolutionary panentheists, whose doctrines resemble those of Hegel, claim that God is present in and continues to develop through the evolving existence of creatures, thereby overcoming the otherworldliness of traditional Christianity.

> Fortunately, the Judeo-Christian tradition can be interpreted panentheistically, in such a way that the tradition calls for humans to do God's will "on Earth as it is in Heaven." For panentheism, obeying the "will of God" on Earth means accepting and respecting all beings as the fruit of God's creative activity.[9]

The sacramentalist or panentheistic view of divinity (or "Christ-reality") in all things is eloquently expressed by Benedictine Brother David Steindl-Rast in an interview with the group Buddhists Concerned for Animals:

> Brother David, I noticed that part of your everyday practice consists of paying great attention to the little critters crawling, flying, and swimming around and helping them when they are in trouble. You also bow when you see a dead animal lying on the highway. What, as a Christian monk, is the basis of your sympathy towards our fellow earthlings?

> *Brother David*: In Christian terminology we would say that you bow to the Cosmic Christ. Everything is created in Him

and through Him and towards Him. That means that we can see Christreality in everything and worship Christ in everything that lives.

You see, we Christians speak of Jesus as the Christ. That means we have come to recognize divine life in the kind of human life Jesus lived. But this life is not limited to Jesus. We find its focal point in him. That makes us Christians. But this Christlife was there before Jesus and continues after his death. He is still very much alive. In the light of Jesus we become aware of the divine light within ourselves, within all other human beings, and indeed in all beings in the whole universe. This is what we mean by the Cosmic Christ.

Ever since the 4th century, we have in Christian iconography, the image of the *Panto creator:* Christ enthroned in glory, the Cosmic Christ visualized. His throne is surrounded by what the Book of Revelation calls "four living beings," continually giving glory and honor and thanks to God. These six winged mythical creatures resemble a lion, a bull, a human, and a soaring eagle. They represent all the awe-inspiring, powerful, intelligent, and swift cosmic forces. It is worth noticing that only one of them has a human face. In God's royal entourage we humans take our place among all other creatures.[10]

The Trappist monk Thomas Merton expressed a similar perception: "We are living in a world that is absolutely transparent and God is shining through it all the time. God manifests Himself everywhere, in everything—in people and in things and in nature and in events. . . . The only thing is we don't see it. . . . I have no program for this seeing. It is only given. But the gate of heaven is everywhere."

From Pantheism and Classical Theism to Panentheism

Unfortunately, belief in an omnipresent divinity in all things has been regarded as pagan and heretical by the classical theism of Christian-patriarchal monotheism.[11, 12] It should not be forgotten that the monk Giordano Bruno and thousands of heretics of like belief were burned at the stake during the Inquisition in the late sixteenth century for teaching that all existence is interrelated, that the microcosm of Earth is part of a spiritual macrocosm of cosmic harmony. In this, Bruno was harkening back to a much older, classical belief system. As Arnold Toynbee observes:

> In popular prechristian Greek religion, divinity was inherent in all natural phenomena, including those that man had tamed and domesticated. Divinity was present in springs and rivers and the sea; in trees, both the wild oak and the cultivated olive-tree; in corn and vines; in mountains; in earthquakes and lightning and thunder. The godhead was diffused throughout the phenomena. It was plural, not singular; a pantheon, not a unique almighty super-human person. Then the Graeco-Roman world was converted to Christianity, the divinity was drained out of nature and was concentrated in one unique transcendent God. "Pan is dead."[13]

The Greeks revered Pan as the guardian spirit of Nature. The Greek philosopher Pythagoras wrote, "The world itself has a soul, the *anima mundi*." Many Native American religious traditions like the Hopi and Sioux worshipped the Great Spirit, and like the pre-Christian Greeks and the Egyptians with their pantheon of animal-headed transmorphic human-bodied gods, believed that animals and plants were ensouled by the breath of the Creator who also created and ensouled the human animal.

The Hopi and Sioux also considered nature sacred, ensouled as the Mother-Provider: Sun was the father, the male, primary material manifestation of divinity. A prayer of Sioux leader Black Elk includes the following visionary passage:

> We should understand well that all things are the works of the Great Spirit. We should know that He is within all things: the trees, the grasses, the rivers, the mountains, and all the four-legged animals, and the winged peoples; and even more important, we should understand that He is also above all these things and peoples. When we do understand all this deeply in our hearts, then we will fear, and love, and know the Great Spirit, and then we will be and act and live as He intends.[14]

Early Christianity likewise revered Nature and all creatures, exemplified as we have seen by the teachings and songs of St. Francis of

Assisi, who saw animals as brethren.[15] A sensory, esthetic theology arose in the thirteenth century, as one scholar, St. Bonaventure, proposed that the mind apprehends the likeness of a perceived object just as the Creator's likeness was generated in Christ: "the manifold wisdom of God, which is clearly revealed in the Sacred Scripture, lies hidden in all knowledge and in all nature. . . . It is likewise evident how wide is the luminous way and how in everything which is perceived or known, God himself lies hidden within."[16] In sum, we can know and love God *in* Nature and *through* Nature.

Yet this Franciscan sacramental panentheistic view was opposed by the Lollards and other reformists later in the Middle Ages because of their distrust of the "flesh and beastly things," thus setting up a division between spirit and matter, body and soul. Yet the Word was made flesh in the incarnation of Christ. Reverence for the things of Nature—God's Creations—was not pagan idolatry, though contrary to their pre-Cartesian views, the Lollards refused to accept the decision of the Second Council of Nicea which had declared centuries earlier "that the honor paid an image is passed on to its archetype."

The beginnings of the "death of Nature" may be traced back to this time in European history, which helped lay the foundations of the Industrial Revolution and the rape of Nature. In order to further political goals and unify diverse cultures and communities under one Church and State authority, pantheism, along with belief in reincarnation, animism and Nature worship (as witchcraft), became anathema, since they were contrary to the authoritarian hierarchy of a patriarchal monotheistic theocracy. However, monotheism is not incompatible with panentheism, because monists accept that all is created within God by God; the One in all. This is comparable to Plotinus' Neoplatonic view of a transcendent and absolute divinity, an intermediate *nous* (mind or realm of ideas) and a world soul which contains and animates the world, within which divinity is immanent and omnipresent.

If divinely revealed truth is the basis of all religion, then panentheism can claim religious authority from what Nature reveals to us emotionally, intuitively, intellectually and ethically about the nature of God the Creator. Henry and Dana Lee Thomas conclude, "The stars, the planets, the trees, the flowers, the oceans, the mountains, the clouds—these are the *body* of God. The spirit that gives them shape and color and motion and beauty is the *mind* of God. Every human body is part of God's body and every human mind is part of God's mind."[17] Belief in the soul or Self as part of or an atomistic (Atman) spark of omnipresent divinity (Brahman) is the basis of Eastern panentheism. This in turn leads to panpsychism in which the soul or self is regarded as the center of conscious awareness. The Sioux Lame Deer calls this the "power" in all natural entities.[18]

Professor J. Baird Callicott observes, "The Indian attitude, as represented by Lame Deer, apparently was based upon the consideration that since human beings have a physical body and an associated consciousness (conceptually hypostatized or reified as 'spirit'), all other bodily things, animals, plants, and, yes, even stones, were also similar in this respect."[19] Persian Sufi Jami (circa 1250) expresses this panentheistic vision as follows:

> The Unique Substance viewed as absolute . . . is the Real. On the other hand, viewed in this aspect of multiplicity and plurality, under which He displays himself when clothed with phenomena, He is the whole created universe. Therefore, the universe is the outward visible expression of the Real, and the Real is the inner unseen reality of the Universe. The Universe before it was evolved to outward view was identical with the Real, and the Real after this evolution is identical with the Universe.[20]

This is the form of monistic panentheism that Spinoza subsequently elaborated, his view being that there is no discrepancy between mind and body, or between ideas and the physical universe. The two are merely different aspects of a single substance that he called alternately Nature and God. Nature is not the agency or product of a supernatural God; God is Nature in its fullness. The universe, a single substance, is capable of an infinity of attributes but knowable to us through two of them: physical "extension" and thought—the material expression and organized, lawful intelligence of Nature.

Christianity versus Pantheism

If we accept that religion is a major determinant of morality, then it would be prudent to examine the role that religion plays in influencing peoples' attitudes toward and treatment of animals and Nature. Harold W. Wood, Jr. observes:

In conventional American religion, things like recycling, energy conservation, not wearing furs, even political action to preserve wilderness or wildlife, ordinarily have no relevance to religion. However, such behavioral modifications from a pantheist perspective can be justified as a religious undertaking. . . . The identification of sacredness in the earth demands reverent behavior. In turn, such behavior necessitates a personal commitment toward living in greater harmony with the biosphere.[21]

Theologian Francis A. Schaeffer dismisses all forms of pantheism. He gives many reasons for his criticism. A detailed consideration of these reasons is warranted, since Schaeffer's views are widely held by many Christians today. First, since he believes in a personal God, all that is of "God's creation" is "external to Himself." Thus, he argues that in pantheism, "One simply does not have a *creation*, but only an extension of God's essence, . . ."[22] so the term "God's creation" has no real place in pantheistic thinking. I would argue, on the contrary, that both pantheism and panentheism recognize that all of God's Creation is imbued with the essence of the Creator.

Schaeffer also opposes pantheism because he believes that "In true pantheism, unity has meaning, but the particulars have no meaning, including the particular of man."[23] This conclusion is illogical, since pantheism recognizes the sacredness of the whole and the sanctity of the individual ("the particulars"). He adds, "Pantheism gives you an answer for unity, but it gives no meaning to the diversity."[24] To a dualistic thinker like Schaeffer, unity and diversity, oneness and individuality are inimical. He fails to accept that pantheism reconciles the dialectic between unity and individuality, that it offers a nondualistic worldview that does not separate God from Nature, human from nonhuman, or the Creator from the created.

Schaeffer's form of Christianity is, like reductionistic scientific materialism, atomistic rather than holistic, since it breaks up the essential unity of Creator and Creation: God is transcendent only and not also coinherent with all things. He takes this hierarchical position, I believe, to preserve what he calls the dignity of divinity and of human individuality, since he contends that "a pantheistic stand always brings man to an impersonal and low place rather than elevating him." He concludes, "Those who propose the pantheistic answer [to improving humankind's attitude toward and treatment of animals and nature] ignore this fact—that far from raising nature to man's height, pantheism must push man and nature down into a bog. Without categories, there is eventually no reason to distinguish bad from good nature. Pantheism leaves us with the Marquis de Sade's dictum, 'What is, is right, in morals, and man becomes no more than the grass.' "[25]

To look for categories within the unified field of being means that classes and hierarchies are fabricated. This is the grand illusion of intellectual reductionism, based on contorted dualistic thinking tinged with hubris. Attempting to further discredit the philosophy of panentheism, Schaeffer reveals his own prejudices by ridiculing the panentheistic reverence for all life in Hinduism, which he blames for India's economic problems, since "rats and cows are allowed to eat up food that man needs. Instead of man being raised, in reality he is lowered. The rats and cows are finally given preference to man himself, and man begins to disappear into the woodwork in economics as well as in the area of personality and love."[26]

It is extraordinary that Schaeffer should believe that panentheism "must push man and nature down into a bog" and say nothing about the fact that some Christian schools do that by regarding Nature and animals as "fallen" as humans themselves. Endeavoring to further discredit the spiritual philosophy of pantheism, Schaeffer contends that it has no answer to the destructive side of Nature, and that from the pantheists' perspective, it would be wrong to fight the plague, since then they would be fighting God. Yet to fight to relieve suffering by taking appropriate remedial and preventive action would be a humanitarian act. Thus, pantheism, as he sees it, has no real answers to the problems that face humanity.

But according to the renowned German zoologist Ernst Haeckel:

> Pantheism teaches that God and the world are one. The idea of God is identical with that of nature or substance. This pantheistic view is sharply opposed in principle to all possible forms of theism, although there have been many attempts made from both sides to bridge over the deep chasm that separates the two. There is always this fundamental contradiction between them, that in theism God

is opposed to nature as an *extramundane* being, as creating and sustaining the world, and acting upon it from without, while in pantheism God, as an *intramundane* being, is everywhere identical with nature itself, and is operative *within* the world as "force" or "energy." The latter view alone is compatible with our supreme law—the law of substance. It follows necessarily that pantheism is the world-system of the modern scientist. There are, it is true, still a few men of science who contest this, and think it possible to reconcile the old theistic theory of human nature with the pantheistic truth of the law of substance. All these efforts rest on confusion or sophistry—when they are honest.

The truth of pantheism lies in its destruction of the dualist antithesis of God and the world, in its recognition that the world exists in virtue of its own inherent forces. The maxim of the pantheist is "God and the world are one." . . . The atheistic scientist who devotes his strength and his life to the search for the truth, is freely credited with all that is evil; the theistic church-goer, who thoughtlessly follows the empty ceremonies of Catholic worship, is at once assumed to be a good citizen, even if there be no meaning whatever in his faith and his morality be deplorable. This error will only be destroyed when, in the twentieth century, the prevalent superstition gives place to rational knowledge and to a monistic conception of the unity of God and the world.[27]

Surely the human-centered worldview of Schaeffer's species of Christianity has done more harm than good to humankind and to the natural world. In his widely circulated essay on this issue, Lynn White, Jr., states:

Christianity in absolute contrast to ancient paganism . . . not only established a dualism of man and nature but also insisted that it is God's will that man exploit nature for his proper ends. . . . In antiquity every tree, every spring, every stream, every hill had its own genius loci, its guardian spirit. . . . By destroying pagan animism, Christianity made it possible to exploit nature in a mood of indifference to the feeling of natural objects.[28]

While Schaeffer concedes that humans, animals and Nature are all part of the same Creation, he contends that all things are equally created by God and are thus equal in sharing the same origin. But for him, humans are superior over all else since only we were created in God's image. Thus, he reasons, "I am made in the image of God; my integration point is upward, not downward; it is not turned back upon creation. Yet at the same time I am united to it because nature and man are both created by God."[29] In pantheism and panentheism, there is no separation and no hierarchy between divinity, humanity, animality and Nature. Initially, Schaeffer agrees that there is no separation; then he says there is because of the quantitative difference between humans and other animals. This latter widely held anthropocentric view is termed *speciesism* by animal rights philosophers. Schaeffer further states, "Man's relationship is upward rather than downward," and then implies that Albert Schweitzer was in some way demeaning himself when he *related himself to the hippopotamus coming through the bush, because Schweitzer had no sufficient relationship upward"* (italics mine).[30] Christians who believe as Schaeffer does reject the view that there is no distinction—or only a qualitative distinction—between animals and other things; and they embrace the view that man is totally separated from all other things. However, Schaeffer does acknowledge that since we and all living things are part of God's Creation, we should respect the things God has made. But this ethic of respect becomes tenuous when we humans believe we are the only beings created in God's image, setting ourselves above the rest of Creation as we begin to play making over the things of Nature for ourselves. And the more tenuous this respect becomes, the more we commit the cardinal sin of assuming dominion over God.

Schaeffer contends that "The man who believes things are there only by chance cannot give things a real value. But for the Christian, the value of a thing is not in itself autonomously, but because God made it. It deserves this respect as something which was created by God, as man himself has been created by God."[31] While this all sounds very reasonable, the notion that animals and other things of Creation have no autonomous or inherent value but exist only as objects of God's Creation can lead to patronage. We then "respectfully" exploit animals and transform Nature into an industrial resource. And when this ethic is linked with the utilitarian Protestant work ethic, the equality of the origin of humans, nonhumans and Nature can be twisted into accepting the equal exploitation of humans as labor, Nature as resource and animals as labor, food, etc.

Schaeffer overlooks these weaknesses in his theology and looks to Christianity to heal the divisions between God, humans and Nature. This is accomplished, he contends, by recognizing that we and all other living things are part of the same Creation. This is all well and good, provided this view can wean humanity from the notion that Nature is property and that the land and all who dwell on it—animals both wild and domestic—can be owned and even patented like commodities and inventions. Schaeffer rightly emphasizes, "When we have dominion over nature, *it is not ours either.* It belongs to God, and we are to exercise our dominion over these things not as though entitled to exploit them, but as things borrowed or held in trust, which we are to use realizing that they are not ours intrinsically. Man's dominion is under God's dominion and under God's domain."[32] This in no way contradicts the panentheist's worldview. Neither does Schaeffer's reference to the Fall, when we began to exercise our God-given dominion wrongly.

Schaeffer insists that Christians are called upon to exhibit their dominion rightly, "treating the thing as having value in itself, exercising dominion without being destructive. The church should always have taught and done this, but she has generally failed to do so, and we need to confess our failure."[33] This failure, I believe, is due in part to the way in which the hierarchical view espoused by Schaeffer can be conveniently twisted to give religious sanction to selfish and destructive dominion over the rest of God's Creation. And when humanity becomes subordinate to the materialistic values of industrialism and secular humanism, the concept of the equality of people, animals and Nature can be perverted to sanction the subordination and exploitation of animals, Nature and people alike, in the service of industrial technocracy under the guise of progress, evolution and the greater good of society.

Pantheism or Nihilism?

Jesuit psychologist-philosopher James E. Royce dismisses pantheism in two sentences: "Since efficient cause [his term for God's creativity and creative instruments] is always distinct from its effect, there is no question of the soul being God, or a part of God. Creation is the antithesis of pantheism."[34] Yet surely since the "effect" and the "efficient cause" are interrelated through the act of creation, the "effect" mirrors something of the divinity that created it. As a painting by Rembrandt embodies something of the artist himself, so Nature embodies and reveals something to us of the Creator. There can be no reasonable grounds, therefore, to support Royce's notion that Creation is the antithesis of pantheism. That which is created is by way of or through God, just as a genuine Rembrandt masterpiece comes by way of or through Rembrandt's genius and divine inspiration. If Royce's reductionistic argument is to be believed, then we must assume that there is no indentification possible between the Creator and that which is created, since the "efficient cause is always distinct from its effect." Thus there can be no Rembrandts for us to cherish (only art as art) and no basis for any apperception of divinity in God's Creations.

Some theologians and others contend that it is wrong to say that God includes the world as part of God's being, because the First Cause cannot be a part of its own effect. Such dualistic thinking fails to recognize that cause and effect are one. From a nondualistic perspective, Creator and Creation are one, part of the same process of being and becoming, where divinity is both transcendent in the Absolute, and immanent and coinherent. As Alexander Pope put it, "All are but parts of one stupendous whole, whose body Nature is, and God the soul."

A conceptual and thus perceptual separation of Creator and Creation, like the duality of mind and body and matter and spirit, is needed in order to dismiss both pantheism and panentheism, which Royce, adhering to Cartesian, if not Catholic orthodoxy, endeavors to justify. The antithesis of Creation is nihilism or destruction, not pantheism. And the antithesis of pantheism is the resultant materialism of transcendental monotheism that gives only humans, and not animals, immortal souls, and "disgods" Creation by confining spirituality to the human soul and a God above.

Such an imperialistic worldview arises from the linear, hierarchical thinking associated with patriarchy and notions of superiority, power, order, etc. Embraced by many religious fundamentalists, it leads ultimately to spiritual fascism. This worldview is clearly dualistic and thus neither unifying, whole nor holy. Hence, the difficulty of organized religion literally to overcome itself, since its very structure and *modus operandi*, as Matthew Fox so eloquently describes, is a hierarchical ladder of power, rather than a vibrant, egalitarian circle of respect and love for all life.(35)

In sum, regardless of the path taken, be it pantheistic, vitalistic or Christian, the differences between them amount to nothing when they converge upon the same ethic of "treating the thing as having value in itself." As G. K. Chesterton once quipped, "There's nothing wrong with Christianity, except that no one has ever really tried it."

To have reverence for all of Creation is, in the final analysis, enlightened self-interest. If we want happiness and fulfillment for ourselves, then the best way is to dedicate ourselves to helping others achieve happiness and fulfillment. We may reach this point via a variety of paths: as Teilhard de Chardin said, all paths that rise, converge. The Christian path of Francis Schaeffer leads ultimately to the same point as does panentheism. His path, as I have pointed out, has certain junctions that can lead one astray. But unlike Schaeffer, I acknowledge that Christianity is not the only path, nor is it the most perfect and certain. The imperfections and uncertainty lie not in any of these paths, but in ourselves.

Esthetics and Affection

For Schaeffer and many thinkers of like vein, esthetic sensitivity is an important subjective human quality that can help us respect and preserve the natural beauty of the world. The beauty of Nature will be preserved because it is believed that esthetic sensitivity will help us exercise our power of dominion properly. But the weakness here is in the fact that fashions, like the perception of what is beautiful, change; and children not raised to appreciate and enjoy animals and Nature are often lacking in esthetic sensitivity toward such things in adulthood. The narcissistic human is likely to fall in love with its own creations, which are perceived as being beautiful, even though they may be detrimental to Nature and defile or destroy that which is truly beautiful. In a profane world there is reverence only for the material things of human creation.

Yi-Fu Tuan reveals how tenuous esthetics can be in ensuring that natural things will be treated with respect.[36] The creation of unnatural landscapes (formal gardens, etc.), deformed trees (bonsai), and animals (bulldogs), though loved by their creators who perceive them as fashionable objects of beauty, are, in the final analysis, unnatural products of a selfish dominion that has warped esthetic values and sense of beauty.

Other Panentheistic Intuitions

The Reverend Dr. John Robinson in *Honest to God* states:

God has been pictured as a super-Self, deciding to act, intervene or send this, that or the other, including his own "Son." As anthropomorphic myth, this is easy on the human imagination and, of course, those who use this language are readily prepared to admit the "as if." But the projection it employs has the effect of locating the action of God as a Being outside, behind or between the processes of nature and history. It gives men today little help towards seeing him as the inside of these processes . . . Somehow we must find a projection which enables us to represent the divine initiative as in the processes of nature rather than as acting on them from without, as exercised through the events of secular history rather than in some sacred super-history.[37]

As the late Swami Muktananda stated, "God is in the forest, God is in the mind, God is in ourselves, we ourselves are in God."

In the apocryphal Gospel of Eve a voice of thunder proclaims, "I am thou and thou are I; and wheresoever thou mayest be I am there. In all am I scattered, and whensoever thou willest, thou gatherest Me; and gathering Me, thou gatherest Thyself."[38]

Akhnaton, the fourteenth century B.C. pharaoh, was apparently unique among the rulers of Egypt in that he discerned "the universal presence of God in nature, a mystic conviction of the recognition of that presence in all creatures," according to the historian J. H. Breasted.[39]

According to Joseph Needham, the ancient Chinese concept of the cosmos is a self-contained, self-organizing organism. He writes: "The harmonious cooperation of all beings arose, not from the orders of a superior authority external to themselves, but from the fact that they were all parts in a hierarchy of wholes forming a cosmic pattern, and what they obeyed were the internal dictates of their own natures."[40] Hence, in Taoism, the Way of Nature is the law of harmony, and this way of right conduct is believed to be inherent in all people. The innateness of democracy and the inherent goodness in humanity is thus recognized.

However, as John Weir Perry points out, democracy is an unattainable ideal until love and brotherhood, personal piety, and moral responsibility arise from *within* the individual: democracy cannot be imposed from without.[41] And just as wisdom is impotent without love, so any social order that is not consonant with ecological order ultimately becomes impotent. The early Chinese philosophers realized this, the essence of democracy being the Way of Nature we humans should follow by recognizing our kinship with all Creation as well as our kingship over the Earth's Creation.

This cosmology—not unlike the modern process theology of Alfred North Whitehead, especially with respect to obeying the internal dictates of one's own nature—is very similar to the traditional Native American concept of "following one's original instructions," what in animals we might call instinct and in humans inborn moral sensibility.

The Confucian scholar Mencius was one of the first to recognize the macrocosm within the microcosm stating, "The myriad things (the whole universe) are complete within us." Being aware of how complete within ourselves we are leads to liberation or self-transcendence. Hence, the relevance of Taoist concepts of *wu-wei* (nonstriving) and *wu-yu* (nonattachment or desirelessness): The self-realization of completeness within ourselves leads to a state of balance or equipoise characterized by *wu-wei* and *wu-yu*. This sense of cosmic incorporation is surely synonymous with experiencing communion, feeling one's kinship with all of Creation. From this apperception we can better appreciate the Taoist-Confucian axiom that to rule is to serve. Kingship and kinship are thus two sides of the same coin whose currency is the Taoist's law of right relationship. Thus, when the ruler is dwelling in the Tao—according to the Way of Nature—the world takes care of itself in peaceful harmony.

In the ancient Japanese religion of Shintoism, which predates Buddhism, there is the saying, "The awe inspiring Deity manifests Itself in all things; even in a single leaf of a tree or a delicate blade of grass." Lao-Tzu, the founding philosopher of Taoism, proclaimed, "To nourish one's spirit is to return to nature." He wrote:

> If we identify our self with the world,
> Then within our self is the world.
> If we love the world as we love our self,
> Then within our self there is only the world.[42]

Henry Beston, in *The Outermost House*, echoes this same sentiment:

Nature is part of our humanity, and without some awareness and experience of that divine mystery, man ceases to be man. When the Pleiades, and the wind in the grass, are no longer a part of the human spirit, a part of every flesh and bone, man becomes, as it were, a kind of cosmic outlaw, having neither the completeness and integrity of the animal nor the birthright of a true humanity.[43]

Such views are not limited to this civilization in these times:

Life is one, said the Buddha, and the Middle Way to the end of suffering in all its forms is that which leads to the end of the illusion of separation, which enables man to see, as a fact as clear as sunlight, that all mankind, and all other forms in manifestation are one unit, the infinitely variable appearances of an indivisible Whole.[44]

Panentheism has long been a part of the Vedantic theological-philosophical tradition in India, as exemplified in the *Bhagavad Gita* (6:30) as "the perception of the Lord in all things and all things in the Lord." Krishna, in the *Bhagavad Gita*, affirms, "The one, yoked in yoga, viewing alike all beings, discerns the Self in all, and all beings in the Self. When he thus perceived me in everything and everything in me, I shall not be lost to him, nor will he be lost to me."[45]

This same spiritual worldview of a unified field of coinherent divinity can be found in other religious cultures. Rolling Thunder described the Shoshone Indian's religion as:

. . . a natural religion, a religion of nature, and that would indicate to us that the Great Spirit is in all things, all things that have life, that all life is to be respected, and all forms of life should be respected including human life, animal life, plant life—and the entire life force. If people were to adhere to that and eliminate the greed which exists in the world today, there'd be no need for the wars and aggression.[46]

Panempathy

Jay McDaniel describes two forms of panentheism, namely, *emanationist* and *dialogical*.[47] Both types can be envisioned by using the analogy of our relations to and experiences of our bodies. By analogy, the world is God's body. Emanationist panentheism sees the world as a direct expression of God's own being, and Nature's creativity as God's creativity: the world is not other than God. Dialogical panentheism sees the world as having some creative independence from God, thus all in the manifest world is not necessarily a direct expression of God's own being: the world, in part, is other than God even as it is in God.

McDaniel notes that just as the living cells in our bodies have sentience and creativity in their own right, so "from a dialogical perspective worldly creatures are like cells in the body of a divine Psyche. They are other than God even as they are within God." Thus, he reasons, "To say that the world is immanent within God even as other than God is to say that God suffers."[48] This leads us to the concept of *panempathy*, empathy with all sentient life as sympathetic understanding and thus divine knowledge. Panentheism and panempathy are consonant and complimentary, the one fostering a reverence for life and the other compassionate concern and feeling for all sentient life. To be made in the image of God thus implies that we have the capacity to be panempathetic.

Panentheism leads us to acknowledge the subjectivity of all creatures. McDaniel states, "God is 'within' the bodies of embodied creatures, human and nonhuman, experiencing the world from their own spatiotemporal perspectives and, as perfectly empathetic, sharing their psychic states. This means that as we humans watch a starving . . . chick, we are watching God."[49]

Theologian A. R. Peacocke reasons that this leads us to an understanding of God as the "suffering Creator." Peacocke stresses that while Creation is an open-ended, continuous process, God is immanent in this process like Bach is immanent within his fugue. He writes, "God is in all the creative process of his creation," and that God is "everywhere and all the time present and active in them as their agent."[50]

Charles Birch concludes, "The position developed by process theology in its ecological model of creation is that of panentheism or what Charles Hartshorne calls neoclassical theism. . . . Its modern development in the light of science is largely the work of A. N. Whitehead and those process philosophers and theologians who have taken the lead from him."[51] And Hartshorne himself states: "All life contributes to the living one who alone can appreciate life's every nuance. He experiences our experiences and that of all creatures. His feelings are feelings of all feelings."[52]

Relational Panentheism

The panentheistic experience of divine presence is perhaps best described as a deep esthetic and spiritual appreciation of Nature. The synesthetic and empathetic transcendental experience of the nature-mystic (as embodied in the poetry of Lord Byron or Wordsworth, the music of Bach or Vaughan Williams, and the art of Landseer or a vibrant van Gogh) is one of relationship with divine presence: a gift indeed. This relational panentheism is experientially equivalent to Martin Buber's nondualistic realization of divinity in the *relational* monad of I-Thou.

In other words, to experience the sanctity of all our relationships and the coinhering divinity of all our relations is the essence of what I would call "relational panentheism." This relational panentheism is evident in the Jain religion (where it is recognized that we and all ensouled beings are equal) and the Native American or aboriginal teaching that the Earth and all our relatives and relationships are sacred.

It is in the profane anthropocentric realm of secular humanism that the sanctity of our relationship with divinity is defiled, as the sanctity of others' being (especially animal-being) is demeaned and subordinated to permit our conscience-free and thus unfeeling exploitation of others. This attitude is rationalized as being natural, necessary and even God-ordained. In this realm the self and nothing *other* is deified. Yet it is through "otherness," the *ganz andere*, that the absolute is realized as the divine presence that is immanent and manifest as both material existence and relationship. Matthew Fox concurs:

> Healthy mysticism is panentheistic. This means that it is not theistic, which envisions divinity "out there" or even "in there" in a dualistic manner that separates creation from divinity. Panentheism means "all things in God and God in all things." This is the way mystics envision the relationship of world, self and God. Mechtild of Magdeburg, for example, says, "The day of my spiritual awakening was the day I saw and knew I saw all things in God and God in all things." Panentheism melts the dualism of inside and outside—like fish in water and water in the fish, creation is in God and God is in creation. Meister Eckhart says that "ignorant people falsely imagine that God created all things" in such a way that they are outside divinity. For "God is in all things. The more divinity is in things, the more divinity is outside of things." (See 1 John 4:16)[53]

Translated into ethical principles, panentheism embraces the principles of *ahimsa* or nonharming; of ethical consistency in our treatment of others; and obedience to the Golden Rule, which is in turn linked with the belief that all living beings are worthy of equal and fair consideration. Politically, therefore, panentheism is the essence of a kind of democracy that is based on concern and respect for others' well-being. And since this concern includes nonhuman creations and species, it implies humane planetary custodianship.

Panentheism therefore represents the spiritual basis not simply of the "deep" ecology and animal rights movements, but also of the global human community. As yet this potential community of spirit is separated by political, religious and other attitudes. Conflicting and competing factions of the world community can be united through panentheism. By virtue of its ecumenicism and evident presence in the basic scriptures of all the world's religions, aboriginal and preindustrial—Buddhist, Judeo-Christian, etc.—this possibility is not beyond the realm of probability. However, in spite of the unifying environmental crises that mandate international efforts of cooperation, this development is improbable unless the profane materialism of secular humanism is transcended. Panentheism may be the key this awakening.

Conclusion

The spiritual worldview of panthentheism leads naturally to all natural entities being treated with equal respect, since they are as much an integral part of the community of life as we are. J. Callicott states:

> In sum, I have claimed that the typical traditional American Indian attitude was to regard all features of the environment as enspirited. These entities possessed a consciousness, reason, and volition, no less intense and complete than a human being's. The Earth itself, the sky, the winds, rocks, streams, trees, insects, birds, and all other animals therefore had personalities and were thus as fully persons as other human beings . . . We may therefore say that the Indian's social circle, his community, included all the nonhuman natural entities in his locale as well as his fellow clansmen and tribesmen.[54]

In recognizing and respecting the kinship and personhood of all natural creations, ethical conduct toward them was a sacred obligation, a duty based not upon some legal or moral code, but upon a deeply felt and experienced spiritual connectedness. This was the conscious basis for lawful and moral behavior. The metaphysical worldview of the Lakotas is expressed by Lame Deer as follows:

> Nothing is so small and unimportant but it has a spirit given by Wakan Tanka. Tunkan is what you might call a stone god, but he is also a part of the Great Spirit. The gods are separate beings, but they are all united in Wakan Tanka. It is hard to understand—something like the Holy Trinity. You can't explain it except by

going back to the "circles within circles" idea, the spirit splitting itself up into stones, trees, tiny insects even, making them all wakan by his ever presence. And in turn all these myriad of things which makes up the universe flowing back to their source, united in one Grandfather Spirit.[55]

In Ghana, a village society's unique reverence for forest deities protects the local wildlife. This tradition dates back over a century, to a time when witch doctors proclaimed the forest monkeys to be children of the gods. These people bury dead monkeys with as much ceremony and adoration as they do their own family members.

Kenneth Laidler believes that for these villages of the sacred forest, respect for all plants and animals is intimately connected to fear: fear of retribution from the gods if they defile the sacred forest or hunt the animal-children of the gods. He concludes:

> In the secular West it is different. It is unlikely that one person in a thousand would "spare that tree" for fear that the gods, or God, might be angry. Yet in the final analysis our beliefs are irrelevant. For we too are subject to the same natural laws that operate on the forest and the people of Boabeng and Fiema. If we fail to respect our environment, misfortune will fall inexorably upon our heads. Gods or no gods, we must learn that uncontrolled exploitation will lead only to extinction.[56]

Here we find a common thread of enlightened self-interest in the rational attitude toward Nature in the secular West and the more animistic attitude of native people. But we have overcome their fear of retribution by our illusory sense of power and control over Nature through instrumental knowledge and technological inventions. Our hubris and lack of reverence stand in the way of enlightened self-interest. Can we have a reverence for all life without fear or animistic superstition? We can surely elaborate a religious attitude toward Nature founded not simply upon anxiety and fear of retribution, but upon understanding, respect and love. Love of life, of the sanctity of all being, is the one religion that is selfless, universal and complete.

Most religions are in part motivated to help us cope with our existential anxiety, fears of death and of the unknown and unknowable. But in the secular West, science and technology have virtually taken over the anxiety-relieving role of religion. Furthermore, they have taken preeminence over those religious values and biospiritual ethics that not only helped us cope with anxiety, but also guided and constrained our actions with respect for Nature's laws, ecology and divinity and our ultimate dependence upon her. But now science, especially the science of ecology, is bringing us full circle to the realization that we must respect Nature for our own good. Such respect, motivated by the anxiety of our own environmental catastrophes, is a significant step toward a spiritually, as well as scientifically, enlightened consciousness.

The natural world will only be more secure when humanity, collectively, treats all of Creation with the respect and ethical sensibility of panentheism. Quite simply, our conceptual worldview must be changed, a paradigm shift in our entire orientation from selfishness to otherness, to living with respect and reverence for others' lives, human and nonhuman. We must look to our hearts and learn to respond to life responsibly and with love, not with fear or anger or power and control gained through new theories, policies, laws, drugs, technological innovations and military weapons. By living in reverence for the sanctity and dignity of all life, of the God within all that is in God, we may become whole and enjoy a healthful and fulfilling life ourselves. In working toward assuring this for others, we may be more certain in securing it for ourselves.

Reverence for life and the necessity to exploit life for our own well-being are not mutually exclusive. Rather our well-being is dependent upon both. A society that chooses to preserve Nature, to protect endangered species or a wilderness area for esthetic or utilitarian reasons is acting out of self-interest, and is perhaps intellectually more sophisticated than the Ghana forest people who, like children, fear that if they don't preserve Nature, they might be punished. The end result, practically speaking, is the same. But a society that chooses to give Nature and the rights of animals equal and fair consideration, out of love and respect—rather than out of fear of divine retribution or of ecological catastrophe—would be very different. Matthew Fox concludes:

> Over the years I have met many serious spiritual seekers who called themselves atheist. Yet I have come to realize that atheism

is a rejection of theism and most atheists are persons who have never had panentheism or mysticism named for them in a culture where theistic relations to divinity are celebrated at the expense of mystical or panentheistic ones. I do believe that if the only option I was given by which to envision creation's relationship to divinity was theism that I would be atheist too.[57]

It is only in a relationship of love and understanding with Nature that we may exercise our power of dominion creatively. And for many, the existential-experiential philosophy of panentheism may be the key. As the *Bhagavad Gita* states:

When a man sees that the God in himself is the same God in all that is, he hurts not himself by hurting others: then he goes to the highest path.

Communion with Animals, Nature and Divinity

C<small>HIEF</small> L<small>UTHER</small> S<small>TANDING</small> B<small>EAR</small> recognized that the essence of communion is as essential for human development as it is for the foundation of a truly civilized culture. He said, "Man who sat on the ground in his tipi meditating on life and its meaning, accepting the kinship of all creatures, and acknowledging unity with the universe, was infusing into his being the true essence of civilization. And when native man left off this form of development, the humanization was retarded in growth."[1]

Albert Schweitzer echoed this wisdom when he observed, "Let a man begin to think about the mystery of his life and the links which connect him with life that fills the world, and he cannot but bring to bear upon his own life and all other life that comes within his reach the principle of reverence for life."[2] This reverence arises spontaneously once we experience the communion that connects us "with life that fills the world."

In accepting the kinship of all creatures and acknowledging our unity with the universe, we experience communion with all of Creation. In this state of being-in-the-world we become fully human and civilized. Since the unity of the universe implies that everything is in communion with everything else, humanity and civilization cannot properly exist separate from the rest of Creation.

Communion with animals entails empathetic identification and objective understanding. In other words, the feelings of animals are appreciated, and their behavior and ecology or natural history are known. Granted, communion was much easier for native peoples living close to Nature than it is for modern urban *Homo sapiens*, many of whom are quite ignorant of the natural history of wild animals. Even their understanding of the behavior of cats, dogs and other domesticated animals (too often, demeaningly referred to as "pets") is limited. Rarely are such creatures appreciated in and for themselves. If they were, we would not have 15 million or so unwanted and abandoned cats and dogs destroyed every year in animal shelters. Nor would society permit the annual suffering and death of some 20 million vertebrate laboratory animals to find cures for human sicknesses. And the cruel incarceration of billions of poultry, pigs and other animals on "factory" farms would not be condoned.

The possibility of communion, except at the most superficial, sentimental level, is further limited by sympathetic, anthropomorphic identification with animals or by such prevalent beliefs that animals are inferior, that they have no feelings, self-awareness, souls or inherent spark of divinity as we ourselves might claim to possess. Such thinking is the height of rational egotism and arrogant anthropocentrism. It undergirds the worldview of modern technocratic society, making communion impossible since it sets up a false duality and a hierarchy that separates and ultimately alienates humanity from animals, Nature and divinity. We are then neither truly civilized nor fully human: as Chief Luther Standing Bear concludes, our human development is retarded.

We may believe that with all the materialistic innovations and conveniences of our technological society, we are "progressive" and far advanced compared with past and present native cultures. But when we fully apprehend how our alienation from Nature and the Animal Kingdom have resulted in serious and possibly irreversible harm to the environment and a veritable holocaust of the Animal Kingdom, we must acknowledge the spiritual bankruptcy of the times, which can be rectified only by reflecting on life and its meaning, accepting the kinship of all creatures, and acknowledging our unity with the universe—through communion.

Matthew Fox has developed a form of Creation Spirituality that emphasizes "original blessing" rather than "original sin."[3] In an interview in the *National Catholic Reporter* (Sept. 13, 1985), he emphasized that "the dualistic spirituality of Augustine has created pain." The false duality of body and spirit is linked with a negative attitude toward the body as imperfect, contaminated with original sin. This attitude is also projected upon all that is natural, including animals and Nature. Fox observes that "the Bible says nothing about original sin"—"And God saw every thing that he made and, behold, it was very good" (Gen. 1:31). He uses the term "original sin" to denote a spirituality that stresses humanity's fall from grace and inherent sinfulness. This theology, he says, was developed in the third century by St. Augustine and pervades Western Christianity today. Augustinian spirituality, according to Fox, is preoccupied with personal sin and is suspicious of Nature, science, the body and passion. In contrast, the concept of original blessing embraces life. It sees Creation as good and fosters a sense of reverence and creative, celebratory participation with Nature and all living things.

We can have communion with animals and Nature when we free ourselves from the constraints of secular humanism so that our spirits and the spirits of all living beings can merge and become one with the Great Spirit's unified field of being. In this way, we come to know God. Communion with animals and Nature is thus a way to experience divinity. We and all sentient beings are really one great family. As individuals, we are all aspects of the one Self and of one humanity. Like other animals, we are manifestations of the same Creation; we have the same origin and kinship in life. We ought, therefore, to respect all living beings as brothers and sisters. This concept is implicit in the teachings of all of the world's major religions. For instance, in Tibetan Buddhism, which accepts the doctrine of reincarnation, Buddhists are encouraged to respect all living beings as their mothers since, at some time in the many incarnations we have experienced, all other sentient beings were mothers to us.

Our dualistic and hierarchical thinking, which leads us to believe we are separate from, and superior to, other animals, also impairs our self-concept and self-image. Body and soul are seen as separate; the body with its mortal frailty and "beastly" passions is regarded as inferior, fallen. In so debasing the body, it is, like Nature and animals, desacralized rather than respected and celebrated. Yet are we not, like animals, living souls whose bodies and spirits are coinherent and inseparable until death, and are but different forms of manifestation of divinity?

Like lovers, body and spirit are one. Walt Whitman expressed this unity in his poem, "We Two How Long Fool'd":

We two, how long we were fool'd,
Now transmuted, we swiftly escape as Nature escapes,
We are Nature, long have we been absent, but now we return,
We become plants, trunks, foliage, roots, bark,
We are bedded in the ground, we are rocks,
We are oaks, we grow in the openings side by side,
We browse, we are two fishes swimming in the sea together,
We are what locust blossoms are, we drop scent around the lanes
    morning and evenings,
We are also the coarse smut of beasts, vegetables, minerals,
We are two predatory hawks, we soar above and look down,
We are two resplendent suns, we it is who balance ourselves orbic
    and stellar, we are as two comets,
We prowl fang'd and four-footed in the woods, we spring on prey,
We are seas mingling, we are two of those cheerful waves rolling
    over each other and interwetting each other.
We are what the atmosphere is, transparent, receptive, pervious,
    impervious,
We are snow, rain, cold, darkness, we are each product and
    influence of the globe,
We have circled and circled till we have arrived home again, we
    two,
We have voided all but freedom and all but our joy.[4]

Donald St. John extends Whitman's poetic expression to our current need for whole-Earth communion:

Communion with Animals, Nature and Divinity

In and through the Earth, humans become aware of their deeper identity. In and through the human the Earth becomes aware of its own spirituality. Human growth in self-awareness is meant to be simultaneously a growth in the Earth's awareness of itself. This dialectic is built into the child and unfolds into a broad ecological consciousness, if not frustrated or misguided by society. The human community itself is a part of the Earth community and is meant to cooperate with the Earth in educating the human. This natural intent of the planet can be seen in the self-transcending dynamics of the child (as described by Walt Whitman):

> There was a child went forth every day,
> And the first object he look'd upon, that object he became,
> And that object became part of him for the day or a certain
>   part of the day,
> Or for many years or stretching cycles of years.[5]

This capacity for intersubjective communion is the essence of ecological spirituality. As the eco-self develops, the sense of isolation and aloneness is replaced by the sense of belonging to a community of beings. Because the self can become other and that other enter into and help form the self, there is no hierarchy between the human and the natural and no basis for, or benefit from, rejecting some beings and accepting others. Just as every part of the body is a miracle and worthy of respect, so every being that forms the Earth body is the subject of praise, admiration and celebration.[6]

This sense of communion opens us to the deep meaning of the natural world. As St. John continues:

> If humans are those beings in whom the Earth becomes aware of itself, they cannot pass judgment on the value of its creatures according to human standards. This attitude allows humans to be accessible to the revelations and messages of meaning that are contained in the complex web of existence. The eco-self intuits these diverse meanings and by absorbing them discovers its own meaning and place.[7]

Such is the redemptive power of communion once we are able to renounce those habitual modes of thought and perception that set up a false, dualistic and anthropocentric worldview that is ultimately harmful to ourselves and to all life. The shape of a leaf, design of a feather, spots on a leopard and antennae of an ant are expressions of intelligent Creation. Mind, as creative intelligence, is manifest and immanent in all things. Likewise, the finest creations of humanity— great art, music, dance and architecture—embody, like a newborn child, something transcendent, beyond empirical analysis. All things so divinely inspired reveal the God within.

Through communion with the song of birds, the shimmering of leaves, the silent grace of leopards and communal endeavors of ants, we discover and affirm our commonality. In the lives, activities and deaths of other creatures, we intuit something of our own humanness, the will to live and a range of emotions—fear, anxiety, pleasure, affection—that are not exclusively human qualities. Through empathy, in sympathetic resonance with all life, we may hear the song of Creation, the music of the spheres, the hymn of the universe.

There can be no true communion with captive zoo animals, performing circus animals and those animals whose furs people wear and whose heads are displayed as trophies and status symbols. Before there can be communion with animals, there must be respect and fellow-feeling. As a culture, we have a long way to go in this regard. The lack of compassionate concern for the plight of animals today is a symptom of our increased alienation from the rest of creation. If this were not so, then the millions of people who visit zoos, circuses, rodeos and even bullfights would rise up and put an end to all forms of cruel domination and exploitation of other kindred sentient beings.

To empathize with the Animal Kingdom today is to experience the holocaust of the animals. One is then moved to do whatever one can to help liberate animals, to restore and protect their natural habitats and to influence their "owners" and caretakers. It becomes an ethical imperative through education, legislation and litigation to change lifestyles and consumer habits in order to minimize our impact upon the environment, to live gently, and to terminate our support of animal-based industries and commercial enterprises that harm the environment and cause needless suffering and death to our animal kin.

According to the Haudenosaunee (Six Nations of the Iroquois people):

Communion with Animals, Nature and Divinity

The people who are living on this planet need to break with the narrow concept of human liberation, and begin to see liberation as something which needs to be extended to the whole of the Natural World. What is needed is the liberation of all the things that support life—the air, the water, the trees—all the things which support the sacred web of life.[8]

Animals are kin to us because they are sentient and because they are a part of the same Creation; they are also part of the same interdependent web of the Earth's ecology. The basic DNA structure of their genes is identical to ours. The double helix of DNA that science has revealed as present in all living beings is like the fingerprint of the Creator.

Living in communion with animals and other living beings does not mean that we should never utilize them. Nor does it mean that our interests will never conflict with theirs. But there is a difference between using animals and wantonly exploiting them or holding the belief that all "nonuseful" animals and plants are competitive pests or weeds. When we must take the life of another living being to sustain or protect our own, we should do so with compassion and regret, and then only on a case-by-case basis after other alternatives have been exhausted. The wholesale slaughter of animals for their meat, skin and furs is unacceptable.

In some cases, environment or ecology create a situation in which killing animals is a survival imperative, such as with the subsistence economies of the Eskimos or Bushmen. For most industrialized societies in temperate climates, however, animal exploitation cannot be justified by situational ethics, since it is wholly self-serving.

It is a cultural norm in the Far East to kill wild animals—bears for their gall bladders, rhinoceroses for their horns and tigers for their bones—for medicinal purposes. Yet this depredation adds to the extinction of wild species, and, regardless of whether purported medical claims are true, the situation is ethically untenable. There are equal if not better alternative medicines. Likewise in the West it is a cultural norm to make laboratory animals suffer in order to test the safety and efficacy of nonessential cosmetics, household chemicals, food preservatives, pesticides, solvents and other nonmedical products.

Licensed vivisection is ethically untenable. The use of animals in biomedical research is acceptable only if we accept a situational ethic that overrides the injunction "Thou shalt not kill" or if not to do so results in the suffering of other sentient beings. The line of reasoning would go as follows: Because the Eskimos and Bushmen live in a difficult environment where the growing of crops is impossible, the exploitation of animals for their survival is ethically acceptable. Thus Western industrialized peoples living in a stressful, overcrowded and chemically contaminated environment are similarly justified in the exploitation of laboratory animals for human health and survival.

But our situation is different. Western society has brought these problems upon itself, and it is surely immoral to make animals suffer as a consequence. To voice such opposition is often misconstrued as caring more for animals than for people by those who fail to see that the correctives to these environmental and health problems are social, political and ideological solutions rather than biological ones that can be identified in the vivisection laboratory or treated in the hospital. Furthermore, even if Eskimos, Bushmen and other native peoples do not live in communion with animals and the environment, which some would contest since their cosmologies speak to the contrary, they have succeeded in living for generations at a subsistence level in balance and harmony with the environment and all its inhabitants. We certainly cannot say that of Western industrialized peoples and their multinational corporations that have caused serious, if not irreparable, harm to the fragile biospheric ecology. It is clearly a supreme challenge and a survival imperative for the Western world to restore balance and harmony by endeavoring to live in communion with the Animal Kingdom whose plight today is an ominous portent of our own. As Chief Standing Bear observed:

> The Indian and the white man sense things differently because the white man has put distance between himself and nature; and assuming a lofty place in the scheme of order of things has lost for him both reverence and understanding.
>
> Kinship with all creatures of the earth, sky, and water was a real and active principle. For the animal and bird world there existed

a brotherly feeling that kept the Lakota safe among them. And so close did some of the Lakotas come to their feathered and furred friends that in true brotherhood they spoke a common tongue.

The animal had rights—the right of man's protection, the right to live, the right to multiply, the right to freedom, and the right to man's indebtedness—and in recognition of these rights the Lakota never enslaved the animal, and spared all life that was not needed for food and clothing.

This concept of life and its relations was humanizing and gave to the Lakota an abiding love. It filled his being with the joy and mystery of living; it gave him reverence for all life; it made a place for all things in the scheme of existence with equal importance to all. The Lakota could despise no creature, for all were of one blood, made by the same hand, and filled with the essence of the Great Mystery.[9]

Separation and Alienation

Being disconnected from life may be regarded as spiritual death. One Christian definition of death is "to be separated from God." Salvation and "eternal life" come when one surrenders, that is, gives up ego-centeredness, to God. One then becomes God-centered.

This Christian view of death is based upon a strictly personalized view of God. In the transcendent nonpersonal view, God is a process and not a person. According to this view, death is separation from Nature or from life and natural evolution. Thus theology and ecology converge in our relationship with Creator and Nature: God is not dead; nor is Nature, but we are dead when separated from God or Nature, because we are separated from life. Vine Deloria, Jr. in *God Is Red*, concludes: "If all things are related, the unity of Creation demands each life form contribute its intended contribution."[10] Separation and alienation occur when we attempt to regard Nature objectively—as a mechanism or as a scientifically measurable and quantifiable system. Our "intended contribution" to Creation then becomes distorted by self-interest and dualistic perception.

Buddhist teacher Tarthang Tulku asks, "When has the traditional religious injunction that 'We are all God's children' (we all have the same parents—Space and Time), not truly moved us? Partly because it has remained an idea, rather than being experienced directly."[11] Hence, the importance of the transcendent numinous reality of communion with all. Tarthang Tulku further states that "instead of recognizing our intimate connection with all others, we create individualized forts of egocentricity which require our constant attention for maintenance and defense. This consolidation and defense of the ego leads to a sense of isolation and imbalance—to a loss of humanity—and thus to a further limiting of our understanding of each other."[12]

Philosopher E. A. Wodehouse proposes, "Man, in the organic synthesis of Man, Nature and Reality, is the living instrument through which Life-as-Creation, awakening into self-consciousness, comes into realization of itself by the creative interpretation of its own works."[13] We and Nature are thus inseparable, and interdependent physically, mentally and spiritually. Our fulfillment lies not in the artifacts, ideas and illusions of our own making, but in the unity of body and mind with Nature—inseparably one Earth, one spirit and one reality. But since every human individual is unique, the process of self-realization will not be identical for all. As Wodehouse observes, "Every such rediscovery of itself through Man is thus, for Life, a fresh adventure. The Book is read a million times, but each time in a new tongue. As Indian philosopher J. Krishnamurti urged, "we can only find meaning and self-fulfillment through the one and only reality of Nature."[14] Modern religion and philosophy have made us exiles from Nature, from the natural order of life. Reality cannot then transmit its meaning to us through Nature, since we negate Nature by believing that we are above it and that our spiritual liberation (or salvation) lies somewhere else. Krishnamurti was one of the few thinkers who reinstated Nature as the link between humanity and divinity. Liberation or self-actualization, as he saw it, is not freedom from life or Nature, but liberation into it. We need not, therefore, look outside Nature for our salvation the meaning and significance of life.

Perhaps the worst heresy of Western Christianity is its denial of the possibility of discovering God through communion with Nature and through attunement to fellow creatures, such discovery being dismissed as pagan pantheism, the idolatrous identification of God with Nature. To see Nature *apart* from God instead of *in* God is to set up a false duality between Creator and Creation, the consequences of which include the desacralization of Nature and destruction of the creative order.

To feel the world through God, one must be consciously *in* God. Such God-consciousness is a nondualistic awareness of the subjective nature of entities both sentient and nonsentient, and of their relational intersubjectivity and objective instrumentality within a unified whole that is complete in itself, yet ever changing. Every organism is perceived as a *fellow being* with a subjectively experiencing Self; a *unique individual* with intrinsic value and interests. Each living being has its own subjective interior and its own objective exterior with respect to the nexus of relationships that together constitute its world-reality. It is from this perception that a holistic spirituality of communion arises rationally, objectively and empathetically. It is a source of inspiration and of a life ethic consonant with the "laws" of Nature; the "great economy" of the biospheric ecosystem; the "will" of God; the Tao.

Joseph Campbell in *The Hero With a Thousand Faces* concludes:

> Man is that alien presence with whom the forces of egoism must come to terms, through whom the ego is to be crucified and resurrected, and in whose image society is to be reformed. Man, understood however not as I but as Thou—for the ideals and temporal institutions of no tribe, race, continent, social class, or century, can be the measure of the inexhaustible and multifariously wonderful divine existence that is the life in all of us.[15]

As Paul Tillich observed, neurosis is a way of avoiding nonbeing by avoiding being. In *The Courage to Be* he states:

> The safety which is guaranteed by well-functioning mechanisms for the technical control of nature, by the refined psychological control of the person, by the rapidly increasing organizational control of society—this safety is bought at a high price: man, for whom all this was invented as a means, becomes a means himself in the service of means.[16]

Christmas Humphreys, in *The Buddhist Way of Life*, points to a way out of this sense of psychological alienation:

As we increasingly become aware of the One Life breathing in each brother form of life we learn the meaning of compassion, which literally means to "suffer with. . . ." "Life is one," said the Buddha, "and the Middle Way to the end of suffering in all its forms is that which leads to the end of the illusion of separation, which enables man to see, as a fact as clear as sunlight, that all mankind, and all other forms in manifestation are one unit, the infinitely variable appearances of an indivisible Whole."[17]

George B. Leonard, in *The Transformation*, echoes Tillich's views when he observes:

Individual consciousness may have suffered a retrograde movement during civilization. For the sake of the efficiency of the ever-expanding social machine, the human individual has in many respects been reduced to a mere component—standardized, specialized, reliable, predictable. Some of the most exquisite capabilities of the hunter's consciousness—ecstasy, communion, even those commonplace skills we now classify as extrasensory—have been censored, punished or simply left to fallow.[18]

The Extended Self

True communion with the natural world becomes inevitable when we recognize that the Earth and its creatures are, in fact, extensions of ourselves. Any sense of separation is an illusion. Biologist W. Jackson Davis, in *The Seventh Year*, states it this way: "We understand in new light the biblical insight that our species arose from clay; the natural sciences have taught us that our very hearts and minds are made of elements in the soil, to which we return when the spirit departs."[19]

Gregory Bateson, in *Steps to An Ecology of Mind*, gives an ecological, rather than evolutionary, view of this inherent connectedness:

The individual mind is immanent but not only in the body. It is immanent also in pathways and messages outside the body; and there is a larger "Mind" of which the individual mind is only a subsystem. This larger Mind is comparable to God and is perhaps what some people mean by "God," but it is still immanent in the total interconnected social system and planetary ecology.[20]

Not only are we connected to all life, but the planet itself, according to some theorists, is a living system like ourselves. James Lovelock, in his book *Gaia, A New Look at Life on Earth*, shows that the Earth is a system that appears to exhibit the behavior and intelligence of a single living organism that is a "master mind" composed of cybernetic processes of the collective intelligence of all life forms on Earth.[21]

Affirming our essential oneness with the natural world leads us inevitably to a wholly different concept of selfhood and relationship to other existences, animate and inanimate. Philosopher J. Baird Callicott describes this new concept of an extended self as follows: "The world is, indeed, one's extended body and one's body is the precipitation, the focus of the world in a particular space-time-locale. . . . One cannot, thus, draw hard and fast boundaries between oneself, either physically or spiritually, and the environment."[22] He relates the following affirming experience:

> For me this realization took concrete form, as I stood two decades and an education later, on the banks of the Mississippi River where I had roamed as a boy. As I gazed at the brown silt-choked waters absorbing a black plume of industrial and municipal sewage from Memphis and followed bits of some unknown beige froth floating continually down from Cincinnati, Louisville, or St. Louis, I experience a palpable pain. It was not distinctly located in any of my extremities, nor was it like a headache or nausea. Still, it was very real. I had no plans to swim in the river, no need to drink from it, no intention of buying real estate on its shores. My narrowly personal interests were not affected, and yet somehow I was personally injured. It occurred to me then, in a flash of self-discovery, that the river was a part of me. And I recalled a line from Leapold's *Sand County Almanac:* "One of the penalties of an ecological education is that one lives alone in a world of wounds."

Australian conservationist John Seed, musing on his efforts on behalf of rain forest preservation in Queensland, has come to a similar conclusion:

As the implications of evolution and ecology are internalized . . . here is an identification with all life. . . . Alienation subsides. . . . "I am protecting the rain forest" develops to "I am part of the rain-forest protecting myself. I am that part of the rain forest recently emerged into thinking."[23]

Ecology thus gives new meaning as well as new substance to the phrase "enlightened self-interest."[24]

This real and affirming experience is an integral part of the teachings of Vedanta, among other religious and philosophical schools. Swami Vivekenanda wrote:

The central ideal of Vedanta is Oneness. There are no two in anything no two lives or even two different kinds of life for the two worlds. You will find the Vedas speaking, at first, of heavens and things like that; but later on, when they come to the highest of ideals of their philosophy, they brush away all these things. There is but one Life, one World, one Existence. Everything is that One; the differences are of degree and not of kind. The differences between our lives are not of kind. Vedanta entirely denies such ideas as that animals are essentially separate from men and that they were made and created by God to be used for our food.[25]

This worldview of a unified field of diversity is also evident in Rolling Thunder's description of the Shoshone religion:

It is a natural religion, a religion of nature, and that the Great Spirit is in all things, all things that have life, that all life is to be respected, and all forms of life should be respected including human life, animal life, plant life—and the entire life force. If people were to adhere to that and eliminate the greed which exists in the world today, there'd be no need for wars and aggression![26]

But if there is to be respect for all entities, there must also be *feeling for them*, not as separate objects but as fellow subjects. Jay McDaniel asks, "Can love of flora and fauna as they exist in and for themselves, rather than as they exist for industrial or economic purposes, be understood as feeling with God? To Western Christian ears, the discovery of God through attunement to fellow creatures has smacked of pantheism and idolatrous identification of God with

---

Communion with Animals, Nature and Divinity

nature."[27] Basing his thesis on process theology with an ecological as well as spiritual orientation, McDaniel offers the following Christian and panentheistic vision:

This universal soul—a whole that is greater than, and yet includes, its parts—is God, understood as the ongoing Psyche of the universe. The totality of creatures in the universe constitutes God's own body.

The divine Psyche feels things as they are, in their inward as well as outward properties, and loves them. A Christian spirituality that sees nature in God will attempt to feel nonhuman organisms as God feels them, that is, with openness to what they are in and for themselves, and with love. It will recognize that nonhuman organisms are parts of the divine body, and it will recognize that humans, too, are parts of that body. Such recognition will not preclude an awareness of the instrumental value various parts can have for one another. It will not preclude a use of the land, of animals in certain ways, and of plants in others. Indeed, it will not be wanton, and it will be complemented whenever circumstances allow by a willingness to let things be, to allow them to flourish in their own right. It will be in Wendell Berry's terms, "kindly use."[28]

Its underlying spirit, like God's own, will be a reverence for life. . . . In different ways and forms, Christ is present within all creatures, human and nonhuman. Within humans, Christ comes as an inwardly felt and continuously present invitation to love life more fully and deeply. When Christians learn to walk lightly on the earth, having cultivated that feeling . . . which in certain ways they have often already cultivated in relation to fellow humans, will then be enjoyed in relation to fellow creatures. Amid such enjoyment they will be responding even more fully to the call of Christ.[29]

Professor Rodney L. Taylor eloquently describes this deep sense of spiritual unity from the perspective of the Confucian religious tradition as follows:

The fact that there is no difference in kind between humans and animals allows Neo-Confucianism to teach the unity of all forms of things. Ch'eng Hao (1032–1085) states that "the humane man forms one body with all things comprehensively. . . . All operations of the universe are our operations." Ch'eng I said, "The humane man regards Heaven and earth and all things as one body. There is nothing which is not part of his self. Knowing that, where is the limit (of his humanity)?" Lu Hsiang-shan said, "The universe never separates itself from man; man separates himself from the universe." And the *Chin-suu-lu* directs one to enlarge the mind in order to be able to enter into all things in the world: "Combine the internal and the external into one and regard things and self as equal. This is the way to see the fundamental point of the Way."(30)

Probably more than any other work, however, Chang Tsai's (1021–1077) *Hsi ming* (Western Inscription) has captured the imagination of Neo-Confucian ethical thought. The first few lines read:

Heaven is my father and earth is my mother, and even such a small creature as I finds an intimate place in their midst. Therefore that which extends throughout the universe I regard as my body and that which directs the universe I regard as my nature. All people are my brothers and sisters, and all things are my companions.

Rodney L. Taylor's commentary on this passage is insightful:

The vision is clear: animals and humans share in the same material force and the same principle. Men embody these in their highest or fullest form, but this only makes greater demands upon our ethical reflections and action. All living things, not just human beings, stand in *moral* relation to man, and man in turn fulfills his own moral nature by standing in moral relation to all living things.

The degree to which this was taken literally as a directive to moral action can be seen in several poignant examples. In a short biographical note about Chou Tun-i (1017–1073), the *Chin-suu-lu* states that he "did not cut the grass growing outside his window." When asked about it, he said, "[the feeling of the grass] and mine are the same."(31)

The Buddhist philosopher D. Suzuki believes that "a kind of chain exists between flowers, animals, people and Buddhas. This chain is called the chain of love—or compassion. Where this chain is perceived and appreciated, there is human serenity and peace."[32] And Sufi Shalistari said, "Each creature that goes before you has a soul and from that soul is bound by a cord to you."

In sum, compassion is our connection with the whole of Creation, and by way of it we enter into a deeper, empathetic communion with all existences. This state of heart and mind was an integral part of primal consciousness, which can be traced down through the ages as a common thread in all the world's major religious and philosophical traditions.

Aboriginal Consciousness and the "Old Religion"

I who was born to die shall live. That the world of animals and the world of men may come together, I shall live.

—Inuit legend

Will you teach your children what we have taught our children? That the earth is our mother? What befalls the earth befalls all the sons of the earth.

—Chief Seattle

Nature is a self-organizing, collective body of intelligence analogous in many ways to human civilization. Both have their own cycles, rates of metabolism, decay and regeneration, and laws of organization, maintenance and self-sustaining economy. Since human civilization derives its sustenance from Nature, it has long been recognized that the first law all of humankind must obey is to live in balance with Nature. Australian aboriginal Bill Neidjie states, "Aboriginal law never change. Old people tell us, 'you got to keep it.' It always stays. . . . We got to look after, can't waste anything . . . if you waste (him) anything now, next year . . . you can't get as much because you already waste. When I was young (was) never wasted (anything) otherwise straight away I get trouble. Even bone not wasted, make soup or burn that bone (as fuel). Watch out . . . that might be dreaming one too."[1]

In Dreamtime awareness, we are connected with the total self-regenerative pattern of Nature. When this unified field is disrupted, even harmed, as when there is waste caused by the ignorance of greed and by indifference to the desecration of Nature, we suffer the consequences.

Dreamtime is the aboriginal spiritual dimension of metaphysical Creation-awareness. In this state of consciousness, one is connected empathetically with the whole of one's biofield, with all one's "relations" from rock to lizard and didgeridoo; with ancestors including original creator-spirits; and with the place one was born and dies into, and where one lives and grows. This nondualistic state is not simply intellectual and cognitive. It is deeply empathetic, such that it often includes what we call clairvoyance, the ability to connect one's feelings with others and with the empathosphere of sentient life.

In this state, there is no separation between human and Nature, as Bill Neidjie observes: "If you feel sore—headache, sore body that means somebody killing tree or grass. You feel because your body is in that tree or earth. Nobody can tell you, you got to feel it yourself."[2] As the !Kung Bushmen see it, we are all part of the same dream that is dreaming us, part of the same Creation. When asked what distinguishes traditional aboriginal religion from all others, Eric Willmot, Australian aboriginal and professor of education at Queensland University, replied, "The spiritual and temporal domains are so connected that any heaven or hell you go through happens during your temporal life span. At death, the goal is to drive the spirit back to its source, the land. It joins with and becomes part of the spiritual component of land. From this component or source, child spirits are reborn—a kind of reincarnation but very different, say, from the Buddhist view."[3]

The complex mythologies, ceremonial rituals and rites of initiation of aboriginal societies are beyond the scope and intent of this chapter. Rather, the intent is to capture the essence of aboriginal "primal consciousness," so as to highlight its affinities with Native American teachings and certain Western and Eastern religious and philosophical schools that foster a sense of oneness with Creation. Here is how this oneness is described in a documentary script on the plight of the Jawoyn group of Australian aboriginals by Sue Arnold and Graham Bicknell:

> To be a traditional aboriginal is to be the land, an ant, a tree, a rock—to identify with a complete sense of oneness, a dedication to maintaining an order, balance. . . . An acceptance of aboriginal thinking is beyond most Westerners, particularly those who have lost their links with the natural world.
>
> The creative Spirit Ancestors of the Dreamtime are not only of the past, but continue to exert influences as a constant presence in the landscape where they determine the seasons and the cycle of all life. So the landscape is a visible imprint and a physical proof of the Dreaming's spiritual energies. When the Ancestors completed their travels they were transformed, some became mountains, rocks and cosmic beings. According to the dreamings, the greatest focus of the Ancestors' powers can be found in places where they left marks, landforms and objects behind. These are the sacred sites, the Romes and Jerusalems of aboriginal people.[4]

While the Dreamings of aboriginal groups are as different as the regions they inhabit and languages they speak, central to their beliefs is the conviction that the whole of earthly Creation, including themselves, originated in the deeds of the Ancestral Spirits. The "time" of these deeds is the Dreamtime.

Dreamtime and Dreamwalking

Dreamtime is no place because it is omnipresent. Nothing is omnipotent over it or separate from it. The Dreamwalker calls the Dreamtime sacred. The basis of aboriginal law is to respect the Dreaming One, the Dreamtime and every Dream Place, and to use kindly and with reverence everything necessary to sustain life and to live in harmony with the Dreams of all. To call this conceptual reality "animistic" is an absurd simplification, as "Goatwalker" and philosopher Jim Corbett makes clear:

> Animism is a technocratic theory attributed to pretechnocratic societies; the savage's awareness that presence is unfragmented and is met in all others is interpreted as a belief that every object has a self in it. Is there more reason for believing that each human body you meet has a self inside it than there is for believing that mountains, trees, and springs do? Are you sure there's a self in your own body? Why do savages refer to spirit as the air we breathe, people living in spirit instead of spirits living in people?[5]

As the deer is the Dream of the wolf, so the wolf is part of the forest's Dream. The Dreamtime of every tree is the Forest Dreaming. The Dreamplace of wolf and deer is the Dream that is Dreaming the forest and all. Tree, wolf and deer are all one within the manifest diversity of their being. The empathic Dreamwalker sees both this unity of being and the uniqueness of every being and, by unifying both objective and subjective modes of perception, becomes a conscious participant in the Dreamtime. Peace, joy and a lightness of being are possible, even within a life of poverty, suffering and death, for there is no poverty of spirit.

The shaman, or healer, is a bridge between two worlds, the physical or material and the metaphysical or spiritual. As Dreamwalkers, shaman-healers bear the wounds of the Earth soul and of a human spirit harmed by ignorance and greed, and they keep the bridge open to the Dreamtime as priests and seers of the Sacred Realm. Traditional cultures respect such healers because they show that where there is the power of love, there is no will-to-power. Often times, a Dreamwalker's first journey entails trading places with an animal and entering its Dreamtime. This feat is recognized as a gift of the animal powers, and many Dreamwalkers take the name of an animal totem. In some cultures, if a shaman helps others take the life of his totem animal for food, he would not eat any part of it himself. This is one of the many laws of the Dreamtime that is meaningless to "civilized" people who have never experienced their first "death," that loss of self and all sense of separation that is the first breath of all Dreamwalkers.

Some Dreamwalkers, as the Sioux medicine man Fools Crow once told me, have Light Beings as their guides, as well as animals. He told me how these Light Beings—angels, if you wish—would guide him to the right herb to use for a healing, show him where a person was sick and help in many other ways.

The first breath of a Dreamwalker, like the first step, the first touch, the first sound and the first taste, is one of communion. This is the experience that empowers the Dreamwalker to make the Dreaming accessible to unborn, not-yet-humane people and those who are in the process of death and transformation via various rites of spiritual initiation, which in traditional cultures usually begin at puberty.

The reality of the Dreamwalker is nonseparate. Like the Buddha-mind and Christ-heart, it embraces and manifests in all; there are no "outside standers," except those not yet born and the uninitiated who believe that they are separate. In the reality of the Dreamtime, there is no separation among Dreamtime, the Dreamwalker and the Dreaming One, just as there is no separation between living beings. Except when there is distorted perception and destructive action, there can be no separation, because nothing arises independently. Everything has the same origin in Creation and is a manifestation of the Creator or Dreaming One, as Dream and Dreamer are one.

Some become Dreamwalkers through prayer, ritual initiation or instruction, while others are able to enter the Dreamtime sponta-neously because of their inborn readiness or because of some intense experience such as a vision, the death of a loved one or a near-fatal illness. A Native American shaman will often tell his white brother, "There is an Indian somewhere inside of you all," by which he means that all people can become Dreamwalkers when they realize the divinity in all things. To paraphrase a !Kung Bushman teaching, everyone is a divine manifestation of the "Dream that is Dreaming us all."

People who have not experienced the Dreamtime and cannot Dreamwalk feel separate from the rest of Creation, even from each other. They often act cruelly and destructively because they have no empathic connection. Their egos are separate. Those who do not feel separation because their ego development has not been arrested and who begin to empathize with the rest of Creation are in the process of becoming Dreamwalkers—humane human beings. But they, along with the Dreamtime and Dreaming Places, are now threatened with extinction the world over because of the collective egotism that supports a fundamentally inhumane global industrial technocracy. This technocracy has done violence against the whole of Creation and now threatens the Dreamtime of the planet Earth itself.

Albert Schweitzer taught that the good healer simply awakens the healer within. He advised that when we have respect and reverence for all life, we will enjoy world peace and the healing of humanity. Inhumanity is the cause of most of the world's suffering. It arises from the misperception of human separateness, of our superiority over other sentient beings—including our own kind—in matters of gender, race or religion. It arises from a nonrecognition of the divinity within. The reconciliation of all dualities—the way of the Dreamwalker—is the way to world peace.

Many children are naturally Dreamwalkers. But today most are the victims of a violent world, being reprogrammed as obedient worker-consumers, or experiencing parental abuse, malnutrition, poverty, war and the degradation of the human spirit. What parents today in industrialized countries Dreamwalk with their children and kindle the divine spark in them so that they can enjoy the fullness of their own humanity, part of which entails relating with compassion to all sentient beings?

The human spirit is the divine spark that can ignite the conscious self to witness the death of the ego's illusory sense of separation, and its subsequent transformation. But this empathic spirit is being snuffed out by the mass culture of industrial materialism, consumerism and rationalized economic determinism. Modern society is more cult than culture, since its artists, mystics and poets are neither read nor understood. The song of Creation grows ever more faint as the forests are destroyed, the seas poisoned and the Earth raped.

To Dreamwalk is to take a stairway, not to some heaven separate from Earth, but to communion with the subjective. It is a state of heart-mind, a spiritual dimension that transcends the realm of an objectified egotistic duality. In some cultural traditions, this state is achieved through prayerful meditation and concentration; in others, through song, chant, dance or the open mindfulness of Zen. In Tibetan Buddhism, this numinous dimension is called *Dharmadatu*—

the reality, according to Buddhist scholar Roger Corless of Duke University, in which, through the clarity of enlightened perception, we see "everything as Buddhas and Buddhas as everything."

Martin Buber termed this state the I-Thou dimension, a nondualistic, compassionate and reverential relationship with human beings. It is also the dimension of the Dreamwalker. Buber was wise not to advocate that people strive to live exclusively in this realm. The unenlightened human psyche cannot tolerate the intensity of the spiritual realm for long. Though it liberates us from human selfishness, separation, materialism and objectification—the I-it dimension of Buber's view—the state of spiritual oneness is only a temporary refuge, since to stay there forever can become yet another form of detachment.

Thus the Dreamwalker must learn to live in balance between the realm of communion with the subjective and commerce with the objective, serving as an interlocutor between the two. In isolation from the numinous and the subjective, the objective realm becomes increasingly separate, voracious and destructive. The Dreamwalker seeks to overcome this separation of the sacred from the profane by helping others to become Dreamwalkers and by working to bring about the healing of humanity and of our relationship with creatures and Creation.

The reality of Dreamtime is often difficult for Westerners to comprehend. Poet Rainer Maria Rilke in the *Duino Elegies* comes close to it, referring to it as "the invisible." He observes:

Transitoriness is everywhere plunging into profound Being. . . . Nature, the things we move about among and use, are provisional and perishable; but so long as we are here, they *are* our possession and our friendship, sharers in our trouble and gladness, just as they have been the confidants of our ancestors. Therefore, not only must all that is here not be corrupted or degraded, but, just because of that very provisionality they share with us, all these appearances and things should be comprehended by us in a most fervent understanding and transformed. Transformed? Yes for our task is to stamp this provisional, perishing earth into ourselves so deeply, so painfully and passionately, that its being may rise again "invisibly" in us.[6]

In other words, the Dreamtime can be equated with the state of mind Westerners call communion. As Thomas Berry observes in his book *The Dream of the Earth*, everything in the cosmos is in communion with everything else.[7] As a consequence of humanity not respecting this holy union, the whole is now disintegrating around us: societies, industries, national economies, the oceans, the forests and planet Earth itself. Devoid of mystery and numinosity, the Earth is no longer seen as sacred, the Mother of us all. The sacred has been made profane: commercially trivialized, industrially exploited and scientifically atomized, reduced to matter, energy and absurdity in the name of necessary progress and profit. Those who do not live cocreatively and coinherently with the Earth and its processes cannot regard the Earth as a numinous manifestation of an intelligently self-organizing cosmos.

The world's populace and its leaders might both benefit significantly from understanding and incorporating the worldview of traditional peoples like the Australian aboriginals, who have evolved over several millennia a more sustainable and less destructive culture and philosophy. But first, an ontological gap between very different worldviews must be overcome. The modern industrial worldview is not only materialistic and secular, it is also progressivist. The traditional aboriginal view, in contrast, seeks neither domination nor progress. Rather, according to anthropologist W. Stanner, "The proper life is one lived under a mood of assent, an assent to the terms of an existence in which there is felt to be a necessary connection between life and suffering. This view is neither fatalistic nor pessimistic. It is accepted as that which is the same forever, and which is protected by natural law from all ecologically harmful forms of human exploitation."[8]

The sacred whole, coinherence and coevolution are thus preserved because the aboriginals have chosen by their attitude of assent to live in harmony with the natural world. In contrast, modern industrialized people, like crazed pariahs, follow the beat of their own drum, believing they can make good by changing the direction of evolution, becoming a law unto themselves. *Homo technos*, technocratic man, changes the direction of evolution by changing the ecological coinherence of animal and plant species, raising only those of immediate use and profitable potential, and killing off the rest.

To the aboriginal, this violent and ultimately self-destructive way is anathema, and they are quite aware that their fate is the fate of other beings and communities, like the great whales, the snow leopard and the tropical forests. The end of the natural world, the Dreamtime, however, is not inevitable if we cherish the forests, the singing swamps and fellow beings—human and nonhuman—equally, and start to share the world, beginning, perhaps, with such a reverence for life that we cease to multiply our kind and those superfluous wants that are fast consuming the Earth.

The Western philosophy that comes closest to the aboriginal view is the Creation-centered sacramentalist and panentheist view, which sees all life as One Life. Anthropologist Peter Sutton underscores the unity that underlies aboriginal belief: "In traditional aboriginal thought, there is no central dichotomy of the spiritual and the material, the sacred and the secular, or the natural and the supernatural."[9] In other words, the aboriginal view, like that of the Native American shaman and the European transcendentalist, mystic, holistic healer, poet and artist, is nondualistic, which relates it philosophically to Zen Buddhism and the praxis of yoga. It is also akin to the beliefs of St. Francis of Assisi, who called other creatures brothers and sisters because they have the same origin as humans. It is the way of Albert Schweitzer's philosophy of Reverence for Life as practiced by Mahatma Gandhi through *ahimsa* (dynamic nonviolence) and *satyagraha* (the power of obedience to the principle of creative but nonviolent action). In the pure and uncontrived simplicity of the aboriginal worldview, this entails an attitude of assent toward life and suffering without progressivist aspirations of power and control; kinship with all life; social democracy and egalitarianism; and strict obedience to conservation, continuity and peace through frugality, self-discipline, spiritual benevolence and gratitude.

This attitude of nondualistic assent affects every aspect of aboriginal life, from art to lifestyle to ritual. Stanley Breeden and Belinda Wright in their book *Kakadu, Looking After the Country: The Gagudju Way* describe how this attitude is manifested in the life of an aboriginal group:

The rocks, pools, paintings and other special places where the spirit ancestors of the Dreamtime now reside still contain their power and creative energy. At these sacred places, the Dreaming sites, the Gagudju can draw on this power through painting, song, dance or other rituals. To maintain the integrity of the life force the people must protect and stay in active contact with the Dreaming sites. These are crucial to the survival of all living things within Kakadu. An animal's Dreaming, a Flying Fox Dreaming, for example, contains the life essence of that species. By performing ceremonies at the site and by painting flying foxes on its rocks, the people energize the creative spirit so new flying foxes will always be "created" and are there as a food source for the people. In this way the Gagudju are tied to nearly all the animals and plants around them.

Each Gagudju person has several totems which are his or her Dreamings. This means that some of the life essence of the Dreaming species resides in the person and has the potential to change him or her into the Dreaming animal or plant. A man might, for example, belong to the Wallaby Dreaming in which case he is descended from the same spirit as the wallaby. Throughout his life he will have a close affinity with the marsupials. He will not hunt or eat them. Wallabies will always be close to him; they are his other self. They warn him of approaching danger, guide him to good hunting places and even tell him of distant events. And when a man of the Wallaby Dreaming paints his body with the wallaby design for a ceremony, he becomes a wallaby. Each Gagudju person is related, in this way, to one or more of the ancestral creator beings.[10]

It should be noted that from early childhood knowledge is acquired through instruction and observation about the biology and behavior of the individual's animal totems, knowledge vital to group survival and conservation. James Cowan writes that the aboriginal:

> . . . sees the land as a metaphysical edifice. He understands its spiritual rhythms. And he accommodates himself to its cyclic transitions. Nor does he ask of it to do more than supply him with life-sustenance and a modicum of well-being. At the same time he refuses to exploit it beyond its capacity for renewal. Beyond that he resists the desire to change the land because he knows that in

doing so he will tamper with its *kurunba* (life essence) and with the Dreaming event that made it. . . .[11]

Cowan describes the Dreaming as "not an alien place populated by unrecognizable spirit-beings, but a place of metaphysical repose for the Aboriginal." He continues:

The Dreaming, moreover, is a fragile place. It remains to be seen whether it will open its gates to a world increasingly inured to the idea of "enchantment" as a prefigurement of grace. For it to weave its spell again, men and women of all creeds and beliefs will need to throw off the cloak of logic and ratiocination, and accept the mytho-poetry of the Dreaming as a supernatural reality. They will have to recognize also that the Aborigines have made the "face of the earth" their *Bhagavad Gita*, their Torah, their Bible or Koran. Indeed the Dreaming is the Aboriginal Ark of the Covenant which they have been carrying about the Australian continent since the beginning of time.[12]

While few of us Westerners would ever consider adopting the aboriginal way of life or living like an ascetic St. Francis of Assisi, it is time that we realize that many of our own kind, even in our own towns and cities, and not out of choice, live in abject poverty of body, mind and spirit. How can we justify living as we do in ways that contribute to others' suffering, to the annihilation of aboriginal cultures from the Amazon and Arnhem Land, to the extermination of the redwood forests in the American Northwest and the once-forever bountiful African savannas and Australian bush? Gone forever is the Dreamtime, what Plato called the *anima mundi*, the soul of the Earth. In America, the Dream of the Buffalo and the Plains Indian is almost all destroyed. What is there left, save doubt itself—doubt that the Western way is right and good? Can we continue to raise our children to accept, serve and thus sustain this way? We are faced with a desperate choice: either end the Dream of Nature through mass exploitation, or restore the natural world through respect and reverence for all beings and the Earth's Creation, and live accordingly.

The aboriginal worldview leads in the sacramental panentheistic direction of St. Francis of Assisi expressed by Jesus of Nazareth in the Gospel of the Holy Twelve:

Verily, these are your fellow creatures, of the great household of God; yea, they are your brothers and sisters, having the same breath of life in the Eternal.

And whatsoever ye do to the least of these, My brethren, ye do it unto Me. For I am in them and they are in Me. Yes, I am in all creatures and all creatures are in Me. In all their joys I rejoice and in all their afflictions, I am afflicted. Wherefore I say unto you, Be ye kind to one another, and to all the creatures of God.[13]

The philosopher Schopenhauer realized a similar vision of the unity of life via the following reasoning:

All variety of forms in nature and all plurality of individuals belong not to the will but only to its objectivity and to the form thereof; it necessarily follows that the will is indivisible and is wholly present in every phenomenon.[14]

Albert Einstein echoed this sentiment in a letter to the *New York Post* (November 28, 1972) in which he wrote:

A human being is part of the whole, called by us the Universe, a part limited in time and space. He experiences himself, his thoughts and feelings as something separate from the rest—a kind of optical delusion of his consciousness. This delusion is a kind of prison for us, restricting us to our personal desires and to affection for a few persons nearest to us. Our task must be to free ourselves from this prison by widening our circle of compassion to embrace all living creatures and the whole of nature in its beauty. Nobody is able to achieve this completely, but the striving for such achievement is in itself a part of the liberation and a foundation for inner security.

As we widen our circle of compassion, empathizing with the Earth as the Body of Christ crucified, or as the Buddha-field or Gaia, we come to feel as the Earth feels and knows, as Lao Tzu wrote:

If we identify one self with the world,
Then within oneself there is the world.
If we love the world as we love our self,
Then within our self there is only the world.[15]

We are incapable of experiencing the natural empathetic Dream-time state of human consciousness if we feel no twinge when we see a tree being felled or a fish caught on a line; when we no longer thank the tree and the fish or seek to avoid destruction and waste in the first place.

From Dreamtime comes the aboriginals' wisdom and first Law: avoid harm and waste. The same law applies to all who are in touch with the divinity in every tree, fish and natural object, including themselves and each other.

The Sacred and The Profane

Religious historian Mircea Eliade has underscored the separation between the religious and secular views of life: "*Sacred* and *profane* are two modes of being in the world, two existential situations assumed by man in the course of his history."[16] He would affirm that the fundamental problem of modern society is that it gives rise to a world that is not in harmony with the natural world or obedient to the laws of Nature because of the prevalent "degradation and desacralization of religious values and forms of behavior."[17] The wisdom of obedience to God, to Creator and the created is seldom appreciated. The materialism of both state and private capitalism, along with industrialism, scientific imperialism and shallow, instrumental rationalism has desacralized the cosmos. If the fruits of the bioindustrial age are to be of any lasting value, its resacralization is now a survival as well as spiritual imperative..

The Earth is resacralized only when we reconcile the false duality of the secular and the sacred by living in communion, following the ethics of nonviolence (*ahimsa*) and reverence for life. We then rise from the realm of the profane, with its many forms of suffering and unnatural destruction, to the sacred, the reality of the *anima mundi*, the soul of the Earth. A tree then becomes, as Eliade would say, a hierophany: a cipher, symbol or material and living manifestation of divinity, the *mysterium tremation*. Eliade writes, "The sacred tree, the sacred stone are not adored as stone or tree; they are worshipped precisely because they are *hierophanies*, because they show something that is no longer stone or tree but *sacred*, the *ganz andere* or 'wholly (and holy) other.' "[18]

A mandala, a cantata and a canyon, like birdsong and the light on leaping whales, put us in touch instantly with the infinite and the ineffable: the "deep otherness" of the cosmos within every microcosm in us and around us. This mundane reality is a synthesis of the secular and the sacred. Within this frame of reference, trees are killed with reverence and only out of human need, as others are grown, nurtured and revered. When we do not live within this frame of reference, we become out of balance, either too worldly or otherworldly, too immersed or self-involved to help restore and resacralize the Earth and all who dwell on it.

Human health and the health of the natural world are inseparable and interdependent, as we are part of Nature and of the One Life. Institutionalized and individual cruelty and exploitation of animals, which deprives them of ever expressing their wills-to-be or of experiencing the fullness of their being, are symptoms and consequences of the diseased condition that arises when we live in the profane realm of a desacralized cosmos. A bioindustrialized and wholly humanized world has no hierophanies, no aspects of natural Creation to link us to the divine realm of the sacred within and beyond the mundane. In a world so disgodded, so devoid of wild creatures and wilderness, filled with domesticated plants and animals that are seen as "our" genetically engineered and patentable creations, we will, as Chief Seattle foresaw, "die of a great loneliness of spirit." That is our choice, the future of Creation and the fate of this Earth.

To some, life is sacred. Others have broken the divine Covenant to dress and to keep Earth's Creation because the Earth is not perceived and reverenced as sacred. When there is no longer communion with life, and when the intuitive wisdom of awareness through feeling is displaced by the destructive dualisms of objectivity and instrumental rationalism, the sacrament is defiled.

We have the ability to split the atom and recombine the genes of various natural life forms. When this knowledge and power are used selfishly, without respect and empathy for the living systems that we are influencing, great harm arises. But when there is vision of the unity of all life and the karmic continuity of harm and suffering, the knowledge and power of dominion can be used to avoid harm, no matter how justified the exploitation may seem from a rational, anthropocentric perspective. When we use our power wisely, suffering is avoided, because to harm another is to harm ourselves.

Mircea Eliade has written, "That the whole of cosmic life can still be felt as a cipher of the divinity is shown by a Christian author such as Leon Bloy, when he writes: 'whether life is in men, in animals, or in plants, it is always Life, and when . . . the inapprehensible point that is called death comes, it is always Jesus who departs, alike from tree and from a human being.' "[19] From this panentheistic perspective, Jesus is the metaphysical cosmic *telos* or manifest and coinhering divinity.

The "Old Religion" Renaissance

Aboriginal peoples who have not been totally assimilated into modern civilization and who, to varying degrees, still follow the traditional ways of their gatherer-hunter ancestors, embrace a philosophy and worldview that I would term the "Old Religion." This religion emerged with the evolution of human consciousness and was common to all aboriginal communities because of their affinity with Nature and shared worldview.

The Old Religion predates Christianity by at least fifty thousand years, emerging with the dawn of human consciousness in the first people who could make fire, tools and bury their dead. It is a religion not easily eclipsed because it is rooted in the racial memories and collective unconscious of our species. At its core, it is a religion primarily of experience, not of dogma, blind ritual or faith.

This experiential core was centered in both the human ego and in the Earth ecos, in the home that was Nature. It was therefore Creation-centered, neither exclusively human-centered (or anthropocentric) nor exclusively Nature or Earth-centered. Creation embraces all and is all: nothing is excluded, least of all the human ego. The Old Religion saw God in all and all in God, though what was variously perceived as God was not necessarily so named. This perception was the result of becoming aware of and experiencing life and death objectively as phenomena within a subjective and material field of being. The ontological quality of this perception was that there was no sense of separation between the observer and the observed, between one's own life and the living presence of a mountain, lake, tree, bear or other brother or sister creation. As a consequence, every being and natural entity was imbued with *mana*, power, spirit or life essence and mystery that the emerging human consciousness, in the process of participation and coevolved interdependence, began to apprehend.

Something greater than self, beyond comprehension yet also inherent in every separate self, was felt at the dawn of humanity. As we entered into the morning light of understanding, the Old Religion gave a sense of security and belonging in the face of our own vulnerability and mortality. The continuity of the seasons and the relative permanence of mountain, lake, forest, bear and eagle gave birth to the feeling of incarnate immortality that lives today in the widespread Eastern religious belief in reincarnation. The Old Religion was surely not based upon mortal fear or bolstered by the promise of salvation and escape from the natural world. Rather it affirmed a divine, numinous dimension to both human existence and all of life. This affirmation was the result of religion as experience. The etymology of the word *religion* is "to bind back or reconnect," implying a re-cognition of the divine in the manifest world revealed to humankind through the evolution of consciousness. As a consequence, religion was not something separate from everyday life and experience, nor was the human psyche separate from Nature. The Old Religion was therefore the conscious affirmation of the sacred unity, presence and interdependence of all life.

The elemental principles and ethics of the Old Religion can be found in the oral traditions and recorded teachings of such peoples as the Native Americans and Australian aboriginals. They are also evident beneath the elaborations of Taoism, Buddhism, Hinduism and the Baha'i faith, and reside at the heart of Christian, Creation-centered mysticism and the Kabbalistic and Sufi mystical teachings of Judaism and Islam. The relevance of the Old Religion to the current global environmental crisis has yet to be fully realized. It provides a common spiritual and ethical basis for an ecumenical unification of the world's more recent religious faiths and denominations. A unity of spirit and will can do much to help bring peace and justice to the world in these times and also help ensure the integrity and future of Creation as well.

THE BOUNDLESS CIRCLE

Initiation, Nature-Reverence and the Vision Quest

In traditional Native American philosophy, animals and all of Nature's Creation are seen as living "according to their original instructions." Such an understanding of nonhuman life is certainly facilitated by living close to Nature and by objective scientific study. But this deeper intuitive wisdom and ethical awareness arise especially when one is part of Nature as a conscious participant without any sense of separation.

This natural state of consciousness has certain childlike qualities as exemplified by the child in one of Walt Whitman's poems who "became everything that he beheld." But to one who stands apart from Nature and by so doing, objectifies the world, this natural state of mind is seen as childishly primitive. And it is often misinterpreted variously as sentimental, animistic, superstitious, illusory and irrational.

Yet from this primitive perception, or rather pure or primal state of mind, we find the wellsprings of empathy and ethical sensibility. These cannot arise from a state of mind that simply objectifies. An objectifying worldview sets up a barrier, both cognitive and emotional, between self and other. This dualistic condition has been long recognized by shamans, healers and teachers as highly destructive and self-limiting. Animals are part of Nature, instinctively following their original instructions. By doing so, the integrity, diversity and vitality of Nature's Creation are preserved. In modern ecological parlance, their relationship is symbiotic—they take from life only as much as they return. It is ironic that many psychotherapists use the term *symbiosis* to denote an unhealthy condition of dependence, and likewise regard visionary experiences as regressive, if not psychotic.

Traditional Native American spirituality has long advanced the belief that since humans are also part of Nature, it is our sacred duty to follow our "original instructions" for our own good and for the good of all. In other words, we should all endeavor to live symbiotically. While for nonhuman animals this is largely unconscious or instinctive, for us it is a conscious choice requiring self-discipline, empathetic sensitivity and ethical sensibility. That we have almost lost touch with this instinct or inherent wisdom is, I believe, a cultural consequence of our valuing intellect or reason over feeling and intuition. It seems at times that our cleverness, willfulness and destructive anthropocentrism have outstripped even the basic instinct for survival and species preservation.

Knowing that these are the cardinal "sins" of adolescence, traditional cultures developed various ways to prevent the individual and the community from remaining in a condition akin to perpetual egocentric or anthropocentric adolescence. Until recently some of these rituals of passage have been misinterpreted simplistically as quasi-sexual initiation rites into maturity, while in fact they were designed to facilitate the psychic transition from adolescence to adulthood. Entry into the world of adulthood included a breaking down of the dualistic worldview of the adolescent ego to provide a glimpse of the nondualistic realm of mature perception and feeling.

The initiation process most familiar to nontraditional Westerners is the vision quest. Adolescents were sent away to fast and pray in complete solitude, often for several days. This Native American tradition is analogous in many ways to the basic training and initiation of Tibetan Buddhist monks and of various Christian contemplative and monastic orders. Successful vision quests, shorn of cultural and personal idiosyncrasies, all had a common quality: a vivid, ego-shattering experience of unity with all of Creation. A psychological barrier was broken, that wall created by the fear of losing one's sense of individuality, which is the cause of egotism and of a dualistic, objectifying worldview that is ultimately self-limiting and harmful to others.

One consistent feature of the vision quest is the involvement of an animal or some other natural phenomenon such as a waterfall or a formation of clouds. The involvement with the animal leads to a realization of the universal nature of the Higher Self and the recognition that we are all part of the One Life. Communion with natural phenomena affirms the presence of a higher power. Subsequently, one may take on the name of the "power" that initiated the visionary experience (i.e., White Eagle, Rolling Thunder, Gray Wolf). The medicine powers of animals and Nature are acquired through incorporation, as in meditation and other disciplines of initiation and empowerment.

These traditions and their practical value and significance cannot be dismissed as primitive animism and superstitious, irrational totemism. They have served preindustrial civilizations for millennia, helping preserve peace, justice and the integrity of Nature's Creation. They foster deep respect for other living beings and reverence for life, more out of love for the Self-in-all than fear of divine retribution. In the mystical, transcendental experience, the object of one's attention becomes the subject of one's apprehension: observer and observed become one. Suddenly you become transparent to that which you behold: be it an icon, your hand, your child, a mountain or an ant. As Hyemeyohost Storm has written, "Any idea, person or object can be a Medicine Wheel, a mirror, for man. The tiniest flower can be such a mirror, a wolf, a story, a touch, a religion, or a mountain top."[20] Anything, therefore, when seen in a sacred way is like a mandala, opening the mind to God or the Great Spirit by way of the coinherent nature of divinity in "all things bright and beautiful, all creatures great and small."

While aboriginal religious cosmologies, rites and rituals may differ from those of the world's more recent religious traditions, the aboriginal experience of the religious is no different fundamentally from any other religious experience that entails empowerment with the knowledge that all is sacred.

Reconciling Duality and Paradox

The deeply empathetic sense of aboriginal consciousness, awakened by the religious experience of the oneness of all life, represents the means whereby the ego as the one and ultimate self is transcended. By identification with the cosmic nature of the Higher Self as universal; by recognition that is neither pagan idolatry nor animism of the coinherent nature of divinity; and by incorporation of some aspect of Nature, such as an animal totem, into the psyche, the boundaries of a self-limiting ego are extended panempathetically, leading to the transpersonal experience of existential coinherence. The neo-Confucianist Shao-Yung (1011–1077) puts this simply: "Letting one's self identify with other beings leads to nature. Nature leads to spirituality. Spirituality leads to enlightenment."[21] Reversed seeing, or *fang kuan*, means not seeing things egotistically, according to the ego self, but according to things themselves. Through such self-identification, we may glimpse the world through the eyes of animals. Such seeing or *kuan* is primal or primordial intuition, seeing in a sacred way.

The following riddles, attributed to Jesus of Nazareth, intimate the kind of paradigm shift or reorientation in our thinking, sensing and feeling characteristic of Dreamtime. We need this paradigm shift in order to bring about a sense of unity between ourselves and Nature so that there can be cocreative participation between the visible (the "outside") and the invisible (the "inside") realms. Jesus said:

I am the light which is over everything, I am the All; from me the All has gone forth, and to me the All has returned. Split wood: I am there. Lift up the stone, and you will find me there.

Jesus said to them:

When you make the two one, and you make the inside the outside, and the outside like the inside, and the upper side like the under side, and in such a way that you make the man with the woman a single one, in order that the man is not the man and the woman is not woman; . . . then you will go into the kingdom.[22]

In Eastern philosophy and religion one can find the same paradoxical logic as expressed in the above quotations. The Taoist sage Lao-Tzu observed, "Words that are strictly true seem paradoxical." Paradoxical logic is the antithesis of Aristotelian logic and the prevalent Judeo-Christian thinking about our place in Nature.

Within the systems and processes of Nature, we find unity within diversity, complexity within simplicity, freedom within interdependence and competition within cooperation. Paradox is the essence of Nature; the paradoxical logic of Taoism and the ethical principles that arise from it are derived from a careful study of Nature. Natural science and philosophy are the cornerstones of sustainable agriculture and other industrial economies, as well as holistic medicine and all appropriate technologies. Natural science and philosophy are inseparable and complementary. They lead to a fundamentally spiritual worldview that contrasts sharply to contemporary bioindustrial science and politico-economic philosophy, which, though complementary, are conceptually divorced from Nature and the spiritual realm.

No industrial society can function for long when it operates as though it is or ever can be separate from Nature. Tragically, many enlightened people who are caught within such a dysfunctional society feel helpless because they have become dependent upon it for their livelihood. It is a tragic irony indeed that a new social order of economic dependence and competition now takes precedence over the old biological order of Nature, which is based on cooperative interdependence. As Chinese philosopher Chuang-Yuan observed, "This is that, that is also this. When this and that are not seen as relative opposites, this is called the essence of Tao."[23]

Lao-Tzu expressed the paradox that underlies cooperative interdependence as follows:

> Reality is all embracing.
> To be all embracing is to be selfless.
> To be selfless is to be all pervading.
> To be all pervading is to be transcendent.[24]

Chuang-Yuan expressed this same paradox in the following words: "In the form of things there is a spiritual reality which is manifested into different particularities. This is called the nature of things. To cultivate this nature is to reverse the attainment. This reversal of attainment identifies with the great beginning. This identity with the great beginning is non-being which is the all-embracing."[25]

Japanese philosopher Kitaro Nishida puts the paradox of self and other another way: "The activity of the self means the subjectification of objectivity and the objectification of the self. But at the same time it means that the object subjectifies itself and the universal individualizes itself. Therein the self is lost, but the true self is found."[26]

Erich Fromm proposes that reality can be perceived only paradoxically, in contradictions. Thus the ultimate reality-unity, the One itself, cannot be realized through thought, but only in the act of experiencing. This paradoxical logic leads Fromm to the conclusion that the love of God or Nature is neither the knowledge of God or Nature in thought, as something abstract or personified, nor the thought of one's love for God or Nature, but rather the *act of experiencing* the oneness of God. In this formulation, Fromm comes close to expressing the participatory experience of the aboriginals'

Dreamtime, an experience which lies beyond belief and rational, objective analysis, and is the heart of the Old Religion.

Erich Fromm notes that "paradoxical thought led to the tolerance and an effort toward self-transformation [in Eastern cultures]. The Aristotelian standpoint led to dogma and science, to the Catholic Church and to the discovery of atomic energy."[27] In the former, the love of God and Nature is the experience of oneness and the expression of this love in every act of living. In the latter, the love of God is essentially the same as belief in God for one's salvation. It is essentially a thought experience, not an intense emotional or mystical experience of divine at-one-ment. It is therefore world-negating, and since God is conceived as transcendent only and not immanent in Nature, Nature is desacralized and becomes another means toward our own salvation and material gratification.

To paraphrase Fromm, the disintegration of the love of God has reached the same proportions as the disintegration of the love of man for humanity—and of our love for animals and Nature. While some claim that there is a religious renaissance today, with few exceptions, it is a regression to an idolatrous and salvific concept of God. Fromm also says:

> Our true self is the basic substance of the universe, and if one knows the true self, one indeed is not only linked with the good of mankind in general but one melts with the basic substance of the universe and one is divinely united with the will of God. Both religion and morality are truly exhausted at this point. The law of knowing the true self and of uniting with God lies only in becoming aware of the force of the union of subject and object.[28]

When the values of people and nations become coherent and consonant with the ethical and spiritual principles of *ahimsa* and respectful reverence for all life, then the numinous power of coinherent divinity will be released into the world through the heart of humanity. This release will mean more than the healing of humanity and its redemptive restoration of this desecrated and disgodded planet. It will also herald the birth of a new humanity and of a new global community empowered by the coherence of spirit and will in accord with the ethical and spiritual principles of a humane and sustainable planetary stewardship.

In the final analysis, it is enlightened self-interest to "follow one's original instructions" by endeavoring to live in reverence and symbiosis. No civilization can be self-sustaining if it operates at Nature's expense, no matter how effectively its short-term technological correctives and innovations may seem to function. That such a self-limiting and destructive industrial society as we have today could ever have evolved is in part due to the fact that it is not a mature society. Indeed, it is not even fully civilized. Only an adolescent society could be so selfishly destructive of the natural world and indifferent to what amounts to a holocaust of the Animal Kingdom. It is now a survival imperative for each and every person to identify completely with the suffering of animals and the destruction of Nature. This process of identification and self-transcendence was the purpose of the vision quest. For without such identification and realization that we are all part of the One Life, there can be no fellow feeling and no empathetic concern for other living beings. And it was well known that "where there is no vision, the people shall perish."

Society and industry have much to learn from Nature. In the economy of Nature, nothing is ever wasted; production and consumption are balanced and complementary, neither excessive nor creating a deficit. Nature never extends credit and is the exemplar of self-sufficiency and of the aphorism "neither a borrower nor a lender be."

Industrial society is organized and operates with virtually no regard for the "laws" of Nature and the rational and ethical tenets of natural science and philosophy. This bespeaks a materialistic form of imperialism that is the antithesis of true civilization; it is a Dark Age that has become planetary in its scope, and which is contrary to the tenets of the world's major religions.

Sin, from a Christian perspective, is seen as "separation from God," which means not living according to God's will. Obedience to God's will is synonymous with obeying our "original instructions," for as Black Elk said, "Nothing will be well unless we learn to live in harmony with the Power of the World as it lives and moves and does its work." According to Baha'u'llah, founder of the Baha'i faith, "Nature is God's will and is its expression in and through the contingent world." Thus, to sin is to be separate from Nature as well as from God, the Power of the World, in thought, word and deed. The false dualisms of materialism and egotism that separate God from Nature, humanity from animality and spirituality from materiality are all symptomatic of the condition that Christianity calls "original sin," and which Buddhism and Hinduism alike attribute to dualistic thought and perception—as distinct from *advaita* or nonduality—that create a world of illusion, suffering and destruction.

We learn from Nature that every living thing takes from life no more than it gives back to the One Life. From this principle we can derive one of the "original instructions" which all who seek to live religiously or to participate in the sacraments of life should heed: take from life only as much as we return, and then only in gratitude.

Obedience to Nature's law entails a deep respect and love for all Creation combined with a biocentric and democratic relationship with the environment and all who dwell in it. Obedience necessitates the adoption of a lifestyle that is the antithesis of the egocentric and technocratic relationship that people of all industrial societies are caught up in today. This new lifestyle sees frugality as a virtue and regards the changing of many consumer habits (such as meat-eating) and cultural traditions (like wearing furs and nonsubsistence hunting) as ethical imperatives.

Such changes should not be seen as giving up or personal sacrifice but rather as personal offerings, giving back by taking a little less from life than we need. And the less we need and want, the freer we and the world will become. The voluntary poverty of the Christian mystic and the Australian aboriginal both share the deep wisdom of asceticism, a spirituality that is incomprehensible to secular materialism because it is not antimaterialistic and punitively self-sacrificial. If it were, it could not be what it is: a nondualistic worldview that does not separate the spiritual from the material and thus treats all things, both sentient and nonsentient, with respect and love.

Ecological and spiritual bankruptcy go hand in hand. Without the ecological and spiritual-ethical sensibility derived from the wisdom of following our original instructions, today's expanding global industrial technocracy will destroy the bioregions that it now exploits and pollutes: in other words, most of the natural world. It may destroy itself in the process, or through human ingenuity succeed in converting the Earth into its own "Spaceship," as Buckminster Fuller foresaw.

THE BOUNDLESS CIRCLE

While some may regard this vision of a Spaceship Earth as progress, we must acknowledge that the probable alternative of "terracide" *and* extinction is unacceptable. But there is a third alternative. And that is to help Nature return to its desecrated places through fostering regenerative ecology. These restored and protected areas are vital to the operation and maintenance of Spaceship Earth, which cannot function for long if its captains, ignorant of natural science and philosophy, do not follow Nature's original instructions. While this and the next generation may see such restored and protected areas of Nature variously as genetic resources, recreational facilities and aesthetic experiences, they will ultimately become recognized by an enlightened and grateful humanity, no longer enchanted by the gifts and greatness of its own technology, as sacred places. We must begin to restore, protect and cherish them now, for the more of them there are, the better the Spaceship Earth of tomorrow will function—unless, of course, we do not care for the well-being of generations to come.

To restore and protect sacred places is as much a survival imperative in the long-term as it is a wise investment for the future. Out of respect and gratitude, we should call these places and all who dwell in them sacred. The word *sacred* implies that which is set apart for the service or worship of deity, implying inherent and inviolable value. Only through such an attitude will Nature be cherished and protected, and the resacralization of the Earth will be our saving grace.

Apotheosis, Resurrection and the New Earth Community

As the spiritual and ethical principles of the Old Religion become increasingly relevant to the crisis we all face, a new Earth community is emerging. Recast in the holistic paradigm of the Old Religion and shorn of pagan superstition and fear, such concepts as apotheosis and resurrection take on a new vitality that links Christian mysticism with an emergent, Creation-centered spirituality.

The apotheoses of Nature, humankind and animalkind are one and the same. While the emergent universe is "unfinished," at every moment, it is perfect in its totality. Thus, our perception of the coinherence of divinity in Nature is not idolatry but rather the apotheosis of the Self and divinity both within and without.

The apotheosis of Christianity is the realization of the Christ within, through love and empathy with the suffering of the world. The essence of Jewish mysticism is in the perception that God is not in the world, but rather the world is in God. Kabbalists accept absolute unity as the basis of their system—a God who is, at one and the same time, the cause, substance and form of all that is and all that can be. To experience oneself as part of this One Life in God is the apotheosis of the Self. It is an experience devoid of self-aggrandizement because it is imbued with the suffering of the world, caused in part by our selfishness and ignorance. This insight gives rise to humility. But there can be no connection and redemption without love, not only of God, nation, family, animals and Nature, but also of oneself and one's enemies.

Each spiritual tradition has its own way of expressing this basic insight. The Buddhists say that when there is enlightenment—purity of perception—everything is a Buddha. One of the inner teachings of the Koran as espoused by the Sufis is that all things are in God and God is in all things. In Hinduism, apotheosis is the realization that the *Atman* (the inner Self) and *Brahman* (God and Creation) are one and the same. When the Christian is "born again" in this way, everything is in Christ as the Christ within. Realization of the unity of Being in God through love is the apotheosis of the observer and the observed. This is the Resurrection of the Cosmic Christ.[29] Part of the Christian apotheosis is to love and empathetically suffer the body of Christ that is now being crucified: the Earth, as our addictive materialism consumes the natural world.

The natural world continues to be desecrated and transformed into an industrialized, poisoned wasteland. Genetic engineering and the patenting of life is accelerating the process of bioindustrialization, and human suffering intensifies. The rich displace the poor. Their sustainable lands are destroyed by nonregenerative agricultural and other industries, along with undeveloped "wilderness" areas, which are now fast disappearing.

Where have all the animals gone? Most are confined in cruel "factory" farms and never see the light of day until we eat them in our own darkness. Many animals are incarcerated in laboratories where they are vivisected. It is ironic that we follow medical practices that demand such suffering. Since the means are the ends in the making, the best medicine surely cannot be derived from a paradigm that endorses the suffering of experimental animals. No good ends can come from evil means.

The few wild animals that have not become extinct from direct competition and habitat destruction are "managed" for the hunter, trapper, fisherman, gene engineer and "naturalist" tourist. And so many of the creatures—domesticated and wild "exotics"—that we keep as "pets" are afflicted by the deprivations of a sedentary existence. Many suffer genetic defects due to inbreeding, which causes serious health problems in many purebred cats and dogs.

These, the children of God, whom St. Francis of Assisi called our little brothers and sisters, are suffering now. They are crying out that we might see, might at last feel their pain as ours. For we are all one in Christ. Liberation of the Animal Kingdom and "the whole of Creation that groaneth and travaileth until now" is conditional upon this apotheosis—the tearing of the veil of the illusion of our separateness from the One Life.

This change in perception and feeling for the world ultimately leads to a radical change in behavior. This change is marked by a very different relationship with Creation, a shift in consumer habits and lifestyles toward voluntary simplicity, and conscientious consumerism (as exemplified by vegetarianism) in order to minimize adverse environmental consequences. This same apotheosis will revolutionize such institutions as health and education, and the agriculture and energy industries, which cannot continue to function at the Earth's expense. These institutions and industries and the economies of the developed and developing nations alike will ultimately fail if we, as a species, fail to recognize our dependence upon the One Life and continue to treat the environment and all who dwell in it without reverence or even equal and fair consideration.

The traditional Christian belief in the Second Coming is the mystic vision of the return or rebirth, in consciousness and in our eyes and hearts, of the Cosmic Christ. Through these eyes we see the numinous presence in all of Nature, as in the eyes of the wolf and the cry of the nighthawk. When the heart of Christianity becomes one with the heart of the world, the Christian Church becomes the Ark of the Covenant to "dress and to keep" Earth's Creation. Through Christ-realization in our compassion for all sentient beings and all of Creation, humankind can be redeemed.

When the heart's eye is opened, it becomes the eye of God, for as Jesus said, "I and the Father are one." For the Buddhist, this is the clarity of perception whereby everything is perceived as a Buddha. In other words, through empathy, the bridge of compassion, we see and feel and become a part of the numinous divine presence that is coinherent in everything.

The panempathetic symbol of the Sacred Heart, when deeply contemplated and incorporated, is the realization of the passion of Christ crucified. This spiritual union, or opening of the heart chakra in Yogic terms, results in the Self-realizing birth of compassion in the human species. And with this awakening of feeling, the metaphysical leap or *metanoia* occurs: we are one in Christ. In Hinduism this is expressed as *tat tvam asi*—"Thou art That." In other words, the awakening of compassion leads to the realization that all of life is one. From the wisdom of this new way of seeing and feeling, the human species at last comes to respect the sacred unity of life and the sanctity of being.

But at the very moment that the beauty and mystery of the divine presence are perceived, the stigmata of Christ crucified are also received. St. Francis of Assisi empathized so deeply not only with fellow creatures and all of Creation, but with Christ on the Cross, upon whom he meditated and with whom he enjoyed holy communion every day, that he received the stigmata. For us it is the same. As we begin to have communion with Nature, we see how much pain and destruction a fallen humanity has wreaked upon the planet and upon itself. Our pain at this realization is the stigmata of Christ as Earth crucified.

"Born again" in this way, the compassionate human soul sees Nature's eternal renewal and transformation as the existential equivalent of the doctrine of spiritual parthenogenesis—the Virgin Birth. Mary, the Virgin Mother, is seen by the new eyes of this awakening consciousness as the Matrix or Earth Mother, and the emergent universe as the Cosmic Womb or plenum void for the coming Cosmic Christ, whom followers of non-Christian traditions variously call the Buddha light, Great Spirit or Brahman.

For monotheistic religions, this means more than a transcendental union with the godhead. It is also a deep empathetic connection with the very matrix or ground of being. Rather than world-negating, it is world-connecting and world-as-Self-realizing. Some "deep ecologists" refer to this connection as "the extended Self," the equivalent of the psychological concept of ego-transcendence and identification. It marks the beginning of a new age on Earth for humankind, now on the threshold of a global socioeconomic and environmental apocalypse. This new age that is dawning as the heart chakra of humankind begins to open can be the beginning of a New Eden. The difficult task today is to begin to restore this raped and vanquished Earth Mother to a semblance of her original beauty, health and vitality. "Ecology," says the Very Reverend James P. Morton, "is the science of the Body of Christ through which we of the Earth community learn our sacred connectedness."

As we heal the Earth by becoming co-participants in intimate, and indeed holy, communion with the processes of planetary and cosmic unfoldment in an emergent universe, we begin to heal ourselves and are made whole. That is the gift of Christ-realization as the redeemer. As Father Sean McDonagh has said, our "redemption, to be complete, must heal and renew the primordial unity and recreate the Earth whenever it has been injured through human greed and vice."[30] And as St. Francis of Assisi advised, it is the duty and fulfillment of every Christian to be the mother of Christ by living according to the Scriptures. We find the basic tenets of these Scriptures in the teachings of all religious traditions; namely, compassion respect and reverence for all life, nonviolence (*ahimsa*), and adherence to the Golden Rule.

As Nature—through God's love and wisdom—incorporates us, so we, in respect for and gratitude to Nature, incorporate God. Such is the nature of God-realization as St. Francis of Assisi and other great spiritual leaders have taught. Ultimately, our attitudes and values, for better or for worse, determine the fate of the Earth and of humankind. In his autobiographical Australian travelogue *The Songlines*, Bruce Chatwin includes the following relevant exchange with a fellow traveler: " 'Renunciation,' I said, 'even at this late date, can work.' 'I'd agree with that,' said Arkady. 'The world, if it has a future, has an ascetic future.' "[31]

Aboriginal Consciousness and the "Old Religion"

While we cannot return to the way of life of aboriginal peoples by becoming gatherer-hunters again, our industrial society may learn something from these people who are living in their own ancestral ways in today's world. Human spirituality, communality, frugality and communion are the basic elements of the "Aboriginal Way" of living in accord with "Nature's Law." By understanding the Old Religion that these people embody in the Dreaming, we may all be empowered to develop a more Creation-centered, Earth-sustaining and fulfilling way of life for the benefit of all to come.

This chapter, therefore, is not to be interpreted as a message urging our contemporary industrial-consumer society to return to some ro-manticized aboriginal way of life. Rather, it argues that we may derive from the old ways of being spiritual inspiration and practical solutions to help our global community live in harmony with the rest of Earth's Creation. By developing ecologically sound, sustainable and thus ethical industries from organic agriculture to solar power, and by learning to live gently on the Earth, modern society may yet discover that living in accord with aboriginal law is the altruistic wisdom of enlightened self-interest that contains the seeds of a potentially global humane society. The following declaration points the way:

DECLARATION OF INTERDEPENDENCE

We the people of the world's ecological community, in recognition of the kinship and interdependence of all life, declare that it is our sacred duty to re-sanctify the Earth by living in reverence of the integrity, beauty, and mystery of Creation; and by living gently, respectful of the inherent value and will-to-be of all living beings, help ensure the future of Earth's Creation and all who shall dwell therein.

Self-imaging: Rediscovering and Recovery of the Sacred

The renowned spiritual teacher, J. Krishnamurti, in his last book, talked about our relationships with trees and other living things.[32] He advised that we would not fear death and, as a consequence, harm ourselves and all life, if we all felt that "killing a deer is like killing your neighbor. You kill animals when you have lost touch with nature, with all the living things on this earth. You kill in wars for so many romantic, nationalistic, political, ideologies. In the name of God you have killed people."(33)

For Krishnamurti, discovering that when we kill the deer we kill a part of ourselves, leads to a new appreciation of life and of death. When we kill a deer we kill a part of our own nature, because we are all of Nature, of the One Life. With this realization, as Krishnamurti writes, "Death isn't some horrific thing, something to be avoided, something to be postponed, but rather something to be with day in and day out. And out of that comes an extraordinary sense of immensity."(34) The Self as love, is indeed immense, illimitable and immeasurable. To experience this sense of immensity, Krishnamurti advised that we "look deeply into the quality of a tree." He wrote:

If you establish a relationship with it then you have relationship with mankind. You are responsible then for that tree and for the trees of the world. But if you have no relationship with the living things on this earth you may lose whatever relationship you have with humanity, with human beings. We never look deeply into the quality of a tree; we never really touch it, feel its solidity, its rough bark, and hear the sound that is part of the tree. Not the sound of wind through the leaves, not the breeze of a morning that flutters the leaves, but its own sound, the sound of the trunk and the silent sound of the roots. You must be extraordinarily sensitive to hear the sound. This sound is not the noise of the world, not the noise of the chattering of the mind, not the vulgarity of human quarrels and human warfare but sound as part of the universe.

It is odd that we have so little relationship with nature, with the insects and the leaping frog and the owl that hoots among the hills calling for its mate. We never seem to have a feeling for all living things on the earth. If we could establish a deep abiding relationship with nature we would never kill an animal for our appetite, we would never harm, vivisect, a monkey, a dog, a guinea pig for our benefit. We would find other ways to heal our wounds, heal our bodies. But the healing of the mind is something totally different. That healing gradually takes place if you are with nature, with that orange on the tree, and the blade of grass that pushes through the cement, and the hills covered, hidden, by the clouds.

Aboriginal Consciousness and the "Old Religion"

This is not sentiment or romantic imagination but a reality of a relationship with everything that lives and moves on the earth. Man has killed millions of whales and is still killing them. All that we derive from their slaughter can be had through other means. But apparently man loves to kill things, the fleeting deer, the marvelous gazelle and the great elephant. We love to kill each other. This killing of other human beings has never stopped throughout the history of man's life on this earth. If we could, and we must, establish a deep long abiding relationship with nature, with the actual trees, the bushes, the flowers, the grass and the fast moving clouds, then we would never slaughter another human being for any reason whatsoever. Organized murder is war, and though we may demonstrate against a particular war, the nuclear, or any other kind of war, we have never demonstrated against war. We have never said that to kill another human being is the greatest sin on earth.[35]

For philosopher Ramachandra Gandhi, not perceiving the deer as a part of our own nature and both as part of the One Life is a kind of distorted self-imaging. He writes: "Life on earth, individually and collective, human and nonhuman, is a mirroring of self—adequately or inadequately, revealing or distorting—mirroring or self-imaging being the deepest impulse of existence."[36]

Chief Seattle expressed the concept of mirroring in different words: "We are part of the earth and the earth is part of us. The fragrant flowers are our sisters, the reindeer, the horse, the great eagle, our brothers. The foamy crests of waves in the river, the sap of meadow flowers, the pony's sweat is all one and the same race, our race."[37]

To Mircea Eliade, self-imaging through openness to Nature is essential to self-knowledge : "An existence open to the world is not an unconscious existence 'buried in nature.' Openness to the world enables religious man to know himself in knowing the world—and this knowledge is precious to him because it is religious, because it pertains to being."[38]

However, what do we gain in terms of knowing ourselves by being open to a world of environmental desecration and degradation, civilizational disintegration and suffering, except the burden of suffering and the pall of pessimism? Furthermore, how can we know our inner nature if outer nature—the natural world—is desecrated or marginalized from our lives and concerns? In other words, as philosopher Ramachandra Gandhi observes, with increasing environmental degradation, our self-imaging becomes increasingly distorted. Any culturally determined norm of collective self-imaging becomes pathological when the mirror of Nature has been defiled. Only when this defilement is apprehended and we see ourselves clearly can our self-imaging lead us to the resacralization of Self and Nature. But a point may soon be reached where Nature's mirror has been so defiled that no self-imaging is possible except from the technological-industrial reality and material artifacts that we have created ourselves. This profane reality is evident today in the narcissism of secular humanism and economic determinism that amounts to nothing more than materialistic self-worship. It is the antithesis of reverence for the omnipresent and coinherent Universal Self in all life.

In the face of environmental degradation and social disintegration, both economically and morally, a sense of helplessness and hopelessness may give rise to the belief that humanity is doomed and that there is no point in trying to save anything. Life seems pointless when there is so much suffering and destruction, and a nuclear war seems a perverse kind of purification.

Do we really want there to be life on Earth? As Professor Ramachandra Gandhi observes, "The dominant contemporary cultures of secular humanism and religious fundamentalism do not provide unambiguously affirmative answers to this question."[39] Professor Gandhi emphasizes the role played by "prestigious scientific and theological doctrines that would have us believe the nature of the universe and earth conditions rule out the possibility of an indefinite continuation of life on earth, that entropic collapse and the apocalypse are inevitable."[40] These nihilistic and defeatist doctrines reinforce the attitude of annihilationism.

Further reinforcement comes from the religious fundamentalists' belief that our real home is in heaven and that the Earth is just some temporary "fallen" place from which we are all to seek salvation. This world-negating belief, coupled with the notion that Nature and all creatures are "fallen" just like human beings, provides no motivational basis for conservation, respect for animal rights or reverence for all life. On the contrary, it liberates humanity from any sense of responsibility toward Nature. By thus desacralizing Creation, all ethical constraints upon industrial expansion and the transformation of the natural world into a polluted, industrialized wasteland are removed.

The annihilationist attitude and its dangerous consequences gain strength and momentum in yet other ways. The ancient metaphysical and theological doctrine of the finite nature of personal existence in which there is only oblivion after death can lead to the attitude that life has no continuity. Thus life has no meaning except in the material realm of gratification and acquisition within the finite span of one's own existence. This devaluing of life, coupled with the attitude that the lives of other beings are not ends in themselves but a means to others' ends adds fuel to an annihilationist-nihilistic worldview.

The demeaning of life and the nihilism that intensifies with the despair of cultural disintegration and environmental degradation lead to a distortion of what Professor Gandhi calls self-imaging. He observes:

> No technological or ideological utopia need be promised by life of earth in its invitation to humanity to the joy of adequate self-imaging, to the adventure of civilization and realization, to the flowering of consciousness and culture. In ecologically and civiliza-tionally impossible conditions of existence there will be possible, if at all, only the most distorted self-imaging. Perhaps that is what hell is—the perversion of the art of self-imaging; and heaven and earth capable of honoring and sustaining that art.[41]

He concludes prophetically, "Let us choose the earth, here and now, as a perfect image of the Eternal Now; and let there be life."[42]

The self-imaging of those who feel hopeless and helpless in the face of escalating environmental degradation and cultural disintegration, and who experience the inevitable sadness and depression that comes with the knowledge of these ills, needs to be enhanced. But there is no easy remedy. An all too common way of coping for caring people is to disengage from attempting to fight for social reforms, for the recognition of human and animal rights and for the conservation of the natural world. A kind of psychic numbing occurs, such that they act as though there are no problems outside their insular lives. And they compartmentalize, valuing and caring for their children or "pets," for example, but not extending these values and concerns to all children and all creatures. Compartmentalization also underlies ethical inconsistency and hypocrisy, like the company executive who sells, and the farmer who uses, harmful pesticides. While such harmful activities are rationalized, these same people claim to care for their children and for the quality of life on Earth. Compartmentalizing as a way of coping leads to a schizoid state in which one's beliefs and actions are inconsistent and often contradictory. It led to the genocidal holocaust of Nazism and today undergirds the biocidal holocaust of industrialism.

Perhaps our last chance to improve our self-imaging lies in our ability and courage to identify fully with the natural world and all who dwell therein. This is an experiential, transpersonal process that necessitates a leap beyond dogma, belief and faith. It entails a change in perception, of seeing a tree, for example, not simply as a resource or aesthetically pleasing object, but as a significant, sentient fellow being that is as much a part of the One Life as we ourselves are. Then no self-respecting person or society would deliberately cause harm to other living beings or desecrate the environment by clear-cutting the forests and dumping raw sewage into the rivers and oceans—unless, that is, there is no feeling for and thus no connection with that which is harmed. There is fundamentally no difference between polluting and destroying a swamp, torturing and killing human beings and vivisecting and "sacrificing" nonhuman beings. Yet distinctions are made on the grounds of morality, superiority and necessity to justify actions which we would protest if done to ourselves, our children or our "pets" and our property. In the process of making such distinctions, therefore, the path to selective and ever-increasing annihilationism is opened up and through rationalization and compartmentalization, the Golden Rule is broken.

The Golden Rule of treating all other living things as we would have them treat us, along with the doctrine of *ahimsa*, of not harming others even if they harm us, becomes increasingly difficult to live by in times of civilizational disintegration. The reflective realization that we are responsible for the world we create because our individual and collective self-imaging is mirrored by the kind of home, society and environment we live in, can do much to help repair what we see in the mirror. There is nothing wrong with the mirror itself.

Aboriginal Consciousness and the "Old Religion"

The distorted anti-life self-imaging of the rising technocracy is accelerating the process of environmental degradation by remaking the Earth's Creation into its own perverted image of an industrialized biosphere. Nothing is sacred except those utopian, materialistic values of power, control, industrial growth, efficiency and productivity. The annihilationism inherent in a technocratic utopia is as real as the concerns of the conservationist and animal rightist, and the distorted self-imaging of such secular humanism needs to be recognized by all who care for the integrity of Creation and the future of all life on Earth.

Ancestor and Nature Reverence and the Fall and Redemption of Man

THE ELEMENTS SUNLIGHT, FIRE, air, earth and water are our primal ancestors, making us the relatives of all living beings. As an old Serbian saying goes, "We should be noble because we are star dust, and humble because we are manure." St. Francis of Assissi acknowledged water, fire and the other elements and forces of nature as ancestral relatives, referring to them as brother and sister in his *Canticle to the Sun*.

Awareness of our ancestral kinship with all of Creation is the essence of religious sensibility, a nondualistic view shared by peoples of different cultures since the beginning of oral history. Lacking such awareness, the human psyche can become an alien, lonely, tragic and often destructive force focused on satisfying its own insatiable needs. This "terminator" species is also a terminal species since, in the process of consuming the world, it exterminates itself.

In earlier times, reverence for ancestors was not a simplistic, superstitious worship of deceased family members. Ancestors were envisioned in myriad forms—animals, rocks and trees, as well as in the elements themselves. In some cultures the elements were anthropomorphized, not out of superstitious ignorance, but as a consequence of a deep sense of connectedness. In this way, Nature's elements and processes became part of a pantheon of gods of rain and fire and goddesses of earth and wind. There were divine forces, benevolent or malevolent, in the forests, waters and mountains. Guardian spirits protected these and other habitats for the well-being of all who dwelt therein. Respect for these unseen forces and for the living creatures, plants and natural elements within their domain, became the cornerstone of sustainability for preindustrial civilizations. Shaped by these forces, each culture acquired its own qualities, traditions and spirit of place. Little wonder, therefore, that when ancient peoples saw their land taken over and obliterated or exploited by "modern" people of the industrial age, they feared the end of their civilization, which was, for them, the end of the world.

We cannot expect people today to revert to ancestor worship or to elaborate a pantheon of Earth's Creation for reverencing. Nor can we expect an industrial society—which sees any constraints on economic growth and expansion as unethical, an affront to the new religion of industrialism and the new morality of economic determinism— to respect the guardian spirits of the land, air and waters. The new religion of the industrial age is fundamentally dualistic, placing the human species outside and above Nature. It stands in sharp contrast to the preindustrial religious traditions of past civilizations which were essentially nondualistic, seeing humankind and Nature as one.

The invention of the clock transformed time into a mechanical and linear, rather than a sacred, natural, cyclical phenomenon. Chronos and cosmos alike were demystified and remythologized by the Cartesian and Newtonian paradigm of a rational, mechanically lawful and thus predictable and controllable universe in which humans were the center. Under the dominion of science (reason) and industry (power), the divinely ordained, wholesale exploitation of Nature became humanity's birthright, to paraphrase Francis Bacon.

Philosopher René Descartes and physicist Isaac Newton, along with Francis Bacon, were the founding fathers of the industrial-scientific revolution. Their legacy burns on today in a consumer-driven economy that is turning the natural world into a global commons for commercial gain. The images of the gods and goddesses of ages past have been defaced. Old mythologies have been supplanted by the myths of progress through global industrialism, material prosperity and competitive individualism—all dualistic concepts that have disgodded the world. Deicide and ecocide are parallel consequences of a dualistic worldview.

Our technologies distance us and alienate us from Nature and from the gods and goddesses of earlier times, who were the mythic Powers of Nature, Cosmos, and of the Animal, Plant and Mineral Kingdoms. Nature, once the norm and the measure of all things, is seen merely as a resource, and its living and nonliving creations exploitable commodities devoid of inherent value. Distanced and alienated, we feel that our power over atom and gene, as over animals and Nature, makes atom, gene, animal and Nature ours to exploit as we choose. But like Prometheus, we will suffer the painful consequences of pursuits that arise from our deification of human life and industry above the rest of earthly Creation.

The converging movements against racism, sexism, speciesism and the desecration of the natural world are appropriate and necessary responses to the harmful consequences of the dualistic mind-set that separates, divides, demeans and exploits. It does not see the individual Self as being both a unique part of life and also connected with all life. It separates the Self from the whole by a process of linear-hierarchic thinking and objectification. The subjective, empathic bond of identification with other sentient beings, human and nonhuman, is thus severed. Compassion can arise only when there is a nondualistic "at-one-ment" with others through empathy. A strong human-animal and human-Nature bond is the antidote to speciesism and environmental desecration.

It is incumbent upon us all to develop a new science of human behavior based upon a nondualistic ethic of respect and reverence for all life. With such an ethical foundation, the possibility of a humane and sustainable Earth community could become a reality for future generations. But until we stop limiting the options of future generations and start to change our attitudes, relationships and lifestyles, as well as our political, industrial and agricultural practices and priorities, there will be no future. Without a radical cognitive and behavioral shift from a dualistic to a nondualistic state of mind, all efforts to make this world a better place today and for generations to come will be futile and only prolong the agony of a dying planet and a fallen race.

The Fall of Man: Anthropological and Psychohistorical Evidence

The biblical Fall is a mythopoetic image shared by many religious traditions. Reference to our loss of innocence and the end of a Golden Age seems to be a significant and shared racial memory in the collective human unconscious. The archetypal Adam and Eve are the dualistic human elements of the Creation myth from whom the first people, most likely gatherer-hunters, arose. This long symbiotic stage of human development represents some 98 percent of the 100,000-year epoch of the existence of *Homo sapiens*. Far more recent is the advent of agriculture and livestock-keeping which resulted in a fundamental shift from symbiosis with the natural world to an attitude of domination and control.

The end of the last Ice Age may well coincide with the end of the Golden Age, since at this time, the transition from gathering-hunting to agriculture is well documented. Within a few generations, urban empires rose and fell through wars and colonial expansion. Since the human causes of flood, drought, famine and pestilence were not fully comprehended, ecological devastations were interpreted as punishments from the gods. In the East, pantheistic religions and belief in reincarnation evolved, while in the Middle East and West, monotheistic religions, with their distinctive components of patriarchy, domination, and an andromorphic god, flourished.

Thus the world over, for a mere fraction of our existence, have we lived in urban communities consisting of different classes, races and religious traditions. In all parts of the world, our ability to adapt and organize ourselves socially and equitably is being sorely tested. Increasing urbanization, unemployment and population growth, coupled with the concentration of wealth and the centralization of control of resources in a powerful minority, are creating a host of problems. If these are not soon remedied, industrial society will become even more dysfunctional and may well take the rest of the world with it.

Some anthropologists report that contemporary shamans and elders in primitive societies are fully aware of how human activities need to be guided to ensure the sustainable use of natural resources. People living close to Nature know the intimate connections between human and environmental well-being. But this empathic wisdom is less evident in more "advanced" industrial societies, where separation from Nature is compounded by an attitude which regards the natural world as an objectified resource and plants and animals as commodities. The patriarchal, linear and hierarchical worldview of preindustrial, monotheistic cultures, whose economic base was livestock, has not transferred well to modern industrialized society.

The thread that connects these epochs—cattle-chattel-capital—originates from the time when our relationship with animals and Nature changed from symbiosis to domination and control. In the process, the natural world was disgodded, divinity was separated, no longer a coinherent aspect of Creation and sentient life. Animism and totemism were thrown out along with pantheism and Nature worship. This mutation in consciousness is our biblical Fall, separating divinity from Creation and humanity from God and Nature. It unleashed upon the world a destructive, arrogant human ego that is developmentally arrested in adolescence. The future well-being of both person and planet are dependent upon overcoming this developmental impasse.

The human ability to objectify—to give names to things and to distance ourselves—and at the same time to be subjective and empathetic makes us a chimeric species. Human beings can be both rational and passionate. Inhumanity arises when we live in one of these modes to the exclusion of the other. In the process of transforming animals, plants and ecosystems into commodities, we have hypertrophied our capacity to objectify and atrophied the subjective, empathic qualities that are the basis for compassion and communion.

The End of Human Evolution—or a New Beginning?

A popular theory holds that human evolution is a progressive process of increasing consciousness (sapience and sentience) involving both brain and social complexity. Evolutionary biologists, paleontologists and geneticists are in general agreement that the chimpanzee (*Pan troglodytes*) is our closest living relative on the primate branch of the evolutionary tree. Our distinctly humanoid lineage goes back only a few million years from modern man (*Homo sapiens*) and Cro-Magnon man, through Neanderthal man, to earlier *Homo habilis* and *Homo erectus*. It is unclear why these earlier humanoid forms died out, but it is clear that human forces are now pushing almost the entire Animal Kingdom into extinction. The Earth's evolutionary process is likewise being terminated, supplanted by the expansionist industrial processes of economic development and technological evolution. These processes are not only destroying the natural world and the Earth's biotic community, but also the atmosphere and other life-support systems of the planet, thus endangering human life.

The emergence of *Homo technos*, technological man, over the past two hundred years could bring the Earth's evolutionary process to an end. Technocrats and those enchanted by technology believe that the current transformation to an industrialized biosphere is a perfectly natural continuance of the evolutionary process. Those of an orthodox religious inclination even believe it is divinely ordained. The supporters of this development fail to see that it is actually a radical departure from the Earth's natural process of evolution which has supported life for billions of years. It is closer to a terminal disease than to the fruition of planetary life. Many people still adhere to the arrogantly anthropocentric view that the purpose of the Earth is human fulfillment; and that creatures and Creation are not ends in themselves with intrinsic value but commodities that exist to satisfy human ends.

But now, as this millennium comes to a close, we see the consequences of a lack of moral restraint and ethical sensibility toward Earth's Creation and our fellow creatures: a dying planet, a disintegrating climate, an increasingly dysfunctional global economy, a sickening and impoverished humanity and a vanishing Animal Kingdom.

These consequences of "technoevolution" cannot be denied except by the most myopic of technocrats and a consumer populace that just wants more. Some even believe that humanity will be able to pull itself up from the brink of extinction by developing new technological substitutes for the now failing planetary life-support systems. But it is becoming increasingly evident that we have neither the time, resources nor ability to accomplish this task on a global scale. Global it must be, otherwise surrogate life-support systems would most likely be dysfunctional and certainly undemocratic if less affluent nation states and bioregions were excluded.

While the desperate effort to save what is left of the natural world from desecration and exploitation is intensifying, some feel that it is already too late. However, it is only too late, I believe, if we do not learn from history and acknowledge that we have been on a path of self-destruction; that if we continue on this path of economic development and industrial growth, we and the natural world will suffer.

Many people fear now that there is no future: Technology seems to be out of control and unable to offer any viable solutions, since new developments almost invariably intensify our species' decline. Nor has organized religion come up with any remedy, while the biomedical industry provides little solace other than the accumulation of corporate wealth. Doomsday prophets contend that neither God nor science nor government can save us from suffering, chaos and ultimate extinction.

However, the antidotes to hopelessness and despair are not to be found in scientific and religious salvation, political solutions or the ravings of doomsday prophets. They are to be found in the deep heart's core of every human being who has the potential and the will to become humane. Through the supreme challenge of saving the Earth and the Animal Kingdom, we will heal ourselves, becoming, in the process, dignified, humane beings.

The possibility of a global Humane Society, an Earth community of humankind that lives in accord with the Golden Rule, is a logical and necessary evolutionary step. But it is contingent upon our collective will and choice to be rational and empathic, truly objective and fully compassionate. This awakening heralds the dawn of a new Golden Age. The hope of the world lies in the survival instinct of an enlightened humanity that realizes that where there is humility that embodies respect and reverence for all life, there is no will-to-power. The quest for absolute power corrupts and demeans humanity absolutely. The only human absolute is compassion. And through compassion, whose bridge is empathy, humanity realizes the true nature of earthliness. Through this realization and the hope that it embodies, the possibility of planetary salvation and personal redemption becomes a viable option.

We create our history and our destiny. Such is the power and responsibility of our dominion over fellow creatures and the natural world. If we learn from history, we will not relive it by repeating past mistakes. The foundation of a community of hope lies, therefore, in the human heart, in our collective capacity and will to live in respect and reverence for all life.

We still have a moment's grace to stop now and build a new global economic order and industries that will protect and restore what is left of Nature's systems that are as integral to our own survival as they are to the evolutionary process itself. If we fail to protect and restore the Earth's natural processes, its biodiversity and its functional integrity, by stopping further deforestation, population growth, global warming, industrial pollution and expansion of livestock and other nonsustainable industries, we seal our fate.

Human beings must recognize that we are a terminal species if we do not take the path of planetary salvation. This recognition entails acknowledgment that we have long deluded ourselves into believing that industrial growth and technological advances are progressive, evolutionary steps. But if we look at the evolution of *Homo sapiens* from a scientific, biological perspective, we see that our evolution has reached an impasse.

As the evolution of pain sensitivity was an adaptive response of sentient beings to avoid bodily harm, so the evolution of environmental sensitivity is an adaptive response to avoid the harmful consequences of damaging it. We are learning today the costs of environmental insensitivity and indifference. The body human is as inseparable from the body Earth as the body politic is from the body of society. As the development of the capacity to empathize with the suffering of our own kind was integral to the harmonious functioning of human communities, so the further development of the capacity to empathize with all sentient beings is integral to the harmonious functioning of human communities within the larger community of the planet.

The Earth will take care of us when we take care of the Earth by extending the right of equal and fair consideration to all creatures and Creation. A consumer society ultimately consumes itself when there is no concern for what people eat or otherwise consume, and what they discharge into the environment.

Perhaps the second Fall—that of industrial society—is the human capacity to harm by turning others into objects of exploitation and commoditization, and the rationalization of the destruction of the natural world as normative, progressive and thus unavoidable. The antidotes of humility and compassion enable us to have communion with the subjective realm, the key to the healing of person and planet. This stance is the only basis for a sound economy, a healthy populace, world peace and a sustainable future. Our redemption lies not in escapist denial of our responsibilities toward the natural world. Rather it lies in our respect and reverence for all Creation, and in our dedication to restore all that we have harmed and defiled. Redemption, therefore, is a matter of saving not only Earth's Creation, but the human spirit from extinction.

The stirrings of an awakening environmental sensitivity and empathy toward all living things are harbingers of a new human consciousness. They represent a necessary developmental and evolutionary step from *Homo sapiens* (and *Homo technos*) to *Homo pansapiens*. Without panempathy and respect for all life, we will continue on the present path of extinction.

It is now simply a matter of personal choice and collective will: ecocide and suicide, or survival and fulfillment. We need not abandon technology, but we must see its myriad misapplications and the progressive ideology of economic development and industrial expansion as evolutionary dead-ends. As our past evolution was integral to the evolution of the biosphere, so our continued evolution is dependent upon the integrity of the biosphere and the development of appropriate ethics, technologies, industries, economies and lifestyles. This new conservative ideology is the antithesis of the liberal ideology of the technocracy. Only on the basis of an awakening of environmental sensitivity and empathy toward all living beings—a Creation-centered spirituality—can we continue to evolve.

Human Evolution and the Empathosphere

A rational, rights-based morality and ethical sensibility is now coming into focus as the human and animal rights movements and the conservation and "deep" ecology movements merge into a unified concern for all of Creation. This, in the final analysis, is the only antidote for the many crises that we face today and the prerequisite for a new world order in which peace, justice and the integrity and future of Earth's Creation will be assured.

Human Evolution and the Empathosphere

Teilhard de Chardin coined the term *noosphere* to express his concept of a world-encompassing reflective dimension of human thought and values. The innovations of computer and satellite communication technologies and the "information highway" are making the noosphere a tangible reality. Less tangible, but no less real, is what might be called the "empathosphere," an all-embracing dimension of human feeling. The empathosphere has a profound effect on human behavior and well-being, and on the well-being of all life forms that are affected by human feelings.

The world-encompassing noosphere created by modern technology will amount to little, however, if it is not reflective. In other words, what Teilhard called the technosphere must be made ethical so that it is reflectively self-regulating to maximize good and minimize harm. The empathosphere can play a vital role in the process of global human integration and evolution. But driven by a technocratic rather than an empathic ethos, the technosphere will never evolve into a noosphere. The empathosphere will disintegrate, along with all human communities under technocratic control. The biosphere itself will become a desecrated wasteland incapable of supporting human life without costly correctives. These trends are evident today, and the urgency of applying reason and compassion, ethics and empathy, to the affairs of state cannot be ignored.

At the 1993 centennial Parliament of the World's Religions, held in Chicago, compassion was declared the lawful sovereign of our age. As the supreme ethical principle, compassion links all religious traditions and makes no distinctions as to age, sex, race or species. Born out of the synthesis of reason and compassion, the evolving human consciousness is collectively on the threshold of self-realization. As St. Paul put it, "We are all members of one another." The realization of the universal nature of the Higher Self is an incremental step in human development. We become conscious of the sacred unity and interdependence of all life as we pass through the stages of unconscious unity and symbiosis, individuation and diversification, and conscious communion and community. The turmoil, suffering and destructiveness of the dualistic stage of egocentrism can serve as a catalyst for the dawning of cosmocentrism—an Earth- or Creation-centered spirituality and a worldview that is fundamentally non-dualistic. This developmental and evolutionary transformation of the individual and of the species is a question of choice, as Teilhard de Chardin saw it, "between suicide and adoration." The virtues and reality of this cosmic worldview have long been recognized. What I have called the empathosphere was recognized two millennia ago by Hinduism as *Dharmadhatu*, the nondualistic realm of universal being. As the *Vedas* teach, where there is fear, there is duality. But when the individuated Self is connected panempathetically with the sentient world, a deep sense of security and belonging is experienced. The empathosphere is the realm of conscious, reflexive realization that sentience is a universal and universalizing principle. As this realization intensifies, we become more panempathic, concerned for the suffering of all beings and committed to seek compassionate solutions wherever inhumanity touches our lives.

When reason and compassion are no longer relevant aspects of society and of individual behavior, it is difficult to live as if there is hope for humanity. Inhumanity erodes humanity like acid rain, erasing the ancient wisdom and ethics of our ancestors that are the structures of a functional community in which compassion and reason are the vehicles of human fulfillment.

Wisdom is the synthesis of reason and compassion. It helps us reconcile ourselves to the paradoxes of life and renounce the habits of dualistic thinking. It helps us realize, for example, that in self-restraint is the freedom we all desire. And in the gentleness of loving kindness is our greatest power. To be reasonable is a virtue. But when reason does not prevail in the name of compassion, justice and a reverential respect for all life, should one then abandon reason? There can be no civil disobedience without violence or rationalized retribution.

Reason and nonviolence must prevail, like wind and water on the mountain, until the fertile ground of mutual respect is found.

Those who destroy and defile Creation and deny such sacrilege are not yet aware of the full dimensions of the sacred beyond their own immediate needs and greed. What is greed, but an addiction to fear? And what are our needs, beyond the pure and simple physical satisfaction of every organism—food, water, shelter, mate and community?

The needs of sentient beings are hierarchical, as the psychologist Abraham Maslow has shown. When our basic needs are met and we are secure and without fear, to what do we aspire? According to Maslow, the aspiration that then arises is self-actualization. He saw a wolf as a self-actualized being, as he saw saints and wisemen and wisewomen who had empathy and compassion. But when our basic needs are not met and our aspirations are perverted to the drive for power and control, possessions, status and wealth, then the corruption of the human spirit and the desecration of Creation begin. Such is the ethos of the industrial revolution, or the Age of Materialism.

A postmodern, postindustrial paradigm, based on a panempathic and reverential respect for all life, and on living in accord with the self-actualizing vision of being human, is beginning to emerge. If we are not to follow the path into self-consumptive chaos, suffering and oblivion, such a paradigm must be the ethos or will, and the telos or final purpose, of the human species.

Conservation and Animal Rights: Reverence in Action

I N SOME CIRCLES IT IS BELIEVED that grass screams when it is cut. Indeed, one Nobel laureate and plant geneticist, Professor Barbara McClintock, described such empathic feeling to her biographer.[1] McClintock's sensitivity is shared by many. Veterinarians who share my empathic feeling for animal patients sometimes feel pain in the same organ or region of the body as the sick animals they are treating.

A similar pain is felt by some conservationists when they see a mountainside devastated by quarrying and strip-mining, or a river choked by a hydroelectric dam. Theologian Matthew Fox sees this empathic feeling for the Earth as the fruit of the boundless compassion that results in the person receiving, in a mystical sense, the stigmata of the body of Christ as the Earth crucified by the human forces of vanity, arrogance, ignorance and greed.

It is these same forces that now threaten the Australian and other aboriginal peoples with extinction, along with the rest of the natural world. And it is these forces that Nobel laureates like McClintock, Schweitzer, Einstein and Martin Luther King rightly feared because they lead people to misuse the power of dominion over the natural world. This power has increased through the material revelations of the sciences, such that humanity has gained considerable technical understanding and control over life, even over the atoms and genes of living systems.

Feeling pain for a dammed river or a blasted mountainside, as for an injured tree or animal or an anguished fellow human being, is a capacity shared by people of diverse cultures and education. It reconciles the false duality between humanity and Nature. We have already noted that St. Francis of Assisi has been recognized as the patron saint of ecologists because he offers an alternative, non-dualistic Christian view of Nature and our relation to it. As historian Lynn White states, "He tried to substitute the idea of the equality of all creatures, including man, for the idea of man's limitless rule over creation."[2] Deep empathy and compassion for fellow creatures and for nature has been long regarded as pagan and as a threat to industrial civilization. The Church, as we have noted, was instrumental in promoting this negative view, as Professor White emphasizes: "By destroying pagan animism, Christianity made it possible to exploit nature in a mood of indifference to the feelings of natural objects."[3]

Shamans, natural healers and priests once taught that we must first be blinded before we might see. They helped our ancestors learn to see in a sacred way. First, they had to see through the clouds and shards of their guilt, rage, fear, greed, confused sincerity, allegiance and unfulfilled longings. Like them, we must first suffer, as shaman, healer and priest once taught, before we can be healed. Our healing is in our suffering through the clouds and shards of our own innocence and despair to a point of centered equilibrium that permits the numinous realm access to our material, mortal and sentient selves.

The awakening of the empathic, compassionate and illimitable Self is the birth of the human spirit, which was achieved in times past through various rites of initiation. Poet Robert Bly in his book *Iron John* contends, "To receive initiation truly means to expand sideways into the glory of oaks, mountains, glaciers, horses, lions, grasses, waterfalls, deer. . . . Whatever shuts a man away from the waterfall and the tiger will kill him."[4] In a disconnected state of mind, one might add, we are more likely than not to obliterate the waterfall and kill the tiger and, in the process, bring about our own spiritual demise. Without the transformative experience of initiation, the individual is truly alienated from the rest of the natural world, from the animal powers and the immanent wisdom and deep mystery of Earth's Creation. Such alienation is now collective and has become the cultural norm, for reasons rooted in the religious, political and economic fabric of industrial civilization.

Now it is time to reconnect in feeling and in spirit with animals and Nature in order to save the natural world from further desecration. This new openness to all living things is an essential evolutionary step for humankind, which if not taken, may well mean extinction for most of Earth's Creation, if not for our own kind as well.

Humankind—Earth Kind

Humankind and all animalkind are part of the same creative process of cosmic unfoldment. Because we share the same origin as fellow creatures, we and they may be called, generically, "Earth kind." Within the biological and cultural diversity of Earth kind, we glimpse the myriad kingdoms or realms of consciousness, from the ant people and the winged peoples of the sky to the dimensions of sapience and sentience within our own species. When we feel so deeply that we begin to empathize with these different realms as aspects of divine manifestation, we realize that it is merely the self-deception of human egotism and anthropocentrism that engenders in us a sense of separation and superiority. Charles Darwin, criticized by some for proposing our biological kinship with animals and accused by others of placing the human species above other Earth species, used to write on his hand, as a daily reminder, "[We are] not superior."

The shamans, priests and healers of earlier times attributed most human suffering to our disobedience of the natural law to live in harmony with all of Nature's cycles and plant and animal communities at all times and in all realms. Some have called these principles our "original instructions." Other less self-consciously willful and clever creatures are constrained to obey this law by the interplay of ecological forces and competition with other species. Only through the powers of reason, humility and empathy can humans find the redemptive constraint and harmonizing balance between exploiting life in order to sustain their own lives and showing respect and reverence for all life. We must also serve and sustain the life that serves and sustains us. When we commoditize and demean animals, we ultimately demean and dehumanize ourselves.

Perhaps, in the final analysis, our original sin, or Fall from grace in a biblical sense, lies in our not following our original instructions to "dress and to keep" the Edenic garden of Earth's Creation in all its beauty and diversity. Our domestication of animals, not as friends and companions, but as commodities—chattel-livestock— was surely a critical event in the history of our species, one that changed our attitude toward nonhuman life. From this perspective, our redemption and atonement must lie in liberating all animals from cruel and unnecessary subjugation and in treating domesticated animals with respect and compassion.

Compassion, the Boundless Ethic

It is philosophically inconsistent to embrace the ethic of boundless compassionate respect for all life and, at the same time, value some animals more than others in terms of their degree of sentience, rarity, aesthetic, emotional or economic value. All these valuations are human-centered extrinsic qualities that we project onto other living beings. They mask the inherent value and significance of living beings, and they turn the boundless ethic of reverence for all life into a conditional and situational morality that undergirds the subjugation, exploitation, suffering and demise of the Animal Kingdom.

In a world where the domestication of animals is a historical tradition for most peoples, few perceive and grieve the loss of wildness, innocence and wilderness. Most people, however, have not lost the capacity to empathize, to show compassion and to enjoy communion with Nature and creatures wild and tame. However, until this compassion becomes boundless and unconditional, the suffering and demise of the Animal Kingdom will continue. We must begin to empathize with all sentient life and embrace even those life forms that potentially threaten our health and well-being. Such openness to the life community entails what some see as a religious conversion or conscious realization of the true nature of the Self that affirms the sacredness of the natural world.

The uniquely human power of dominion was not significantly abused when animals were kept as companions, totems, allies and for physical as well as spiritual sustenance. But this power was abused when our ancestors began to tame, herd, selectively breed and commercially exploit certain species at the expense of the health and welfare of these species and at great cost to other species, especially large predators, as well as the wild lands their expanding flocks and herds occupied. Today we find wastelands—not natural deserts—where cattle, sheep and goats were first domesticated.

As in times past, so today animals are an integral part of our lives and economy. The fact that, as in times past, we incorporate an animal such as a "pet" dog, cat or exotic bird into our lives for nonfinancial reasons and, by so doing, experience a glimmer of unconditional love, does not atone for the continued and intensified exploitation of animals. The patronage extended by industrial society today toward a few animals, like homeless and abused "pets" and endangered species, will not suffice. The only atonement for our original sin and Fall from grace is to liberate all animals from the tyranny of our inhumane dominion that arises in part from our capacity to objectify and commoditize nonhuman life—life that is more vulnerable, yet no less sacred, than our own. Chief Luther Standing Bear gives us insight into the wisdom that is gained when we extend friendship and reverence toward other animals:

If the man could prove to some bird or animal that he was a worthy friend, it would share with him precious secrets and there would be formed bonds of loyalty never to be broken; the man would protect the rights and life of the animal, and the animal would share with the man his power, skill, and wisdom. In this manner was the great brotherhood of mutual helpfulness formed, adding to the reverence for life orders other than man. The taking of animal life for food and clothing only became established, and frugality became regarded as a virtue. Animal life took its place in the scheme of things, and there was no slavery and no torture of four-footed and winged things.[5]

Initiation

Rites of initiation are embedded in the mythology, spirituality, sense of place and social life of every culture. They play an integral role in the development and metamorphosis of both individual and culture. A culture that has no such rites is in danger of losing its collective vision and sense of the sacred identity of each individual. Such a lack of identity leads to conflict and great suffering, which is carried from one generation to the next if there is no anchoring of the individual Self into society through ritual rites of initiation.

Our industrial-consumer society sorely needs such rites in order to begin to mature beyond its destructive, adolescent dualities of perception and conception. These rituals cannot be simply co-opted from other cultural traditions, like the Native American, Australian aboriginal, Tibetan, or African. Nor can they be based solely on imaginatively revitalized pagan rituals of old Europe and ancient Egypt, like those of the Druids, the Wicca and Freya cults, or the rites of Dionysus and Isis. These potential and potent sources for ritual initiation and mythic wisdom are best integrated, where appropriate, into the psychohistorical context and religious tradition or belief system of our own sphere. Most people have some connection with at least one religious tradition. Any tradition can provide a foundation and reference point for exploring and integrating other cultural traditions and for finding the moral and religious basis for a new connection to the natural world and its creatures.

But why should anyone bother to do this in the first place? Anyone who wishes to see world peace would want to find some solutions. Likewise, those who suffer the injustices committed against traditional peoples and their ancient cultural ways should want to question those aspects of their own lives which may be contributing to the demise of the natural world and its traditional peoples.

The causes and consequences of cultural genocide and ecocide, the accelerating extinction of plant and animal species, as well as

the increasingly dysfunctional condition of the biosphere and the
economy of most nations, are founded upon a worldview that is
accepted as normative by an ignorant consensus and powerful elite.
This norm is the reference point for millions of people who are
beginning to see the common sources of suffering that afflict all of
Creation. Many people also experience a sense of deprivation, a vague
longing or inexplicable emptiness that makes life seem as if it has no
meaning or promise of fulfillment.

It is no coincidence that traditional peoples are beginning to voice
their plight and speak out against the demise of the bioregions they
have nurtured and respected for millennia. As they share their spiritual teachings and ethics with the people of the industrial world, a
movement of profound significance is taking place. We are starting
to discover that we will be incapable of finding the right solutions to
the problems we have brought about if we do not follow the advice
of the elders of civilizations more ancient and wiser than our own:
to live gently in balance and harmony with Creation, to cultivate
an attitude of humility, compassionate respect and reverence for all
life. Until this advice is respected for its practicality as well as for its
spirituality, we will not be, as the native peoples say, "in right heart
and mind" to find and apply the right solutions.

Those of us who suffer with the Earth and who come to see
that compassion is the highest power, and that humility and service
are its channels, can begin to heal the world—and ourselves in the
process. Then industrial civilization will evolve out of its voracious
adolescent stage, like an all-consuming parasite, into the maturity
of a fully human, global society. When we lack empathy for other
sentient beings, variously objectifying them into racist, sexist, ageist
and speciesist categories, treating them as resources, pests, capital
and chattel, we are not yet fully human.

Ancient civilizations have much to teach us. Their sustainable
ways of being have been all but obliterated by the arrogant presump-
tions and powers of patriarchy, colonialism and industrialism. Those
who can experience, empathetically, the suffering of these people,
and of all fellow sentient creatures, plant and animal, feel the rage
of gross injustice toward a culture that condones the plunder and
destruction of natural communities. In the name of progress and
necessity, industrial society in its adolescent stage does violence to

Creation, even claiming that its actions are God-ordained, scientifically valid, socially beneficial and therefore just.

It is important that those who share an alignment of heart and mind with the elders of preindustrial civilizations not despair, or burn out in a frenzy of concern and extreme reaction. If we harm ourselves in the process of caring for others, if our burden of empathy makes us bleed too much, then we must distance ourselves in order to protect ourselves, so that we might continue to live meaningful lives that cause more good than harm. Living in a way that minimizes harm to others and to the environment, but which maximizes the good of all is a difficult challenge. However, this mode of living is the ethical and spiritual basis for a just and sustainable society, a mature industrial civilization that is a celebration and affirmation of the creative power of the universe, which we humans experience through the power of compassion.

Any rite of initiation that leads toward a compassionate realization of the interdependence of all life and of the universality of individuality enables us to experience the sacred within and beyond our everyday dualistic view. But if our motivation for participating in such rituals is personal power and control over others, our initiation will join us only to a cult of destruction, and the power, control and security we might believe we have attained will be illusory. The mass deception and indoctrination by such cults, whether scientific, materialist, military or religious, has been the tragic affliction of humanity from one generation to the next. As we move toward a global community, it is essential that we be fully aware of the pitfalls of our arrogant and ignorant adherence to cultish traditions, "truths," and values that are not based upon the boundless ethic of respect and reverence for all life.

A ritual of initiation that is based upon an ethic of compassion, on the other hand, will enable and, in the process, ennoble every member of society to become a creative participant in the life community. Through such initiation, one's past life outside the boundless circle of panempathy is renounced. Such spiritual anarchy and metamorphosis is a normal developmental progression for our species.

Moreover, as Mircea Eliade notes, such rites are essential to reestablishing our lost connection to the natural world; through the shamanic tradition of friendship with animals, knowledge of their language, and the ability to "transform" into animal bodies, Eliade writes, "modern shamans re-establish 'the paradisal' situation lost at the dawn of time."[6] According to anthropologist A. P. Elkin, Australian aboriginal "men of high degree" communicated with their totemic animals to the extent that they gained knowledge of potential danger and far-distant events.[7] The Native peoples of Central America call their guardian animal spirit the *nagual*, which may be an individual animal or an entire animal species; the shaman engages in communion so deep that he or she can change into an animal familiar. Anthropologist Ake Hultkrantz notes that the *nagual* is first encountered during the shaman's initiation ritual.[8] As Native American medicine man Black Elk has said of this intimate connection: "Peace . . . comes within the souls of men when they realize their relationship, their oneness, with the Universe and all its powers, and when they realize that at the center of the Universe dwells *Wakan-Tanka* [The Great Spirit or Creator] and that this center is really everywhere, it is within each of us."[9]

The sense of unity of the human with the whole of Creation was also a central teaching of Confucianism. One Confucian teacher, Wan Yang-Ming, held that:

Everything from ruler, minister, husband, wife and friends, to mountains, rivers, heavenly and earthly spirits, birds, animals and plants, all should be truly loved in order to realize my humanity that forms a unity, and then my clear character will be completely manifested, and I will really form one body with heaven, earth and the myriad things. This is what is meant by "fully developing one's nature."[10]

Echoing the Confucian worldview, physicist Paul Davies has reasoned that modern physics can initiate us into the sacred dimension of Creation because it supports the concept of "a natural, as opposed to supernatural God" who exists *in* matter without being *of* it, just as our brains consist of atoms, though our minds transcend them. Davies makes this analogy explicit: the "brain is the medium of expression of the human mind. . . . Similarly, the entire physical universe would be the medium of expression of the mind of a natural God."[11]

Animals are particularly easy for shamans to identify with—being less impersonal than trees and mountains—hence, their importance in many cultures as allies or totems that connect the individual to a broader dimension of reality and, in the process, help in "fully developing one's nature." Historian Kenneth Clark believes that "we can never recapture the Golden Age, but we can regain that feeling of the unity of all creation. This is a faith we must all share." He rightly concludes, "What is needed is not simply animal sanctuaries and extensive zoos, but a total change in our attitude."[12]

For theologian Thomas Berry, this feeling of the unity of all Creation is integral to planetary survival and progress. He proposes that:

> the natural world about us be recognized as the primary manifestation of the world of the sacred; that creation concerns have priority over salvific concerns; that the integral community of life, earth, and the entire universe be accepted as our primary referent as regards reality and value; that our sense of progress be primarily concerned with progress in the purity and life-giving qualities of the air, the water, and the soil, and that the habitat of every life form be accorded its due recognition as sacred and inviolable; that the Christian sense include the sense of Christ as a dimension of the universe, of the planet earth, and of all living forms as well as a dimension of the human.[13]

Through communion with Nature and other living beings, a sense of kinship is awakened. Such sensibility empowers us to avert the harmful consequences to life and environment that arise when we live without respect for the essential unity and interdependence of Self and world. Wherever there is sentient life, there is suffering, as well as forces that can harm, even obliterate, life. But where there is sapient and empathic life, there emerges a desire to alleviate suffering and a determination to minimize the harm that *Homo sapiens* has done to the environment, to kindred sentient creatures and, consequently, to itself.

Time is running out for humanity to become an integral member of the Earth's life community. We are destroying that community. When it is gone, it is unlikely that we will have either the cleverness or the technology to enable the planet to function normally and meet our many needs and growing numbers. Human biology and psychology must be changed. Our biological and psychological characteristics, honed through millions of years of evolution, have enabled us to expand and dominate the planet like no other species. We are a highly adaptable, competitive, aggressive and fecund species, whose survival and proliferation were enhanced by these traits and also by our capacity to communicate and cooperate in social groups. As we move inexorably toward a global economic community, we face the biological and psychological difficulties of adapting, cooperatively and creatively, within a much larger community than ever before. This community includes other cultures, as well as other plant and animal species and their communities and natural ecosystems. If we are to succeed in this inevitable process of evolutionary transformation, from which there is no turning back, we must equate success with the vision of a biologically and culturally diverse, humane, socially just and sustainable planetary community. As Father Thomas Berry has stated, "In his deepest subjectively, man is the earth, as the earth in its conscious phase is man."[14] In order to make this vision a reality, we must renounce those aspects of our biology and psychology—both genetic and cultural in their roots—that underlie our competitiveness, aggressiveness, arrogance, insecurity, fear and destructiveness, and nourish those qualities and values associated with cooperation, nonviolence, humility and creativity.

People can be resensitized once they are informed about how we harm animals and Nature. And students can be educated, not simply to appreciate philosophic aspects of animal rights and ecology, but also to use their emotions as a compass for compassion and as a source of deep wisdom, wonder and appreciation, as well as spiritual redemption and self-realization.

Through empathetic understanding and esthetic appreciation of Nature, we come to reverence the Creation as a sacred whole and to see the divinity of every creature, relationship and process. Ethical and spiritual concern for endangered plant and animal species can thus be the catalyst to unify a diverse humanity to serve and save the world. Moreover, the experience of each living moment of Nature has the possibility of being a religious experience. The religious or ethical and the secular and material then become one in spirit, and each individual human life becomes a conscious part of the spiritual dimension. The illusory duality between spirit and matter, human and animal, Self and other dissolve, shattered by the realization of the omnipresence of divinity in every part and process of Nature, and of our connectedness with it all.

The Question of Animal Rights

While it may be both ethically and ecologically sound to exploit certain animal species, their commercial use at the scale employed by major industries today is incompatible with their overall welfare. The reasons are many and are documented in this book. The industrial system is driven by an ideology that has come to place economic interests and the law of supply and demand over the autonomy, intrinsic value and interests of the individual. This ideology purports to serve the greater good of society and, in totalitarian societies, has been used to justify oppression and the violation of individual rights. It is also the rationalization used to justify animal exploitation. For example, while it is recognized that modern intensive farm animal husbandry systems designed to maximize production do not contribute to the well-being of individual animals, it is argued that such ethical and health costs are offset by economic gains and by the ability of such methods to provide society with a cheap and plentiful supply of farm animal products.

In the human sphere, we are burdened with the consequences of this ideology. The symptoms of our cataclysm include poverty, unemployment, environmental degradation, pollution, human sickness and spiraling inflation. In the animal domain, we find suffering, disease, habitat destruction and accelerating extinction of species, portents of a global crisis. Examples of major commercial animal industries include "factory" farming; fur ranching; "managing" wildlife for trapping and hunting recreation; the "exotic pet" trade; sealing, whaling and fishing; horse racing; rodeos; biomedical research and the testing of new drugs, consumer products, agrichemicals and other hazardous industrial chemicals and pollutants; and the most recently developed industry, "puppy mills" for the mass production of purebred dogs. As the scale of any of these enterprises is directly proportional to the magnitude of capital investment, so the size of each industry is correlated with a quantitative increase in potential and actual animal suffering. This can be attributed in part to the fact that the intrinsic value and interests of animals as individuals are secondary to the economic necessity of maximizing returns on investments—an objective that is euphemistically termed "efficiency" in the livestock industry—and to the ideology of purported societal benefits, such as furs to wear, meat to eat, deer to shoot and "safe" levels of pesticides and radiation in animals.

The "Values" of Sentient Beings

Many animal rights philosophers have emphasized the importance of recognizing the value of animals in encouraging a deeper respect for nonhuman life. The intrinsic value of animals is contrasted with the perceived extrinsic value from the point of view of human utility. Animal rightists regard an animal's intrinsic value as taking precedence over its extrinsic value, because, they argue, all creatures are ends in themselves rather than the means of satisfying others' needs.

However, we should not dismiss the fact that in Nature, animals do serve others' needs. A deer has an inherent value and a life of its own but is also a means whereby the needs of predator species such as the wolf are satisfied. However, it is a naturalistic fallacy to rationalize human exploitation of animals from the fact that animals prey upon and kill each other. Predator species are few in number. But six billion animals with the size and appetite of *Homo sapiens* on this small planet would have undeniably devastating ecological consequences when they behave as predators.

In recognizing the extrinsic value of animals and other living beings in their contribution to the harmony, beauty and diversity of the biotic community, the animal rights activist moves conceptually toward a more holistic, ecological view. This has been lacking too long in the animal rights movement, as has respect for the inherent value of animals as individuals by the environmental and conservation movements.

Some philosophers, reflecting a fairly prevalent social consensus, believe that domesticated animals that we have "created" for our specific use have less inherent value than wild animals. This is also fallacious, I believe, because it is indicative of an anthropocentric attitude toward nonhuman life.

Another fallacy is the belief that a being that is more intelligent and self-aware than another has greater inherent value. However, this view is also based upon anthropocentrism and, further, has racist and speciesist overtones. Moreover, in focusing upon inherent value to the exclusion of extrinsic value, or vice versa, we fail to appreciate the natural paradox inherent in such distinctions: Organisms, such as soil bacteria and fungi, which, from an anthropocentric perspective, have less inherent value than, say, a wolf or human, actually have a greater extrinsic or instrumental value, since they make major contributions to the integrity of the biotic community. Nothing will grow in sterilized soil devoid of microorganisms!

Similarly, the individual potential of nonsentient or, more correctly, pre-sentient forms of life is enormous. The inherent potential of an individual human being seems finite when compared to a plant or bacterium that can multiply asexually and clone itself, and the potential importance of rocks and water is infinite, since they embody trace minerals that are the basic elements of all life forms.

Thus when contemplating what St. Francis called "sister" water, we become aware of an existence that is devoid of consciousness, sentience and intrinsic value in terms of having a life of its own. From that limited perspective, water is "inferior" to *Homo sapiens*. But by virtue of "her" inherent potential, water is clearly superior. And in terms of her extrinsic value to all life, she embodies the saintly virtue of selfless giving. When we begin to perceive other existences from the panentheistic perspective of St. Francis or from the instrumental yet holistic view of intrinsic and extrinsic value and potential, the notion of human superiority is shattered.

An appreciation of the integrity of Creation consists, according to philosopher Charles Birch, of the recognition of the "intrinsic value of every living creature and the maintenance of the integrity of the relations of each creature to its environment."[15] Thus the extrinsic-existential value of each creature is defined in relation to other members of its biotic community, as distinct from any human-instrumental values that we might place on them. Jay McDaniel concludes that practicing a biocentric ethic involves reverence for life, which is respect and concern for the well-being and ultimate fulfillment of all sentient beings.[16]

Thus it is important, I believe, to consider both the value and potential of all existences in arguing the case for animal rights and conservation. While "rights" language has its limitations, and some prefer to speak in terms of human obligations and duties, a greater appreciation of the extrinsic value of natural organisms and of their place and role in Nature will bring a needed ecological-environmental perspective to the animal rights philosophy. Perhaps we should ask our fellow members of the human species—the most sapient and sentient Earth species with the greatest inherent value—what extrinsic value it has in terms of contributing to the integrity, stability and beauty of the biotic community. Had we the simplicity of bacteria, the humility of the deer and the wisdom of the wolf, we humans might be of more value to the natural world!

Animal Rights and Human Responsibilities

Ironically, while accepting that animals have souls, Jesuit James E. Royce shows his prejudices when he writes:

> [Saying] "Be kind to the birds because God has created their souls" is sentimental nonsense, as is much antivivisectionist propaganda. God is, of course, ultimately the First Cause of all being, but not in any special sense of plant or animal souls. The reason why we should avoid wanton cruelty to animals is not because of their dignity, but our own. Animals have no personal rights and are for man to use. When a man abuses them, it is wrong because he is acting in a manner unworthy of his rational nature, which is the norm of morality.[17]

The "special sense" Royce refers to here is the intellectual, rational aspect of the human soul, but is this a morally relevant distinction? Royce clearly implies that rationalized inhumanity toward animals is morally acceptable. He denies that "brute animals" possess rationality, intellect, personal identity and self-reflectiveness because, since humans possess intellect, it would mean that we would have to be "logically consistent, and give animals the rights and responsibilities proper to an intelligent being."[18]

Yet the possession of rights is surely not contingent upon having responsibilities: children, the mentally defective and comatose persons have rights independent of any responsibilities. Nor is belonging to the human species a relevant qualification for the entitlement of rights, since animals, like humans, do possess intelligence and sentience, the capacity to feel and to suffer physically and emotionally.

The idea that only morally responsible beings can have rights—that is, interests that should be given equal and fair consideration—subordinates ethical and spiritual principles to moral-legal codes. There is no such thing as an absolute moral law, and to paraphrase Professor John MacMurray, the notion of obedience is not a moral conception.[19] The concept of legality is inappropriate in discussions of ethics and causes confusion. The application of moral principles cannot be defined by a system of law, since the moral responsibility for the application of these principles rests upon the agent. For the same reason, obedience is not a moral but a legal concept.

When Royce states, "Animals have no personal rights, and are for man to use," he commits the ethical fallacy of seeing personal rights in a legal sense and not in the moral sense that the ethics of our Christian heritage would have us do. This prejudicial attitude has implications of "biological fascism." In confusing ethics, morals and legal codes, Royce illustrates, as MacMurray emphasizes, how the legalistic morality of our Roman heritage has confused, confounded and ultimately subordinated the ethics of Christianity. The fact that animals cannot be morally responsible agents means that they cannot be persons in the legal sense, and while they might thus be denied legal standing, this does not mean that they have no rights in terms of our ethical duty toward them. Cardinal John Heenan, Archbishop of Westminster, makes this point clearly:

> When I was young I often heard quoted a piece of Christian philosophy which was taken as self-evidently true. It was the proposition that animals have no rights. This, of course, is true only in one sense. They are not human persons and therefore they have no rights, so to speak, in their own right. But they have very positive rights because they are God's creatures. If we have to speak with

absolute accuracy we must say that God has the right to have all his creatures treated with proper respect.

Nobody should therefore carelessly repeat the old saying that animals have no rights. This could easily lead to wanton cruelty.[20]

Reverend Andrew Linzey concurs:

Animals are valuable in themselves by virtue of their creation by God. It is not just that injury to animals reinforces a low view of their value (though it certainly does that) but that it is a practical denial of their intrinsic value. Animals belong to God in a way that makes their significance and value more fundamental even than human artistic creations—inspiring though the latter may be. . . .

They do not simply exist in some utilitarian relationship to humans whereby they can be seen as fodder for furthering human purposes of life enhancement or enjoyment or happiness. The doctrine of creation stands in opposition to all such wholly anthropocentric notions. Man, as we have indicated, cannot claim to be the total measure of good as regards other living creatures.

This view is likewise affirmed by the Archbishop of Canterbury, whom Reverend Linzey cites as proclaiming:

It [Creation] exists for God's glory, that is to say, it has a meaning and worth beyond its meaning and worth as seen from the point of view of human utility. It is in this sense that we can say that it has intrinsic value. To imagine that God has created the whole universe solely for man's use and pleasure is a mark of folly.[21]

And one should add that this "folly" places the future and integrity of Creation in grave jeopardy.

Animal Selfhood

It is quite evident that more highly differentiated species possess unique traits and individual personalities. *Homo sapiens*, the great apes and the wolf are prime examples of this phenomenon. All social species show evidence of behavioral complexity, flexibility and diversity linked to the evolution of individual selfhood. Reminiscent of Aristotle's great chain of being, all social creatures can be placed on a continuum of increasing selfhood, from the ant in its colony and the fish in its shoal, where there is little individuation or differentiation, to the domesticated dog and civilized human, where individual differences are self-evident. However, it would be incorrect to regard more individuated beings as superior and less individuated ones as inferior, as all beings are part of the One Life, manifesting with varying degrees of differentiation. Nor should we regard less individuated creatures as more expendable. Rather, it is simply easier for humans to identify with more highly differentiated members of nonhuman species and thus easier for us to mourn their deaths and empathize with their suffering than it is with "lesser beings," like ants and worms, who all seem to look the same.

Our anthropocentric bias leads us to value nonhuman life according to the yardstick of individualism and similarity to humans. It blinds us to the fact that every living being has inherent value and a life of its own no matter how poorly individuated it may be. The denial of selfhood to "lower" organisms who lack individual personality leads to speciesism, which is analogous to racism. Selfhood is universal and universalizing; it cannot be denied since it is an attribute of being, no matter whether the being is a lake, tree or animal. Overemphasis on such qualities as sentience and sapience can create false distinctions, when other shared qualities, such as the will-to-be, the capacity to be harmed, existence within time and space and interdependence within the unified field of being, are ignored or discounted.

Eastern philosophy holds that selfhood is transient and mutable, existing relatively in space and time, yet void of independent origin and existence. In the *Bhagavad Gita* it is written: "He who sees that the self in himself is the same self in all that is, he becomes selfless. . . . It is the highest of mysteries." For consciously reflexive beings, knowledge of self and other arises from this sense of interdependence, and from this knowledge, the universal nature of the self is realized.

In Buddhism, realization of the true nature of selfhood is a quality of the enlightened mind. All beings, according to Buddhist teachings, have an inherent core of beauty and value called Buddha nature that is hidden by the illusion of duality and separation which characterizes the everyday realm of *maya* (deceptive appearance). Buddhahood is awakening from this illusion and appreciating the true nature of all beings. For Christians, this state is often described as being "born again"—Christogenesis—from the dualistic realm of "sin" into the nondualistic realm of "heaven." In both traditions, and in other spiritual paths as well, awareness of the sanctity and unity of all being brings with it a profound change in perception, feeling, thinking and behavior, characterized by humility, respect, compassion and loving kindness.

Several secular philosophies express a similar holistic understanding of the dynamic interconnection between the human self and the selfhood of all other forms of being. Eco-feminist philosophers such as Elizabeth Dodson Gray have described the "new understanding" that arises when all life is held in loving and nondual communion. In *Green Paradise Lost*, Gray writes: "The new understanding of life must be systematic and interconnected. It cannot be linear and hierarchical for the reality of life on earth is a whole, a circle, an interconnected system in which everything has its part to play and can be respected and accorded dignity."[22] Gray's statement is supported completely by the findings of ecological science, quantum physics and molecular biology. Given this, it would be wise for us to think, feel and act accordingly, with a unified sensibility that is Creation- or Earth-centered rather than self-centered and disconnected from the whole and the holy. Gray concludes, "Some day, perhaps, we shall have an identity that can enjoy the earth as a friend, provider, and home. When that happens, we will know that when the earth hurts, it will hurt us. Then the environmental ethic will not just be in our heads but in our hearts—in the nerve endings of our sensitivity."[23]

Recognizing the selfhood of animals has legal as well as moral and philosophical implications. When animals are seen as individuals, legal and moral rights are a natural consequence, as philosopher Bernard Rollin shows:

The animal rights advocate argues as follows: If the concept of rights is embodied in our legal system as a protection for the individual human being on the basis of his or her being a moral object, then some such protection must be granted to animals as well, for we can find no difference between humans and animals that is morally relevant! This is not to say there are no differences between human beings and animals. There are of course myriad such differences. The point is that these have nothing to do with morality; the entire history of our moral and legal systems may be seen as a process of recognizing the irrelevance of such differences.[24]

From Dehumanization to Creative Participation

The unsoulment of animals and the denial of their rights—what might be termed "deanimalization"—is no less a violation of ethics than the analogous process of dehumanization. Denying animals soul and personhood and violating their rights for some purported social good is on a continuum with social philosophies such as fascism or bolshevism that subordinate the rights of individuals to the "rights" of society and industry and, in the process, demean the sanctity and dignity of human life. Under such social systems, the human condition is characterized by alienation and exploitation rather than creative participation. Sadly, this is becoming the moral foundation of our modern industrial-consumer society, despite its claims to be democratic and Christian.

Renowned animal-experimenting psychologist B. F. Skinner expresses the kind of thinking which supports these dehumanizing values with great clarity in his autobiography, *A Matter of Consequences:*

> If I am right about human behavior, an individual is only the way in which a species and a culture produce more of species and culture. . . . The question is whether we have reached the point at which we can accept a scientific view of human behavior and use it to solve our problems.[25]

Biological fascism is implicit in Skinner's ideology:

> My answer to Montaigne's question has shocked many people: I would bury my children rather than my books. But I would give the same answer to myself. If some Mephistopheles offered me a wholly new life on condition that all records and effects of my present life be destroyed, I should refuse.[26]

For Skinner, immortality is achieved by serving a greater good—producing more of a species or a culture. He applies this definition to himself as well, quipping, "A scientist is only science's way of making more science," and admitting that if he is right about human behavior, he has "written the autobiography of a non-person."[27] Skinner's scientism and rational egotism is surely the essence of dehumanization. Little wonder, then, that Skinner and scientists of like mind regard any questioning of their use of animals in their laboratories as misguided and heretical—against the creed of self-sacrifice and dedication to the benefit of society. Though ideologically seductive—since more knowledge promises more power and control—this scientistic worldview is destructive of the sanctity and dignity of life.

Seeing the life of individual humans or animals as solely for the service of society is surely unethical, though this view has become an article of faith in our moral life as well as the basis of our social, political and economic systems. However, as religion and ethics decay, our fear and insecurity increase, and we put our faith in the power and authority of politics and science—the new priesthoods of a dehumanized world. Other equally devastating consequences follow. As our sense of ethical sensibility and responsibility decline, more laws and regulatory controls are needed to enforce the new order. But government cannot be the conscience of society, nor can science and technology solve the problems that will inevitably arise from such flagrant disregard for the value of life. As John Rodman observes:

> The distinction between Man and Beast is at bottom a political rather than a scientific distinction. It is ultimately an act of domination rather than knowledge: or rather, it is an act of knowledge—as domination—the imposition of a rigid dichotomy that authoritatively assigns roles but cannot be scientifically defended.[28]

In this regard, we would do well to recall Albert Schweitzer's words from *The Teaching of Reverence for Life:*

> To the truly ethical man, all of life is sacred, including forms of life that from the human point of view may seem to be lower that ours. He makes distinctions only from case to case, and under pressure of necessity when he is forced to decide which life he will sacrifice in order to preserve other lives. In thus deciding from case to case, he is aware that he is proceeding subjectively and arbitrarily, and that he is accountable for the lives thus sacrificed.[29]

Not surprisingly, Native Americans have long seen the practical and ethical consequences of dehumanizing and "deanimalizing" life on Earth. Vine Deloria, Jr., in *God is Red*, states the Native American moral position clearly:

> Entities are themselves, because they had been made to be so. Any violation of another entity's rights to existence in and of itself is a violation of the nature of creation and a degradation of religious reality itself.[30]

Modern life, according to the Hopi people, is out of balance, a condition that they term *Koyaanasqatsi*. When the Hopi people hear Christian evangelists speak about the coming apocalypse, they view the catastrophe to come as a necessary purification of the Earth, through which a proper balance will be restored. Our supreme challenge today is to find ways short of apocalypse to restore this balance, a quest which is as much a survival necessity as it is a spiritual imperative.

We can no longer deny or rationalize away the tragedy and the plight of the Animal Kingdom under our dominion. The apotheosis of Nature's inherent divinity, the recognition of animals' rights and a return to organic, regenerative agriculture and industries that do not exhaust and poison the biosphere are auspicious beginnings. The late Sioux spiritual leader Black Elk echoes Albert Schweitzer's warning that without a reverence for all life, we shall never have world peace: "Nothing can be well until we learn to live in harmony with the Power of the world as it lives and moves to do its work."[31] To deny this prophetic vision is to deny a self-evident trend. Faith in technological, political, economic, military, medical or any other form of power maintains the ideological illusion that external solutions to the problems of the world are possible. The solutions we seek cannot be external, for the problems are internal: ideological, cognitive, emotional, ethical and spiritual.

The prelude to the excellent book, *Earth Keeping: Christian Stewardship of Natural Resources*, edited by Loren Wilkinson, clearly expresses the need to move away from a human-centered theology:

> When Christians affirm that God loves the world and that Christ died for the life of the world, they are speaking of not just

humanity, but of the whole planet—indeed, the whole creative universe. Thus, of all people, Christians should be concerned for the future health of the planet—both for the "narrow world" of humankind and the "broader earth" of complex and living eco-sphere.[32]

With a few, important exceptions, Christians have shown little concern for the well-being of the world, because the emphasis in Christian thought has been upon personal, rather than cosmic, salvation, as Wilkinson notes:

> Indeed one narrow use of the word "world" is in declarations that Christians have been saved *out of* the world. That idea has been interpreted by many to be a sort of license to neglect the world in order to care for the soul. This interpretation, when combined with a radically individualistic trend in western thought, has produced what is the prevailing mood among Christians with regard to their involvement in the planetary environment: we are concerned first of all with the relevance of the gospel for our own salvation; second, with its relevance for the salvation for the rest of humankind. But for most, the concern stops there: that vital human center is also the circumference of any feeling of responsibility for the rest of creation. We have seen the rest of the world merely as a background for the human drama of salvation.[33]

However, individual humans are an inseparable part of Nature, as Nature is inseparable from us. Thus, we cannot be saved from or out of Nature, as Wilkinson continues:

> We are redeemed in nature, not apart from it. Thus, Christians should include the rest of creation in their own salvation. . . . If, then, we are to choose among different ways of using the planet's wealth, we must, as Christians, consider more broadly the consequences of that salvation we have understood too often as a private and otherworldly gift. For we are saved not only *from* the consequences of our sinning, but *for* that continued task of stewardship once given Adam. Unless our understanding of redemption extends to our stewardship of the earth, it is incomplete; and without redeemed persons, humanity will only destroy the rich and beautiful planet it inhabits.[34]

Conservation and Animal Rights: Reverence in Action

James Berry has joined in condemning the current Christian attitude and its devastating consequences for the world. In an essay promoting the 1987 North American Conference on Christianity and Ecology, Berry writes:

> If human society cannot conform to the demand that creation be treasured and nurtured and cooperated with, then the earth is doomed. The human is a non-viable species in a homocentric context. The planet itself is non-viable in a homo-centric context. It has become plain as day that the consumer society, the materialistic society, is turning a paradise into a stinking mess. If the whole Christian Church were to come to see our society the way the writers of these (conference) papers see it, life styles would change. . . . Our churches have not made significant efforts to disabuse us of the false myths of productivity, growth and progress through technology—myths that disregard the interests of the non-human world. Setting these perceptions straight is a task the Christian community is best suited to take on, probably the only community capable of it.
>
> The conferees must consider the implications of what they will be proposing. Agony is associated with withdrawal from addiction, and this society is addicted to consumption. Recognition that this agony is nothing compared to the agony of living in a world that looks like present-day Ethiopia will strengthen the Christian resolve, for that is surely where we are headed if we do not withdraw.[35]

Forward-thinking spiritual leaders of all traditions have raised their voices in support of a united international and pan-spiritual movement for a new ethical awareness. In *The Assisi Declarations: Messages on Man and Nature from Buddhism, Christianity, Hinduism, Islam and Judaism*, His Holiness the Dalai Lama issued a ringing call for change:

> As we all know, disregard for the natural inheritance of human beings has brought about the danger that now threatens the peace of the world as well as the chance to live of endangered species.
>
> Such destruction of the environment and the life depending upon it is a result of ignorance, greed and disregard for the richness of all living things. This disregard is gaining great influence. If peace

does not become a reality in the world and if the destruction of the environment continues as it does today, there is no doubt that future generations will inherit a dead world.

Our ancestors have left us a world rich in its natural resources and capable of fulfilling our needs. This is a fact. It was believed in the past that the natural resources of the Earth were unlimited, no matter how much they were exploited. But we know today that without understanding and care these resources are not inexhaustible. It is not difficult to understand and bear the exploitation done in the past out of ignorance, but now that we are aware of the dangerous factors, it is very important that we examine our responsibilities and our commitment to values, and think of the kind of world we are to bequeath to future generations.

It is clear that this generation is at an important crossroad. On the one hand the international community is able now to communicate each other's views, on the other hand the common fact is that confrontation far outweighs constructive dialogue for peace.

Various crises face the international community. The mass starvation of human beings and the extinction of species may not have overshadowed the great achievements in science and technology, but they have assumed equal proportions. Side by side with the exploration of outer space, there is the continuing pollution of lakes, rivers and vast parts of the oceans, out of human ignorance and misunderstanding. There is a great danger that future generations will not know the natural habitat of animals; they may not know the forests and the animals which we of this generation know to be in danger of extinction.

We are the generation with the awareness of a great danger. We are the ones with the responsibility and the ability to take steps of concrete action, before it is too late.[36]

In conclusion, when everything seems to be falling apart, the center will still hold provided we remain clear. As balance is existential and psychophysical, so harmony is dynamic and relational. Our sensitivity and awareness of life in balance and harmony enable us to live in closer accord with the Golden Rule: to find our measure, live well and heal or be healed as the need arises.

Conservation and Animal Rights: Reverence in Action

Educational and Developmental Concerns

IN EXPLOITING THE NATURAL world for commercial purposes, industrial society marginalizes and ultimately alienates people from animals and Nature. While much concern has been expressed over the adverse impact of such exploitation on the natural world, little thought has been given as to how alienation from Nature and the Animal Kingdom adversely affects human development and overall well-being.

Among the theorists writing on this topic, Paul Shepherd observes, "If all creatures are possible ideas, relationships, emotions, feelings, the habitat is for us the outward form of the whole space of the mind. . . . Our manmade landscapes are caricatures of the rational mind, the external extension of civilized thought."[1] Shepherd's observation leads us to an important question: Is it possible that human landscapes, often so unnatural, are detrimental to our mental development and psychological health?

Children show a natural interest in animals and Nature. Shepherd proposes that this interest may be a normal developmental stage essential for the emergence not only of sensitivity and compassion, but of self-awareness. We know that the development of human intelligence rests upon a child's exposure to a richly diverse environment. Moreover, self-awareness and the distinction between self and other arises out of socialization. If a child's social environment is restricted, its awareness of self in relation to others will be shallow. This deprivation may be aggravated further if the child is deprived of contact with Nature and nonhuman creatures. Contact with the natural world helps a child to define the boundaries of the self and to develop a deeper and broader "inscape."

A simple analogy will help prove this point: Since we define ourselves in terms of our relationships, a child raised only with adults will have a narrower definition of self than one raised with both adults and other children. Thus it is reasonable to assume that a child who is given the opportunity to socialize with animals will have much greater sense of self-identity than one who is raised with only human contact. In this way, animals make us more human by teaching us what is human and what is not.

Experiencing living beings who are different yet fundamentally similar also teaches a child empathy and understanding. A child who lives in a purely human world, with domestic "pets" that may be actually or conceptually no more than animated toys, is surrounded by a mirror of sameness. Such a lack of diversity, like the regimentation of factory-farm fields and the homogeneity of orderly suburban housing developments, add to the current crisis of alienation. Without other-species diversity and a firm grounding in the natural world, we risk losing our self-identity in the collective species-identity of global humanization. The resulting loss of self-awareness may lead to greater degrees of disconnectedness and psychic disturbance later in life.

Thus human socialization with a wide variety of nonhuman species, ideally in their natural environments, is essential for normal development. Paul Shepherd endorses this view, contending:

> The physical reality of animal differences and multiformity are in some way prior to the development of companionship among

people, an experience of animals without which strictly human interactions give us crowding rather than fellowship. It is felt as a loss of harmony in the self or within society or among nations, but it has its source in a failure of the primitive sources of energy for bringing a disparate world together.[2]

Anthropocentrism is thus a kind of self-denial rather than a self-in-the-world affirmation. The world which results from this loss of connection is clearly diminished, as Shepherd notes:

> Modern technology makes everything a product of man. Order in nature, according to the philosophy of this view, offers no guiding wisdom, no heuristic design, no relationships with hidden analogies to culture. It offers only molecular order, to be rearranged for our consumption, species order to be tamed for our amusement, and stellar order to be the arcane playground of mathematical games and spectator rocket sports.[3]

The wholesale domination, exploitation and de-naturing of Nature may well be "civilized" society's most de-humanizing and biocidal error.

Modern industrial society also gives children a distorted view of Nature. Socialized with placid "pets," animal picture books and fables and anthropomorphic Disney-type movies, the modern child has little chance to relate meaningfully to real animals. Such restricted and impoverished socialization may manifest in insensitivity towards animals and Nature later in life, and indifference towards their "rights" and conservation. It may also be related to the objectification of animals so common in our culture which, as we have noted, is having disastrous social and ecological consequences. Thus humans need animals for far more than their practical uses, as Shepherd notes:

> The only defense of nonhuman life . . . is one close to human well-being. . . . It might be called "minding animals" . . . the human mind needs animals in order to develop and work. Human intelligence is bound to the presence of animals. They are the means by which cognition takes its first shape and they are the instruments for imaginary abstract ideas and qualities, therefore giving us consciousness. They are the code images by which language retrieves ideas from memory at will. They are the means to

self-identity and self-consciousness as our most human possessions, for they enable us to objectify qualities and traits. By presenting us with related—otherness—that diversity of non-self with which we have various things in common—they further, through our lives, a refining and maturing knowledge of personal and human being.[4]

Given the importance of animals to human development, we must ask ourselves some hard questions. What can help a child who has only indirect and vicarious contact with animals distinguish between a real animal and a humanized "pet" or stuffed toy? How can we help a child distinguish between real wildlife and the idealized versions filtered through books and movies or glimpsed in circuses and zoos? The measure of what our children learn of the natural world is a function of our cultural awareness and sensitivity. There are no easy answers to these questions; however, we can begin by working to see that "pets," zoos, wildlife parks and the like will not become anesthetizing and desensitizing surrogates, substituting semidomesticated facsimiles for real animals and replacing a real understanding and appreciation of Nature with something that seems authentic, yet is wholly illusory.

Nature-deprivation pathology is, I believe, associated with a deep sense of rootlessness; it fosters an identity crisis based on the lack of a spirit of place and a real sense of community. This pathology, which is all too common today, is aggravated by our lack of contact with many of our life sources. How many adults know the river or lake or watershed from which they get their water? How many nurture the Earth and know the plants they eat? How many have raised, killed, skinned and dressed the animals they eat? Part of this detachment has led to "civilized ignorance": How many modern men and women, given an acre of good earth, could raise enough food to sustain life? This detachment has also led to a weakening of power, awareness and control over what we eat, and what, in general, is being done to our lives and to the world around us.[5]

Moreover, without the fullness of relationship with the natural world and a concomitant fullness in the development of self-awareness, there can be little depth or fulfillment in human relations. As humanity becomes increasingly separated and alienated from Nature, and as we "de-animalize" and "de-naturize" all that is nonhuman, so we become increasingly alienated from each other. We and Nature are inseparable in a oneness of diversely integrated otherness. This is the key to a healthy biosphere and a healthy body, mind and spirit for all human beings.

To destroy our kinship with all life is also to weaken our cosmic perspective, which diminishes our ethical development and restricts our access to the coordinates by which we may chart our future. It is ironic that a personified "pet" will be totally indulged by its owner and yet that same owner will happily wear the furs of wild animals caught in steel-jaw traps and eat an inhumanely raised calf or pig because it has been conveniently depersonalized into veal, pork or bacon. Humane and ecologically sound ethics derive from a science that has as its coordinates a sensitivity to animals and Nature. Without these as a basis, we find ourselves alone in the world, inhabiting an impoverished humanosphere in which our own creations reflect a monotonous infinity of sameness. In such a humanized world of self-glorification and gratification, there will be little room for divinity. Thus the survival of human beings, not simply as a species but as spiritual beings, necessitates a radical change in our attitudes, values and actions: a liberation of humanity, animals and Nature from the tyranny of technocratic imperialism.

To accomplish this goal, children must be taken beyond the world of domestic "pets," farm animals and genetically engineered animals (many of which have been given human genes[6]) that reflect infantilism, dependence, conformity, obedience and utilitarianism. These humanized, human-exploited animals dilute the child's experience of nonhuman otherness and lead them to hold erroneous conceptions of animals and Nature in general. Conversely, contact with natural ecosystems and their diversity of species develops an ethical appreciation of otherness and fosters the healthy spiritual self-concept.

Morality and Education

I am uncomfortable about teaching, preaching and legislating morality. Teaching school children to be kind to animals by telling them that cruelty is morally wrong is an exercise in futility—a quick way to turn children off, except for the few unquestioning conformists in the classroom. Children will not need to be taught *why* they should be kind to animals if they are taught instead that animals can suffer, that animals have many needs and emotional states similar to, if not identical with their own, and that animals are part of the same creative process and the same seamless ecological web of life. Knowing these things as rational, scientifically verifiable facts is surely more compelling than moralistic "shoulds" and "should-nots" that have tended to foster prejudice, bigotry and conformity, rather than compassion and understanding. Morality is a poor substitute for empathetic identification and sensibility, for the wisdom of the open heart. Empathetic knowledge about the ways of animals is the key to right action and the essential prerequisite for compassion. Children learn that moralistic injunctions such as "Thou shalt not kill," and "Thou shalt not be cruel," are hypocritical and unrealistic as absolutes when they discover that grownups are cruel to animals and to each other, and that humans kill animals and each other for a variety of reasons. Teaching, preaching and legislating morality is, in the final analysis, a poor substitute for empathetic understanding from which ethical actions arise spontaneously.

British education specialist Peter Kelly, writing in *Orion Nature Quarterly*, reflects on how accepting many animals are of young children and how well they seem to relate to them. He believes that this rapport exists because young children understand animals intuitively, a natural affinity of mind that is lost as we mature and become more rational and objective (separating cognition from emotion) and more dependent upon verbal rather than prelinguistic communication.[7]

Kelly goes on to show that through carefully observing how animals behave, and understanding their behavior, perceptions, fears, desires and conceptual world, we might regain our lost childhood affinity of mind. He terms this affinity *biological empathy*, as distinct from anthropomorphic (humanized) and behavioristic (dehumanized) and mechanized attitudes and relations. He states that in biological empathy, one imaginatively projects "one's own consciousness into the lives of others and attempts to conceive the world through their senses, emotions, and responses and their relationships with their environment."[8] Kelly proposes that in order to become familiar with the animal's mental world, "communication with an animal needs to be conceived as a process of gradually adapting to the animal's own system of signs, perceptions and behavior."[9] On this basis, he draws the following important conclusions:

Observation and communication are two stages in the development of empathy. Together they help to achieve what one might term a *transfer of being*. This occurs when we acquire a confident sense that we have got near to experiencing what it is to be a cat, a dog, a horse, a bat, or whatever species is studied. This empathetic understanding is not solely intellectual in nature; it involves intuitive insight and respect for the animal's integrity and uniqueness. Neither is it an absolute condition, for I doubt if one can ever fully comprehend the psychological nature of another being. But one can come into significant proximity, I would hope, to the truth.

In a world becoming more and more urban and technological and showing only a few signs of losing its anthropocentric orientation, the need to heighten awareness of the variety of life becomes a matter of survival and even of morality. Such awareness is part of the perspective that will allow us to appraise the significance of what we do to ourselves and to our environment. Society as a whole must acquire a deeper sense of the reality of nature— of animals, of the environment, and of people. The development of the capacity for biological empathy is a measure that must be taken to meet that requirement. In making this point, I am not arguing against urban life and technology, and certainly not against the idea of human beings looking after the needs of human beings. It is an argument for a balance in our affairs to avoid the inevitable problems that alienation from the natural world produces.[10]

The importance of biological empathy is not a new idea. In a book on animal rights published in 1892, Henry Salt relates the following relevant anecdote:

Let those who think that men are likely to treat animals with more humanity on account of their dumbness ponder the case of the fish, as exemplified in the following whimsically suggestive passage of Leigh Hunt's "Imaginary Conversations of Pope and Swift." "The Dean once asked a scrub who was fishing, if he had ever caught a fish called the Scream. The man protested that he had never heard of such a fish. "What!" says the Dean, "you an angler, and never heard of the fish that gives a shriek when coming out of the water? 'Tis the only fish that has a voice, and a sad, dismal sound it is." The man asked who could be so barbarous as to angle for a creature that shrieked. "That," said the Dean, "is another matter; but what do you think of fellows that I have seen, whose only reason for hooking and tearing all the fish they can get at, is that they do *not* scream?"[11]

If fish could scream, or if we could learn to understand the emotions and nonverbal language of animals, the world would be very different, not just for people who like to fish but for all of us and for the animals that fall under our dominion. When we cannot sense in our hearts the silent suffering of fish as they struggle desperately in the net or on the hook, we view their death throes as merely mechanical and, in so doing, discount their very being.

Empathy and Compassion

Empathy is defined variously as the intellectual identification with or vicarious experiencing of the feelings, thoughts or attitudes of another; the power of projecting one's personality into and so fully understanding the object of contemplation; and the imaginative projection of one's own consciousness into another being.

Sympathy and empathy are distinctly different phenomena. *Sympathy* is the sharing of another's emotions, especially grief and anguish, involving pity and compassion. *Empathy* (from the Greek term meaning "affection," and a more recent German term *einfühlung*, which means "a feeling in"), entails the power of *understanding* and imaginatively entering into another's feelings. While the two are not mutually exclusive, empathy implies some level of objective knowledge and therefore a greater accuracy of perception and affect than are seen in sympathy. Because sympathy is more subjective, it may be a less accurate and more intuitive way of perceiving and responding to another's emotions. In our relations with animals, as with each other, sympathetic concern may be misplaced, while empathetic concern, since it includes both objective understanding (of the animal's nature and our ethical responsibilities) and emotional involvement, is likely to be more accurate and less often confounded by anthropomorphic projections.

Empathy is motivated by *concern*, the accuracy of that concern being a condition of rational, objective or "scientific" knowledge. From right understanding, right action, manifested as compassion and responsible stewardship, arises. The sympathetic experiences, feelings and imaginings that come from empathizing—the introjection of one's projections—become more accurate with experience and rational understanding. This is the key to good human relations and to the humane treatment of animals.

Some people question whether it is really possible to experience emotional rapport or empathy with an animal. Sympathetic concern for animals is often judged, sometimes correctly, as a sentimental, anthropomorphic projection. Sheer subjective sympathy toward an animal, without objective understanding of its behavior and needs, can lead to erroneous assumptions as to its well-being, and to misjudgment of others' treatment of animals as cruel. Empathy is possible only when the "feelings, thoughts or attitudes of another" can be vicariously experienced.

There are those who believe that since the subjective world of animals cannot be objectively weighed and measured, it does not exist. Furthermore, empathizing seems pointless since, they argue, animals do not really have emotions or an inner subjective mental world, except as governed by unconscious instincts. This animal-as-machine attitude, which we have called Cartesian after the philosopher René Descartes, who gave this attitude scientific respectability in the seventeenth century, is not the only factor that impairs our ability to empathize. The ability to empathize may be inborn as an adaptive component of our sociobiology and, as Alice Miller has shown, lack of mature parental love and understanding can severely impair a child's empathetic development.[12]

The experience of parents' empathetic understanding, expressed as the ability to deal supportively with the child's suffering, anxieties and growing independence, has a significant influence upon a child's ability to love and empathize. In our patriarchal society, males may show more cruelty toward animals, or justify the same, because they are socialized to close off empathy when faced with others' help-lessness and suffering. Miller believes that males' intense, existential anxiety and reduced ability to empathize, and their greater need to assume dominion over others through power and control, may be rooted in little boys' greater sense of insecurity and separateness from the mother in early life. This is less intense in little girls because they have the security and connectedness of maternal gender identity. Hence women may be better able to empathize and cope with others' suffering, as exemplified by their greater nurturing ability, which thus may be more than a culturally determined sex-stereotype. The greater the sense of personal security, the less the need for such dis-tancing defense mechanisms to cope with anxiety as rationalization, denial, sublimation, objectification and reaction formation.

Those adult males who are less "feminine," empathetic and nurtur-ing are not necessarily less sensitive than women. Their apparent in-sensitivity may be attributed to emotionally closing down to varying degrees when faced with others' helplessness and suffering. Seeing others suffer may awaken unbearable feelings of vulnerability, fear of being hurt and of losing control or of being controlled. Thus fear and empathy are linked, as empathizing evokes the awareness and terror of one's own ultimate nonbeing. These fears of losing power and control are the greatest obstacles to our being and becoming humane. To judge people who are deficient in empathy as deliberately cruel or intrinsically insensitive is surely unjust, yet this is a common reaction in the humane, animal welfare and rights movements. Defensive ideologies such as patriarchal domination and machismo are, perhaps, pathologically maladaptive reaction formations in the service of the insecure male ego.

The ability to empathize is also affected by cultural attitudes and values: in this culture, emotions are generally put down by instru-mental rationalists as irrational and subjective. Self-serving religious and political ideologies also impair the ability to empathize, espe-cially ideologies which support God-given human dominion over women, animals and Nature or the belief that God is transcendent and not also omnipresent in all living things. Beliefs that animals have an intrinsic right to exist, are ensouled or possess a spark of inherent divinity, have been dismissed by many as "Eastern" philosophy or pagan pantheism. Yet as we have shown, respect and compassion toward all of God's creations are also an integral part of Islamic and Judeo-Christian tradition.

The moral foundation of our industrial civilization's relationship with animals and nature is clearly flawed by its lack of reverence for all life. Belief in human dominion and in animals having no inherent rights, divinity or capacity to suffer emotionally are used to rationalize away and deny empathetic feelings of compassion, guilt and responsibility in order to further the exploitation of animals by the biomedical, farming and wildlife "resource" industries.

There are other reasons why empathy toward animals is impaired. First, we lack objective, scientific knowledge, as opposed to applied production-related information, about the behavioral requirements and emotional, subjective world of animals. Farmers, animal scientists and others involved in livestock production also have little or no formal training in ethology. A stockman who knows his animals, who can "think like a pig," for example, usually does a better job than one that lacks this basic and essential knowledge of animal psychology and behavior.[13]

Second, a blunting of sensitivity occurs naturally as a defense mechanism when one has to perform various painful procedures upon animals and must ultimately kill them or send them to slaughter. Empathy is withdrawn because the burden of responsible compassion that comes with feeling another's suffering and helplessness awakens one's own sense of vulnerability and death awareness, which can be unbearable. Many people seem to confuse empathy with an inappropriate anthropomorphic sympathy because they are repressing their own true feelings behind a defensive screen of intellectual rationalizations to justify and protect vested interests in animal exploitation and to alleviate feelings of guilt. Closing off empathy, especially in laboratory animal research (with its scientific "objectivity") and in "factory" farming and wildlife exploitation (with their objectification of animals as "stock," "food converters," "resources" and "trophies"), ultimately distorts perceptions and feelings and becomes a primary source of needless animal abuse and suffering.

Third, the empathetic burden of responsibility is lightened further by economic and other rationalizations used to justify certain procedures. Suffering is necessary and unavoidable, the standard argument runs, if any societal benefits are accrued.

What may be termed "protective objectification"—the distancing from and denial of others' subjectivity in order to avoid closeness, responsibility and the burden of empathy—is another obstacle to empathic response. This pattern is exemplified by women treated as sex objects, medical patients as mere cases, and animals as trophies, status symbols, research tools and livestock. Many persons in a paradoxical or conflicting relationship with animals will mobilize this distancing defense, since emotional involvement can lead euphemistically to "burn-out": for instance, farmers who nurture animals that will be killed; animal shelter personnel who are concerned about animal welfare but must euthanize them; biomedical researchers and laboratory technicians who care for animals but cause them to suffer, and mutilate, kill and dissect them; physicians and nurses attending terminally ill patients. While such persons must be realists in dealing with the paradoxes of life, the difference between a nurturing and supportive person and one who is disconnected is the difference between humaneness and indifference, compassion and inhumanity. The distinction is not between intrinsically kind and cruel persons, but between those who can bear the burden of empathy and those who fear it. The distinction between a humane farm and a large "factory" farm is surely based upon the operator's capacity to empathize with the realities of suffering.

Protective objectification is analogous to Judaic philosopher Martin Buber's I-It relationship. From Buber's perspective, empathy enables us to break out of the objective, detached I-It mindset into the trans-subjectively objective realm of I-Thou. The objective and subjective realms of each I and Thou are mutually inclusive: every entity is a dualistic monad. The subjective, intrinsic value or worth of one entity is part of the objective, instrumental realm of other interdependent monads, be they atoms or living beings, that are bound in relationship that may be purely physical, ecological, social or emotional. In Buber's terms, the subjective "I" of one monadic entity is the objective "It" of another. But when there is respect for the "I-ness" or subjective realm of another's being, and empathetic love and compassionate understanding, the objective "It" becomes another subjectively resonant, spiritual "Thou." A monadic relationship is then made, through respect and love, which is, for human beings, the emotional, spiritual and ethical manifestation and experience of a unified field of being. This state of relatedness does not, I believe, as Buber suggests, exclude or transcend the I-It objective duality but rather enfolds it in compassion, such that the objective instrumental realm is still an intrinsic part of the relationship but does not govern it.

Buber's concept of I-Thou embodies the spiritual and political principles of reverence for all life, humane stewardship, respect, nurturance, "reciprocal maintenance," co-evolution and *agape*, as self-giving love. Objective instrumental rationalism and love are not mutually exclusive, but rather they reconcile, at the conscious, ethical level of reality, the dialectical, paradoxical antinomies of life. The exclusion of love from objectivity brings evil and suffering into the world, which cause increasing anxiety, which in turn leads to more power and control over others or to emotional withdrawal and more evil and suffering.

Buber eloquently describes the "otherness" of an animal when he writes of stroking a horse at his grandparents' estate:

> I must say that what I experienced in touch with the animal was the Other, the immense otherness of the Other, which, however, did not remain strange like the otherness of the ox and the ram, but rather let me draw near and touch it . . . and yet it let me approach, confided itself to me, placed itself elementally in the relation of Thou and Thou with me.[14]

Buber emphasizes that an I-Thou, rather than an I-It, relationship is therefore possible in the absence of reciprocal observing ego, as when one contemplates a rock or Nature or interacts with an animal. It is possible in such moments of openness with the nonhuman world to actualize and encounter the spiritual essence of being that inheres in all animate and inanimate forms. We humans may then discover, if not actually bestow, meaning and significance—not as objective knowledge or some projected ideology of animism or panpsychism—via a panentheistic gnosis of the divinity or spiritual quality within all, and thus experience an expanding state of panempathy.

Buber writes that the unity and living wholeness of a tree is manifest to those who say "Thou" and is present when they are present. It is they who grant the tree the opportunity to manifest its being, but most often our habitual attitudes, ways of thinking, perceiving and relating, deny us such a relationship. In Buber's words:

Spirit become word, spirit become form—whoever has been touched by the spirit and did not close himself off knows to some extent of the fundamental fact: neither germinates and grows in the human world without having been sown; both issue from encounters with the other.[15]

That most animals are capable of experiencing and expressing affection and of enjoying life in their way, as we do in ours, and—like us—have interests, means that they are emotionally and cognitively and, some would say, spiritually, little different from us. That we are different in terms of our power of dominion over them does not mean that we can ignore the ethical relevance of those similarities. We differ in degree and not in kind: we are not superior, but our objectifying of the world leads us to believe so, and no longer to perceive the unified field of All Being.

Comparative sciences such as zoology, ethology, physiology and psychology reveal how sapience and sentience—intelligence and conscious sensitivity—evolve. The only differences between humans and other animals, which create no discontinuity but build upon the phylogenetic and ontogenetic sequence, are our powers of self-contemplation, creative imagination and verbal conceptualization and communication. The two axes of sapience and sentience reach their highest expression phylogenetically and ontogenetically in humans as understanding and compassion, as the will is consciously motivated by the subjective force of love and directed by the objective power of knowledge. Knowledge applied without love is as self-serving, self-limiting and destructive as the ignorance of narcissism. Empathy, the synthesis of concern and sympathetic understanding of others, a quality not lacking in other animals, is the very essence of humane being.

Psychologist Carol Gilligan links empathy with moral maturity. When both intellect and empathy are integrated in our thinking, "it joins the heart and the eye in an ethic that ties the activity of thought to the activity of care."[16] Without such integration, purely intellectual, rational thought is objectifying and potentially alienating, since it limits empathetic understanding. A purely sympathetic response is a subjective projection, potentially inappropriate, and no less damaging than a purely objective response. Informed sympathy is empathy, expressed as compassionate understanding. Rational empathy is the only basis for ethically responsible behavior.

We live in two worlds: the objective and the subjective. When we make the two worlds one, and put the inside on the outside, as Jesus once said, we will discover the Kingdom of Heaven, or in modern parlance, reality as a unified field of being. As animals, we live in our subjectivity, and as rational beings we stand apart from the world in our intellectual objectivity. In the one is kinship; in the other, power. Joined together, we have mature, responsible relationship and planetary stewardship. Apart, we have delusion, oppression and destruction, creating the imbalances that we perceive as evil and experience as suffering. By inhibiting empathy and using power and control over life in order to avoid feelings of vulnerability and helplessness in the face of life's burdens, we cause even more suffering. The barrier between these two worlds, which Buber terms I-It and I-Thou, is neither objectivity, nor subjectivity. Both are essential attributes of our Being and becoming. But they must become integrated with the unified field of our own being that embraces animals and Nature, for we are both. To perceive and think otherwise is to remain unintegrated, which is the ultimate barrier to self-realization and moral maturity. We, animals and Nature are one. In order to change the world, we must first become as one with the world in peace and harmony. And since peace comes from within, we must first see to ourselves before we can change the world. Then the way of empathy is clear.

When there is objective knowledge about what an animal's overt behavior signifies, and what emotional states, intentions and expectations such overt behavior reflect, empathy is possible. Without such objective knowledge, we have sympathy and varying degrees of anthropomorphization. Understanding and sympathy combined make empathy possible.

Empathy is a perceptual and cognitive phenomenon, not simply an anthropomorphic "humanizing" projection. It is analogous to what phenomenologist Merleau-Ponty terms "lateral coexistential knowledge" as distinct from objective, "vertical" knowing and perceiving. Professor Carlton Dallery illustrates this mode of perception as follows:

THE BOUNDLESS CIRCLE

This is not the place to summarize Merleau-Ponty's magisterial work, *The Phenomenology of Perception* (1946). For our purposes, it is important to note that perception is described as the complex, always open, temporal "access" between world and perceiver. It is neither a causal process nor a process distinct from social relations, speech, or understanding (as it would be if perception were a "thought of seeing"). So in perceiving a snake, for example, I do not simply receive an impression of a sinuous form having a certain mottled pattern; I do not see a cold, indifferent fact, or have a bunch of impressions to which I might or might not endow some value depending on my feelings; I see the snake, which is to say that I see its behavior in an environment proper to it and that I "appropriate" the snake's way of being, the snake's perception of certain things around it. But I am free to regard the snake as an object and admire its beauty, or to loathe its slithering.[17]

For those humanists, atheists, agnostics and others who do not adhere to any particular religious tradition, it must still be self-evident that the more we distance ourselves emotionally from animals and from others' suffering, the less human we become. As rationalism supplants compassion and our anthropocentrism increases our distance from the nonhuman Creation, we are losing our sense of humanity. This loss of humanity has become a major threat to the survival of the human species as *humane* beings. And it has likewise become a threat to the integrity and future of Earth's Creation. In an essay on the common road, George Orwell acknowledged the vital importance of experiencing Nature in childhood when he wrote:

I think that by retaining one's childhood love of such things as trees, fishes, butterflies and—to return to my first instance—toads, one makes a peaceful and decent future a little more probable, and that by preaching the doctrine that nothing is to be admired except steel and concrete, one merely makes it a little surer that human beings will have no outlet for their surplus energy except in hatred and leader worship.[18]

There are those who have put their faith in science and technology and in human will and ingenuity to solve these problems. Some of them also believe that it is part of the normal evolutionary process—if not divinely ordained—for *Homo sapiens* to exploit all of life and to turn the natural world or biosphere into a humanized and industrialized technosphere. They have distanced themselves so completely from animals and the rest of Creation that they represent the germinal core of a new race of humanoid that I have termed *Homo technos:* technocratic man. But as Father Thomas Berry has advised, if the human species is to avert this cultural mutation, for the good of humanity and of the natural world, we must become instead "biocratic"—intimately involved, emotionally and intellectually (as well as spiritually), in the Earth's creative processes of which, as *Homo sapiens,* we are still an integral and interdependent part. There can be no distance, and indeed ecologically (and spiritually), there is none: we are all part of the One Life and of the Earth community, and to think and act otherwise will ensure our own demise. But as we come to empathize with the world's suffering—to have what I call panempathy—and to heal this sick and dying planet and ourselves in the process, humanity will indeed evolve. *Homo sapiens* will become *Homo pansapiens* through compassion and reverence for all of Creation.

However, I do not wish to end with such simplistic optimism, even though I still have faith in the inherent goodness of the human heart—when it can be reached, that is. I reiterate that the greatest threat we face today, archetypically embodied in the concept of *Homo technos,* technocratic man, is the loss of heart, of fellow-feeling and of an attitude of reverential respect for all sentient beings, and with this loss, the inability to love and unwillingness to suffer the world's pain.

To feel at one with Nature, the Body of Christ, and to experience the world's pain, is to receive the stigmata of the Earth crucified. To be at one with the Earth, through the beauty and mystery of Nature's Creation, and through love for every created thing, is to know the divine Self or One Life. This realization of the Christ, Buddha-nature or Universal Self for the theist, atheist and agnostic alike, is the source of hope and inspiration for our redemption and for the healing and resurrection of the Earth.

"Rainbow People": Restoring the Covenant

Animal liberation, which at its heart is a call for a shift from an ego-centered to an eco-centered spirituality, also implies human liberation, for it frees us from an idolatrous concept of God.
—Rev. Gary Kowalski

As Nature, through God-wisdom, incorporates us, so we, through Nature-reverence, incorporate God.

—Anonymous

IN OUR CITIES, DORMITORY SUB-urban developments, industrial "parks," monoculture fields and forests, there is no place for what aboriginal people—the First People —call the Dreaming, or Great Spirit, and for the natural expression of the creative process. It is variously defiled, coerced, perverted, degraded and extinguished almost everywhere.

Like the First People of the Dream, who lived in harmony with the Great Spirit by obeying their original instructions, the People of the Rainbow today, those of all colors, nations and creeds, are coming together in one spirit. Their task is as simple as it is monumental. It is to resacralize the Earth; to restore the Covenant long broken by those human beings who, in assuming dominion over Creation, forgot their original instructions and the Law of Nature and Creator to live gently, in harmony and reverence with all life. Peace, justice and the integrity of Creation are the supreme goals in these times of wanton desecration of the Earth's Creation and flagrant violation of the rights of all sentient life to equal and fair consideration.

The seeds of a planetary spiritual democracy are being sown now by the People who recognize this as a survival imperative of planetary restoration and resurrection and as a redemptive act for the original sin of breaking the Covenant; of our willful and ignorant separation from the Creation, Creator and creative process. Nothing will be well until the Animal Kingdom is unfettered and given sanctuary in the wildlands and waters ravaged by human ignorance and greed, destroyed and poisoned with agrichemicals and industrial pollutants, which we must now restore and preserve.

It is a matter of human dignity—and spiritual pride—to oppose those unnatural human forces that continue to desecrate Earth's Creation. We might think about this opposition, fought against the consensus worldview of the times, as tantamount to World War III. It is the war not to end all wars, but to end the annihilation and transformation of the natural world into the technocratic materialist's own utopian dream of an efficiently productive, highly industrialized biosphere.

We have now reached the point in our biological evolution where, to quote Teilhard de Chardin, we have one final choice: suicide or adoration. Beginning to see and feel and suffer the holocaust of the planet and its Animal Kingdom crucified is the first step toward responsible, redemptive action. This is as much a part of the process of our own healing and wholeness as it is for the Earth and all who dwell on it. Teilhard de Chardin's term for this process is the *hominization* of the Earth. Because of our numbers and global impact, this process is now intensifying. There is no turning back.

Indeed, over the few generations in which we have started to coerce rather than control the creative process and to industrialize the biosphere, the process of hominization has gathered momentum. But, as with the evolutionary process itself, there are choice and chance. We have freedom of will and one last chance—to help ensure that the hominization process, which is paradoxically as natural as it tends to be unnaturally destructive of all that is natural, is accomplished with the minimum of stress and distress and without further destruction of sentient beings and of the living matrix of Earth's Creation, the biosphere. The more this matrix is destroyed—natural ecosystems industrialized, polluted and obliterated; the food chain broken, while we foul the air all life breathes and the water all life needs—the more we sicken in spirit, mind and body.

The remedy lies not in conventional allopathic medical and technological fixes. Most address symptoms and consequences and do not address the causes so as to find preventive solutions. In other words, it is not a matter of trying to prevent the hominization of the Earth, but rather of treating the disease which promotes inhumane and destructive industrialization under the ethos of secular humanism.

Industrialization that does not facilitate hominization, because it excludes linking concern for the health, well-being and other basic rights of every human being and has harmful effects on Nature and the animal and plant kingdoms, must be opposed. Self-control is an integral part of the hominization process, especially in the development of new technologies and industries. Otherwise, techno-involution will occur. This kind of "progress" is the antithesis of the hominization of the Earth. It is biocidal—destructive of the natural world—and potentially also a suicidal path leading to human extinction in spirit, if not in body. What survives would be genetically and culturally mutant life forms: humankind in the form of *Homo technos*, and other species genetically engineered to enhance their adaptation to proliferating human needs. For hominization to proceed smoothly, the sage advice of Mahatma Gandhi needs to be followed: "Civilization should not be the infinite multiplication of human wants. Science should not order human values. Technology should not order society. Civilization should be the deliberate limitation of wants to essentials that could be equally shared."

The synthesis and synergy of consumerism and industrialism have become the cultural equivalents of what in Nature we know as parasitism and predation, and what in medicine we recognize as disease. This state is the antithesis of natural symbiosis and commensalism—what in medicine, we call health—and it is as biologically and socially absurd as it is ecologically catastrophic. The arrogant anthropocentrism and secular materialism of the times have so distorted our perception of our place in Nature that we are evidently incapable of recognizing the difference between health and disease, between what is natural and what is abnormal. How else can we explain making animals suffer to find "cures" for primarily self-induced human diseases or justify poisoning our air, food and water with industrial pollutants and agricultural chemicals in the name of necessity, progress and profitability?

The belief that we can profit at Nature's expense and that good can come from harming other sentient beings is as absurd as the belief that human health and well-being is somehow independent and separate from a whole and healthy natural world. Indeed, the secular anthropocentrism and scientific imperialism of the rising technocracy is ethically blind to anything outside the material realm of human gratification. It is based upon a pathological worldview that is dualistic, hierarchical and patriarchal. As such, it is a disease in itself, one that is fast becoming a threat not only to humankind but to all life on this planet.

We are slow to realize how greed and fear arise when we begin to objectify the world. Then we feel increasingly disconnected and insecure, feelings that intensify our greed, fear and destructiveness. Greed, under the guise of efficiency and productivity, has led to an overproductive agri-industry, with its chemical poisoning of the biosphere; exhaustion of nonrenewable resources, especially topsoil and deep-water aquifers; extinction of rural communities and traditional sustainable low-input farming practices, as well as the cruel incarceration of animals in intensive livestock and poultry "factories."[1] Making farm systems more humane, while not promoting vegetarianism or at least a 70 percent reduction in the farm animal population and a decreased use of pesticides in an already pesticide-soaked environment, is counterproductive, since such half-way solutions do not get to the heart of the problem—a change in the human heart.

And where is the human heart when it comes to society's acceptance of animal experimentation as necessary and justifiable? This feeble rationalization is an example of how our fear of sickness, death and the loss of our loved ones—not to discount the greed of those who profit in the medical industry—has led us to condone vivisection as a conventional norm. Rudolph Bahro, leading philosopher of the German Green Movement, states:

> We are a species so far excluded from communion with itself or with the forms of life closest to us that almost any one of us can be trained to carry out torture without feeling anything. The bridge between our rationality (of which Goethe says: "He calls it reason and uses it to be more bestial than any beast") and the bosom from which it springs is so broken that we hardly hear the warning voice of our own unconscious as representative of nature any more. Science toughens its priests and servants, as well as its clients, even more reliably than the dragon's blood toughened Siegfried in the *Niebelungenlied*. In my opinion animal experiments, quite regardless of whether or not their results can be transferred to humans and whether or not they help us in some direct or indirect way, are in principle part of the logic of self-destruction. It is the same as with the army. The principle of "security first" which underlies these dealings with disease and death, as indeed almost all their practices to date, will only lead to destruction.[2]

It would be wrong to say that no benefits have come in the past from animal research. But now there are new diseases of civilization, related to our lifestyle and to our habit of poisoning and impoverishment the environment, that no amount of animal research will prevent. And we need no more animal experiments to prove the obvious: that pesticides, alcohol and drugs are harmful to our health and cause cancer, birth defects and genetic damage. To justify continued animal research to find *cures* for these self-induced diseases is not only unethical; it is also bad medicine, since the best medicine is prevention.

At the beginning of the Industrial Revolution more than three hundred years ago, John Donne wrote, "Nature is the common law by which God governs us." If we do not obey this common law and continue instead to be parasites on Earth and to exploit its inhabitants, allowing scientific materialism to order human values, and technology to order society, the hominization process will be aborted. Supplanted by a highly destructive, dehumanizing global industrialization, humanity as *Homo sapiens* will disappear, along with the natural world, and for a finite period, *Homo technos* will rule the Earth. This scenario is not inevitable, provided the hominization of the Earth includes the preservation and restoration of the natural world. From a Christian perspective, this entails restoring the Covenant with the Creator "to dress and to keep" the Earth.

The collective development of human consciousness and conscience has progressed from a primal unconscious symbiotic stage into an adolescent phase of omnipotence, in which the external world is objectified as something "other," to be controlled and exploited. Symbiosis has given way to objectification, a dualistic, fundamentally materialistic and instrumental worldview. Objectification of the world went along with the industrialization of the biosphere and the commoditization of Earth's Creation. As John Mohawk observed in *Creation Magazine*, "When land became a 'commodity' and lost its status as provider and sustainer of life, Western civilization began its history of subjugation and exploitation of the earth and earth-based cultures." The next evolutionary stage—"panempathy," which implies the birth of *Homo pansapiens*—entails the conscious, empathetic psychic interiorization of the world as an objective other, with the emergence of a nondualistic consciousness and conscience. This process might lead to the emergence of what Thomas Berry calls the ecozoic era.[3] It is exemplified by extending the empathetic field of ethical sensibility and moral concern to embrace creatures and Creation through applying the Golden Rule to all our relationships, human and nonhuman.

Animal and Environmental Protection and Human Well-Being

The sciences of ecology, quantum physics, economic theory and holistic medicine affirm that everything is interconnected and thus interdependent. This essential unity has been recognized in the teachings of Creation-centered religions, but not by those that are human-centered. The unity of the cosmos and Creation, symbolically represented by the Tao in the embrace of yin and yang, is called the Sacred Hoop or Medicine Wheel by the Native Americans. To break the wheel is bad medicine. Anthropocentrism destroys the wheel, the sacred unity and harmony of life.

As history should teach us, the many crises that humanity faces today are symptoms and consequences of an anthropocentric attitude that is blind to the sanctity of all life. This way of feeling, perceiving, thinking and behaving is the cause of most of the suffering and disease we cause to ourselves and to the animals and the natural environment. We compound this tragedy by deliberately and indifferently poisoning the environment with agricultural chemicals and industrial pollutants and by using animal research to find profitable cures for the diseases we bring upon ourselves. If we understood fully the complexity and significance of disease, we would recognize that experimenting on animals for purely human benefit is itself part of the disease complex.[4] The suffering and death of a chimpanzee to find a cure for AIDS is no different from the suffering and death of a red fox caught in a trap for its fur or of a dolphin or seal dying in the ocean that we have polluted. The end is the same—suffering and death. Is it ethically sound to reason that the suffering and death of a laboratory animal for medical advancement is more justifiable than the suffering and death of a wild animal that is a "pest," a "harvestable" resource or a trophy for a hunter? This kind of thinking sees the implantation of a chimpanzee or baboon heart or a genetically engineered pig's liver into a human patient as justifiable, since, after all, people eat the hearts and livers of other animals anyway.

In the final analysis, such reasoning is human-centered and leads to a hierarchy of utility. The more useful the animal is to humanity, as a medical model or organ donor, the more justified its exploitation, suffering and death. Human selfishness has no limits. Myriad defensive rationalizations and misconceptions are used to condone it, such as the naturalistic fallacy that it is not unethical to exploit and kill animals because they kill each other in Nature. We, however, have a choice; predators do not. The rationalization that human beings are superior because they are created in God's image, coupled with the belief that the natural world is for our exclusive use, completes the evil continuum of ignorance, arrogance and greed.

The Jain doctrine of *ahimsa*—avoiding all forms of violence toward other beings and the natural Creation—may appear as an impossible ideal or the tenet of religious cult, but it requires neither self-sacrifice nor some esoteric theology to put it into practice. What may seem to be self-sacrifice, not eating animals or wearing their furs, is in fact self-giving benevolence. One need go no further than the theology of God-as-love to realize the profound simplicity and wisdom of *ahimsa*. Its foundation is reason and compassion; its practice is recognizing that an act of cruelty toward an animal is a spiritual problem, requiring concern for the victimizer as well as the victim.

Through that deep empathy that makes compassion boundless and reverence for life nondiscriminatory, we can weep for the slaughterman and for the people with guns, harpoons, whips, clubs, chains, goads, halters, harnesses, traps, lures, nets, hooks, poison baits, scalpels, electrodes and all other means used harm, debase and kill animals. We weep because they harm, debase and kill a part of themselves and thus a part of ourselves, since empathy informs us that we and all our relations are part of the One Life.

But how patiently can we wait for people to begin to acknowledge their earthly relations and obligations, their sins of omission and commission? How long can we endure the dying of the Earth, the suffering and extinction of other creatures and cultures and the spreading cancer of a diseased humanity? Until the end of all suffering wrought through ignorance of the sacred unity of all life that we acknowledge through respect and reverence for all existences.

From Global Anarchy and Exploitation to Sustainable Cooperation

Toward what ends will our appetites and passions lead us? Hopi and other ancient prophesies warn of our becoming a people dark with rage in an age of destructive anarchy. This demonic malady is more risk to humanity and the planet than AIDS or any other epidemic. Omnipresent is the related potential of thermonuclear or biological warfare, which may yet come to pass.

As we have noted, the Hopi foresaw two thousand years ago what is now happening to the Earth and the human race and called it the "purification." Australian and other surviving aboriginal societies have not lost the wisdom of living simply within the carrying capacity of the land that sustains both them and the creatures and plants that make up their biological and spiritual community. The biospiritual ethic of living in harmony within Nature's holarchy guaranteed the security and future of these peoples with far greater certainty than we might anticipate since we began to see the Earth not as a community of subjects but as a set of products of varying degrees of utility. Our fear, insecurity and greed intensified as we multiplied, along with our livestock, and cleared more land to meet our needs.

The spiritual degradation of humanity wrought by industrialized exploitation of Nature is understandable and tragic. Indeed, it is a tragic perversion of our once noble survival instincts and biological wisdom when people can find reasons to torture, mutilate and kill each other, and engage in genocide and ecocide. We may yet redeem ourselves and regain our dignity, but only when we make peace with each other and with the Earth by ensuring that our appetites and passions are fulfilled without violating the Golden Rule.

Reporter Robert Kaplan observes, "Those peoples whose cultures can harbor extensive slum without decomposing will be, relatively speaking, the future's winners. Those whose cultures cannot will be the future's victims."[5] With 90 percent of the doubling of the human population occurring in the Third World over the next generation, national security will be eroded by environmental degradation, disease, internecine conflict, tides of refugees and urban immigration. There will indeed be many victims in the years to come, and war over access to and control of vital natural resources, especially water and fossil fuels. Kaplan predicts, "Future wars will be those of communal survival, aggravated or, in many cases, caused by environmental scarcity. These wars will be sub-national, meaning that it will be hard for states and local governments to protect their own citizens physically. This is how many states will ultimately die."[6]

Geopolitics and population dynamics are determined by environmental resources which, in turn, shape the social evolution of the human race. The tensions between northern and southern hemispheres and between rich and poor, inflamed by ill-conceived aid and development programs that fuel overconsumption and overpopulation, necessitate immediate, concerted international cooperation. But the best laid plans of people of good intent will amount to naught if we do not curtail further overconsumption and overpopulation. In the absence of enlightened self-control, humanity will continue to be the victim of Nature's indiscriminate controls and, rather than being obedient to natural law, will seek liberation in violence against its own kind. We will continue to blame others—rich or poor, capitalists or religious fundamentalists—until we accept our powerlessness and begin to make amends by renouncing those appetites and passions that are the cause of our spiritual and biological demise.

In the final analysis, it is too simplistic to blame poverty and ignorance, especially in the Third World, for all environmental degradation. While rapid population growth and migration to fragile ecosystems have been major factors in such degradation, we should not forget that colonialism and many World Bank and American international development programs have helped to destroy traditional sustainable agricultural, agriforestry and fishing practices and to further the interests of a minority of rich land owners, many of whom run the governments of the countries in question. It is clear that multinational corporate interests and related government agencies from the industrialized northern hemisphere have done more harm than good to the peoples of the southern hemisphere and to the environment. Environmental degradation will be abated in poorer countries only when the control of natural resources is fully democratized so that communities can manage them sustainably.[7] Equity and social justice are the political components of the Golden Rule, which should be the ethical framework of the newly formed World Trade Organization, with the goal of helping to foster global cooperation and biocultural diversity. Sustainable development through economic growth will not be possible if the rights and interests of indigenous peoples are marginalized and a reverential attitude toward all life is seen as an obstacle rather than the right path to progress. What sustains the spirit sustains the nation.

Toward a Nonviolent Society

Social justice should include eco-justice, and adhering to the democratic principle, include all minorities and fellow creatures as beings worthy of equal and fair consideration. Human industry, not industrialism, should first restore and protect the ecology and the rights and interests of animals and other minorities. Without such industry, there is no enduring peace or prosperity, and all power is simply relative. The only absolute power which is incorruptible is the power of that spiritual love we express in our respect and reverence for all life. It is desire that corrupts, and the desire to have absolute power corrupts absolutely. Nonenduring wealth is the treadmill of materialism, which industrialism serves. Greed, fear and desire can never be satiated. Their transmutation is our liberation from this treadmill; and as the sages of all ages have always taught, liberation from self-delusion. The challenge of the times is to develop industries based upon benevolence and service rather than power and greed; upon the security of operating ethically with respect for the environment; upon the rights and interests of consumers, minorities, family, native and peasant farmers and sustainable rural communities.

The Valdez principles of corporate industrial responsibility drafted after the devastating Exxon oil spill in Alaska, and the Green Label concept launched after Earth Day to label products that are "environmentally friendly" are auspicious beginnings. But it will be too little too late if the multinational corporate oligopolies, all nation-states, private entrepreneurs, politicians and the voting public do not realize the urgency of these measures. We must begin to develop immediately the means by which every individual, community and nation can function in a humane and sustainable way, or we relegate these promising initiatives to the garbage pile that the Earth is fast becoming. We must rise above corporate irresponsibility and personal indifference and seek every means to achieve a better world for generations to come. Not to do so means violence against the integrity and future of Creation.

When the harm done exceeds the good that may be derived from a violent act—when it fails to preserve or enhance the beauty and diversity of the biotic and human communities—then such an act is ethically wrong. However, we do not yet have a socially responsible and *responsive* judiciary in the United States or a consensus in the United Nations or in the newly formed World Trade Organization that recognizes that respect and reverence for all life is not only an ethical and survival imperative but the only economically sound and environmentally viable choice we can make. The only other choice, to paraphrase poet T. S. Eliot, is to go out with a bang or a whimper.

Without ecological awareness, we will continue to see U.S.-based petrochemical and pharmaceutical corporations export products that are banned or not yet approved for use in the United States, and a host of other corporate crimes justified falsely on the grounds of economic development, progress and necessity. There can be no real United Nations until all nations are united in one spirit under the same green flag of respect and reverence for life.

The human population of 5.6 billion is consuming life at a faster rate than the Earth can sustain. The harm we do collectively to the Earth is unlike the minimal harm done to the environment by natural predators and past and present sustainable gatherer-hunters like the Native Americans and Australian aboriginals. Minimal harm and "kindly use"—living simply so that others may simply live—are ethical imperatives; it is an ecological maxim and a natural law that we must not live beyond the carrying capacity and resource-base of the environment. Species that cause irreparable harm eventually become extinct or few in number because they overpopulate, over-consume and limit the options for generations to come.

English philosopher Francis Bacon helped sanctify the Industrial Revolution four centuries ago: We should "have commerce with Nature" and "vex her" in order to gain control over her powers; this, he maintained, was God's will. In two centuries, we can see how this attitude has decimated and desecrated the United States of America. Built on slave labor and immigrant need and desire for a better life, this attitude has poisoned its rivers from source to outlet, cut down ninety percent of its original forests, virtually exterminated the vast herds of buffalo that once roamed the Great Plains and subjected Native Americans to no kinder fate. Our greed is an example to the Third World, which cannot be chastised for making deserts from raising too many livestock, since we did the same in our own southwest. Our historic indifference to ecological democracy and social justice is also evidenced by the virtual extinction of the wolf and grizzly bear.

The paradigm of industrialism, with its intellectual, religious and scientific trappings and cleverness, is a disaster and a threat to the continued existence of life on this planet. The affluent of industrialism's technopolus—the power elite—may be able to afford the technology to build a new world, but if respect and reverence for life are not reflected in appropriate technologies, aid and development programs, and in a sustainable and cooperative World Trade Organization, the new world to come will be barren and unrecognizable. Until we begin to serve rather than vanquish the Earth by incorporating these principles into a life and Creation-centered spirituality, the Earth will be unable to serve us much longer.

As a spark of divine Creation, the spirit ensouled in human form gives humanity the possibility of understanding the sacred as well as the material dimensions of the life we experience. The human soul is linked with the souls of all the plant and animal kingdoms because all life has the same divine and earthly origin. While humans differ from plants and animals in many ways, we are part of the same fabric of interdependent existence that once functioned as an integrated whole, the biosphere or planetary ecosystem.

The spirit in us elevates us above the rest of Creation only so we may realize that, since lower beings in the great chain of life serve higher beings and ends, so higher beings should serve lower beings and the same ends: to protect, nurture and celebrate the fullness of life on Earth in its myriad forms of divine expression, beauty, diversity and functional harmony. We might believe that, unlike other creatures, we have freedom of choice and self-determination. This is true, but when we violate the laws of Creation by destroying the fabric of life to satisfy our own exclusive ends, we fall from grace and suffer the consequences.

Is our place in Creation to vanquish the Earth or "to dress and to keep it"? The ethical sensibility that arises from the spiritual insight of our kinship with all life must guide us to make those enlightened choices that cause the least harm to other living beings and to the functional integrity of the biosphere. In the process of facilitating our own self-determination, we find that the path of nonviolence includes social justice and eco-justice. The most spiritual of all human industries is the life of service, individual and collective, aimed at realizing the full potential of being human by living closer to the ideal of reverential respect for all life.

To end this chapter and to close this book without offering some practical ways of living ethically and spiritually would be a serious omission. Since agriculture is the primary economy and sustaining basis of society, how we farm and what we eat are important components of a humane, socially just and sustainable society.

"Rainbow People": Restoring the Covenant

Farming Without Harm and Choosing a Humane Diet: The Bioethics of Sustainable Agriculture

No other society past or present raises and kills so many animals for their meat. No other society past or present has adopted such intensive systems of animal production and nonrenewable, resource-dependent farming practices. These methods have evolved to make meat a dietary staple and to meet the public expectation and demand for a "cheap" and plentiful supply of meat. An agriculture that raises and slaughters billions of animals every year primarily for meat depends on costly nonrenewable natural resources and precious farmland to raise the feed that these animals convert into flesh, land that could be used more economically to feed people directly. Such conspicuous consumption is a poor model to emulate. According to the U.N. Food and Agriculture Organization, in the United States, some 800 kg. of grain are used to feed livestock to meet the average annual per capita consumption of 42 kg. beef, 20 kg. pork, 44 kg. poultry, 283 kg. dairy products and 16 kg. of eggs.

Supporters of intensive animal "factory" farming claim that America has the cheapest and most productive agriculture in the world and that humane reforms would increase costs and put an unfair burden on the poor. Critics of factory farming are accused of being more concerned about animals than people and against progress. Both of these erroneous conclusions need to be dispelled.

The real costs of factory farming have been well documented, ranging from price supports and subsidies at taxpayers' expense, to the demise of family farms, rural communities, waste of natural resources and animal stress, disease and suffering. Coupled with corporate monopoly, these hidden costs have aggravated rather than alleviated poverty and malnutrition nationally and internationally. The fact is, the real costs of factory farming are not accounted for by agribusiness, and its high productivity is neither efficient nor socially or ethically acceptable.

Those who believe that farm animals do not play a vital ecological and economic role in sustainable crop production and range management are as wrong as those who claim that intensive livestock and poultry production are bioethically acceptable because they cause no harm. Now is the time for openness and objectivity and a coming together of all sectors of society involved in the production, marketing and consumption of food to support the development, adoption and market viability of humane and ecological farming practices that enable farmers to farm with less harm.

The industrial factory-scale system that the animal component of modern agriculture has evolved is bioethically unacceptable. Making the retail price of meat cheaper through tax subsidies and price supports, better vaccines and biotechnology, irrigation projects and further deforestation and draining of wetlands, makes it even less acceptable. So will innovations in meat safety inspection, handling and processing, including food irradiation, since a full and fair cost accounting will still show that producing meat as a dietary staple causes too much harm.

However, the rightness or wrongness of meat eating and of killing animals is not the central concern of the humane bioethics movement. Its focus is the need to implement less harmful alternatives to contemporary animal agriculture: Intensive livestock and poultry production systems, aimed at producing affordably priced meat as a dietary staple, cause harm to farm animals in terms of environmental and production- or husbandry-related stress and disease; to the agro-ecology, wildlife, biodiversity and natural ecosystems; to family farms and rural communities; and to consumers and indigenous peoples of the Third World. The antidote is public support for the adoption of organic and other alternative, sustainable crop and livestock production practices that are humane and ecologically sound.

Reverential respect for life and for the land is the guiding bioethical principle of a just and sustainable agriculture and society. Questioning agricultural practices, including new developments in genetic engineering biotechnology, should not be judged as unscientific or obstructionist. Surely the essence of progress is to apply science and ethics in the development of agricultural and other industries so as to cause the least harm and do the greatest good to the entire life community. We cannot sacrifice the good of the environment or of rural communities for the short-term good of the economy, for society will suffer, now and in the future. Likewise, we cannot sacrifice the good of farm animals or the soil in the name of productivity and labor-substituting technological innovation and marketing without ultimately harming the economy and the health of everyone.

To farm with less harm, each of us must consume and live in ways that support bioethical principles. This means a *reduction* in the production and consumption of meat in those countries where meat is a dietary staple. It also means *refinement* in terms of how animals are raised, transported and slaughtered, and *replacement* of animal protein and fat with cheaper vegetable fats, oils and proteins. The Earth's human population of a soon-to-double 5.6 billion (of which 1.6 billion are malnourished) will necessitate an increase the current livestock population of some 4.5 billion just to maintain current public demand for meat. If we begin to apply bioethics in the public and corporate policy decision-making process, we will have a better chance of predicting and preventing harmful increases and of visioning a positive future.

Even conventional agriculturalists are beginning to recognize that a farming policy based on using good land to raise feed for livestock is not sustainable. In 1994, the conservative Council for Agricultural Science and Technology published a landmark report by agronomist Paul E. Waggoner entitled *How Much Land Can Ten Billion People Spare for Nature?* In the introduction Waggoner writes:

> Today farmers feed five to six billion people by cultivating a tenth of the planet's land. The seemingly irresistible doubling of population and the imperative of producing food will take another tenth of the land, much from Nature, if people keep on eating and farmers keep on farming as they do now. So farmers work at the junction where population, the human condition, and sparing land for Nature meet.[8]

With this premise, and using the latest data from around the world, Waggoner proceeds to show how "smart farmers" can harvest more per plot and thus spare some of today's cropland for Nature—if we help them with changed diets, never-ending research and encouraging incentives. Among the points the report makes are the following:

- Calories and protein equally distributed from present cropland could provide a vegetarian diet to ten billion people.
- The global totals of sun on land, CO_2 in the air, fertilizer and even water could produce far more food than ten billion people need.

- By eating different species of crops and more or less vegetarian diets, we can increase the number of people who can be fed.
- Recent data shows that millions of people do change their diets in response to health, price and other pressures, and that they are capable of even further changes.
- Given adequate incentives, farmers can use new technologies to increase food productivity and thus keep prices level despite a rising population. Even better use of existing technology can raise current yields.
- Despite recurring problems with water supply and distribution, there are opportunities to raise more crops with the same volume of water.
- In Europe and the United States, rising income, improving technology and leveling populations forecast diminishing use of cropland.

The first step for every caring person to take is to choose a humane diet. This should be on top of every nation's agenda, as it is on the agenda of both The Humane Society of the United States and Humane Society International, with their 2.2 million members and constituents, and which I am glad to serve as Vice President, Bioethics and Farm Animals. Choosing a humane diet is a bioethical imperative if we are to prevent further human and animal suffering, the loss of biodiversity and nonrenewable resources and, indeed, preserve the life and beauty of this planet.

Eighteen national agribusiness groups representing the interests of farmers and ranchers have publicly attacked our Choosing A Humane Diet project. These groups include: American Farm Bureau Federation, American Feed Industry Association, American Meat Institute, American Sheep Industry, American Veal Association, Animal Health Institute, Animal Industry Foundation, Egg Association of America, Holstein Association of America, Livestock Marketing Association, National Broiler Council, National Cattlemen's Association, National Livestock Producers Association, National Milk Producers Federation, National Pork Producers Council, National Turkey Federation, United Egg Association and United Egg Producers.

They claim that "This campaign for the first time really places The HSUS [Humane Society of the United States] squarely in the lead of animal rights groups seeking a vegetarian society by using emotionalism to induce the public to both reduce and replace animal products with other foods." These groups seek to discredit the legitimacy of our concerns and to protect their vested interests in maintaining the existing system of factory farms and feedlots. Their criticisms also cast The HSUS as the enemy of farmers and ranchers. Yet the real enemy of farmers and ranchers is agribusiness, which has contributed to the loss of over 425 thousand family farms over the past decade, as animal factories and feedlots have proliferated and put smaller producers out of business.

But there are farmers and ranchers who support The HSUS, many of whom are listed in The HSUS book, *The Humane Consumer and Producer Guide*. A revolution in agriculture is gaining momentum nationally and internationally to make it more ecologically sound and environmentally and consumer friendly. The watchword of this revolution is organic *sustainable* agriculture, which we see as humane agriculture as well. With the support of caring consumers, our ultimate goal of farming without harm is attainable, provided that the farmers, ranchers, food wholesalers and distributors who care are supported by all of us choosing a humane diet.

Many of the national agribusiness groups who oppose the humane sustainable agriculture movement today will support it tomorrow when they gain a clearer understanding of our motives and of the bioethics and profitability of farming nonviolently. Such understanding will lead to a shared vision of a brighter future for all, beyond the short-term goals and imperatives of the world marketplace.

In addition to opposition from the agricultural industry, many academicians, politicians and others still believe that factory farms and feedlots help America lead the world in producing meat at low cost and that to abolish them would hurt the poor who would not be able to afford more humanely and ecologically raised, organically certified meat and poultry. We can only hope that as they come to adopt a bioethical perspective, they will recognize that factory farms and feedlots are neither efficient nor sustainable ways of producing food for human consumption.

Bioethics should also be used to evaluate developments and current practices in agriculture. All new agricultural products, processes and policies should be subject to rigorous bioethical evaluation prior to adoption in order to promote the "farm-without-harm" ideal and the goal of sustainability. The criteria for bioethical evaluation include safety and effectiveness; social justice; equity and farm animal well-being; environmental impact, including harm to wildlife, loss of ecosystems and biodiversity; socioeconomic and cultural impact, especially harm to established sustainable practices and communities; and accord with established organic and other humane sustainable agriculture practices, standards and production claims. Farming without harm and choosing a humane diet are coins of the same currency that will forge a strong alliance between urban consumers who care and rural producers who share the vision of a humane and socially just agriculture and society.

Reincarnation and the Immortality of the Spirit

WHEN WE DIE, THE BODY IS recycled into matter and reincorporated into other living things. This is a biological fact. It is logical to assume that the human spirit is also discorporated upon physical death and is subsequently reincorporated into an appropriate creative relation to other living beings: our myriad future selves. In essence, these tenets make up the doctrine of reincarnation. Accepting reincarnation changes the way we look at death and at the way we live. It gives us a sense of the continuity and oneness of all life, as compared to the egocentric and potentially nihilistic effect of belief that we have only one life in linear and finite time, a life that begins at birth and ends forever at death, or continues in Heaven, Hell or Limbo.

This limited understanding of the nature of the afterlife is not scriptural; Jesus taught that the Kingdom of Heaven lies within. In *My Religion*, Leo Tolstoi emphasized that Jesus never promoted the doctrine of personal resurrection but said, rather, that whoever lives in God, in the truth of divine teachings, will be united with God. Tolstoi held that the doctrine of Jesus consisted in elevating the son of man, that is, recognizing that all human beings are the "son[s] of God." He wrote, "Only the son of the father who obeys the will of the father shall have eternal life."[1] A complementary verse in Mark states that those who are worthy of resurrection will remain like the angels of heaven (7:21–24). We might usefully understand the word *resurrection* to mean the spiritual transformation of an enlightened soul already embodied.

The material body is mortal; the immaterial body, the spirit, is immortal. This we know from such books as Ian Stevenson's *Life After Death* that describe the out-of-body, "death" experiences of people who are "brought back to life" and from Professor Stevenson's compilation of well-documented studies of spiritual reincarnation.[2] It seems evident that the spirit is resurrected, reincorporated with a body to form a new living soul. This process of organic transformation is a physical reflection of spiritual creativity and is the basis of biological evolution, a point that Darwin almost realized. Conscious life is witness to the continuity and revelation of an emergent cosmos. Professor Stevenson, whose pioneering work was conducted through the Division of Parapsychology at the University of Virginia, is one of few people in the West actively researching the phenomenon of reincarnation. He has recorded some two thousand cases of past-life recall throughout the world and has investigated and analyzed some eight hundred occurrences. A British newspaper, *The Observer*, quotes Stevenson as saying, "But I do get a fair number of what I'd call poison pen letters, from—of all people—Christians, who are angry and think that I'm in league with the devil. Or they try to save my soul."

What is angering these Christians? According to many authorities, reincarnation was accepted by the early esoteric Christian Gnostics, who were probably influenced by Hindu and Egyptian (Osirian) philosophy. But in 553 A.D., the exoteric Church Council of Constantinople repudiated the concept of reincarnation, decreeing, "Whosoever shall support the mythical doctrine of the preexistence of the soul and the consequent wonderful opinion of its return, let him be anathema." The abolition of the reincarnation doctrine from Christianity helped strengthen the belief in only one life on

Reincarnation and the Immortality of the Spirit

Earth, holding out Heaven as a "reward" for believers who conform to the moral standards and legal codes of the times. Since people had only one lifetime to prove themselves worthy of Heaven, rather than an eternity of potential incarnations, followers of this orthodox doctrine had to be subservient to the political authority of Church and state.

As Church and state were joined as twin authorities, obedience to which assured one of an eternity in Paradise, the sacred was made profane. The doctrine of reincarnation can help reconnect the sacred and the secular, and link both with a sense of the biological continuity, kinship and mutual dependence of all life. But like the notion of resurrection, the doctrine of reincarnation can be misused to support an egotistical and hierarchical worldview. The belief that human beings who do not live according to the "rules" will be reincarnated as pigs or snakes is demeaning of such creatures. This belief is as perverse and judgmental as the contention that if we do not believe exclusively in Jesus as a personal savior we will not be born again, or we'll go to Hell rather than Heaven.

Such perversions begin and end in dualism. As the spiritual process and dimension of an emergent universe of divine manifestation, reincarnation is the antithesis of a nihilistic view that either denies divinity or makes human beings into God. On the contrary, reincarnation opens up the possibility of our realizing that we are that aspect of divinity that can apprehend itself, not as omnipotent and separate, but as coinherent, omnipresent and transcendent: resurrection indeed. Reincarnation negates the dualistic concepts of "Heaven" and "Hell" insofar as there is no Final Judgment Day. An eternity of lifetimes enables us to make choices that either maintain the status quo—what Eastern philosophers call *samsara*, the eternal round of the causal universe—or liberate us into the cocreative, nondualistic dimension of *nirvana*, the Kingdom of Heaven within.

The doctrine of reincarnation leads us to a point of universal self-reflection/realization and to the acknowledgment that through our every incarnation, we create what we experience: Heaven or Hell, *nirvana* or *samsara*. According to Buddhist thought, the distinction between the two states is, in essence, illusory: *nirvana is samsara*. The trick is realizing that even within the realm of causal or conditioned existence (*samsara*), one can experience inner Heaven. Teilhard de

Chardin termed this state of being the omega point, the point of planetary Reflection, seeing it as:

> a sudden blaze of brilliance, an explosion in which Thought, carried to the extreme, is volatized upon itself. Having once become reflective, it cannot acquiesce in its total disappearance without biologically contradicting itself. In consequence, one is less disposed to reject as unscientific the idea that the critical point of planetary Reflection, the fruit of socialization, far from being a mere spark in the darkness, represents our passage, by Translation or dematerialization, to another sphere of the Universe: not an ending of the ultra-human but its accession to some sort of trans-humanity at the ultimate heart of things.[3]

Reincarnation is not an illusion. Only a worldview that maintains *samsara* by, in part, denying the sublime unity, continuity and universality of body and spirit in an emergent cosmos could deny its reality. Little wonder, therefore, that the concept of reincarnation is inconceivable to secular materialists and to human-centered religious traditions that deny the kinship of humans and animals and the essential continuity and universality of spirit between civilization and wilderness.

Some Westerners reject the notion of reincarnation because they think that it means that even a pesky mosquito might be the reincarnation of a deceased relative. However, it is possible to accept the idea of human reincarnation without accepting the belief that human souls can transmigrate into animal forms. W. Y. Evans-Wentz, in his translation of the *Tibetan Book of the Dead*, describes as a folkloric belief the idea that a person who commits murder might be reincarnated as, say, a beast of prey, or that a person who overindulges in sensuous activities might be reborn as a pig or a dog. A belief in transmigration to animal forms suffused with negative anthropomorphic attitudes toward "undesirable" humanlike traits in "lower" animals severely undermines an esoteric understanding of the doctrine of rebirth and increases our alienation from the Animal Kingdom. The *Bhagavad Gita* states, "Wise people see the same soul [Atman] in God [Brahman], in worms and insects, in the outcasts, in the dog and the elephant, in beasts, cows, gadflies and gnats."[4] Thus it is not surprising that Hindus are strict vegetarians.

As Evans-Wentz understands the doctrine of reincarnation, the human soul undergoes many human incarnations in its evolution, while the body, as matter, eternally transmigrates through all organic and inorganic kingdoms. (This latter idea is well-documented in studies of ecology and molecular biology.) If a human soul does not continue to evolve but instead regresses, it acquires more "beastly" traits; thus references to animal-like traits in human character should be understood as symbolic rather than literal. Accordingly, a "bad" person will not be reborn as a thieving monkey or lustful pig.[5]

Vedanta, a philosophical branch of Hinduism, proposes that individual animal and human souls are the myriad reflections of Brahman, the Absolute Being or Oversoul. Vedantists teach that the evolution of the soul is accomplished by escape from the folds of materialism, or *maya*, by means of numerous rebirths until it manifests more and more of its divine nature, culminating in union with God. This is analogous to the Buddhist view of *nirvana*, which can be seen as an escape, through reincarnation, from the desires and attractions of materiality. Buddhists also hold that an individual's subtle mindstream—what we in the West might call the soul—is reincarnated along with its karmic burden of deeds from past lives. A line from the *Bhagavad Gita* expresses the concept of the soul's immortality beautifully: "Verily the Real Man—the spirit of Man—is neither born, nor doth it die. Unborn, undying, ancient, perpetual and eternal, it hath endured, and will endure forever."[6]

Other traditions have complementary beliefs. Some historians of theology believe that the Druids had a doctrine of reincarnation. They termed the immaterial and immortal part of human beings *Awen*, which proceeds from a universal spiritual principle of life. This *Awen* animated the lower forms of life—mineral, vegetable and animal—before incarnating as human, from which point it evolved on to *gwynfid*, or the Circle of Bliss. Beyond this was the Circle of the Infinite, or *Ceugant*.

The Greeks also had a mystical concept of Union with God. Pythagoras (570–470 B.C.), one of ancient Greece's most ardent teachers of the doctrine of reincarnation along with Plato, had a significant influence on early Christianity. Early Greek philosophers, such as Empedocles, Plutarch and Porphyry, also endorsed the concept of reincarnation and linked it with vegetarianism.[7] Interestingly, the justification given by Greeks such as Pythagoras for vegetarianism was the concept of transmigration. He argued that since animals could be reborn as humans, their souls were of the same nature or essence as ours. Since by this line of reasoning, humans and animals were of equal moral worth, humans should eschew killing animals for food. Empedocles expressed this same idea when he wrote:

> For I was once already boy and girl
> Thicket and bird, and mute fish in the waves.
> All things doth Nature change, enwrapping souls
> In unfamiliar tunics of the flesh.

Plotinus, a third-century Neoplatonist, elaborated further the concept of an animating force in animals which was no different from the vital principle in human; both were radiations from the One or the All-Soul.

Other early philosophers contributed to the debate on this question. Celsus, a second-century critic of the Judeo-Christian view that human beings were the center of the universe, argued that animals, not humans, were at the center, because all things were created to contribute to the order and harmony of the world, not solely to fulfill human interests. This view contrasted that of Origen, who contended that animals were made exclusively for human use. However, other thinkers, including Plotinus and other Neoplatonists, Jewish Kabballists and the early Christian Essenes adopted the doctrines of reincarnation and the immortality of the soul.

On the other side of the world, Lao-Tzu, whose third-century B.C. writings in the *Tao Te Ching* are the basis of much of Taoist philosophy, held firmly to the doctrine of reincarnation. He wrote:

> To be ignorant that the true self is immortal, is to remain in a grievous state of error, and to experience many calamities by reason thereof. Know ye, that there is a part of man which is subtle and spiritual, and which is the heaven-bound portion of himself; that which has to do with flesh, and bones and body, belongs to the earth; earthy to earth—heavenly to heaven. Such is the law.[8]

Modern Western esotericists, including Theosophists and followers of the Arcane school agree that reincarnation is a true teaching, and that "the Law of Rebirth embodies the practical knowledge which men need today to conduct rightly and correctly their religious, political, economic, communal, and private lives, and thus establish right relations with the divine life in all forms."[9]

It is significant, in relation to the Church of Rome's later attitudes about reincarnation and the souls of animals, that in contrast to the Greeks, the Romans had no clearly defined ideas about the survival of the soul. Ancestor worship and a collective ancestral soul was as far as they went, with the exception of a few philosophers such as Ovid and Virgil, who did believe in reincarnation. Ovid says, in his narrative poem on Pythagoras, *Metamorphoses XV:*

> The heavens and all below them, earth and her creatures, All change, and we, part of creation, also Must suffer change. We are not bodies only, But winged spirits, with the power to enter Animal forms, house in the bodies of cattle. Therefore, we should respect those dwelling-places Which may have given shelter to the spirit Of fathers, brothers, cousins, human beings At least, and we should never do them damage—Kill, if you must, the beasts that do you harm, But, even so, let killing be enough; Let appetite refrain from flesh, take only A gentler nourishment.[10]

Islamic mysticism (Sufism) also embraces the concept of reincarnation. The thirteenth-century Sufi poet Jalaluddin Rumi gives an evolutionary picture of the soul's journey in the following verse:

> I have again and again grown like grass: I have experienced seven hundred and seventy moulds. I died from minerality and became a vegetable; And from vegetativeness I died and became animal. I died from animality and became man. Then why fear disappearance through death? Next time I shall die Bringing forth wings and feathers like angels: After that soaring higher than angels—What you cannot imagine. I shall be that.[11]

Nineteenth-century American poet Walt Whitman, who was influenced by Hindu philosophy, captured the essence of reincarnation in the following words from *Song of Myself:*

And whether I come to my own today or in ten thousand or ten
   million years,
I can cheerfully take it now, or with equal cheerfulness I can
   wait . . .
And as to you, Life, I reckon you are the leavings of many deaths,
(No doubt I have died myself ten thousand times before.)[12]

Francis Bowen, in *Christian Metempsychosis*, reasoned that since
our physical bodies are being constantly reformed at the molecular
level, such that we inhabit essentially different bodies in one lifetime,
it is logical to accept that the soul may inhabit a succession of bodies
from life to life. He writes:

Why should it be thought incredible that the same soul should
inhabit in succession an indefinite number of mortal bodies . . . ?
Even during this one life our bodies are perpetually changing,
though by a process of decay and Restoration which is so gradual
that it escapes our notice. Every human being thus dwells succes-
sively in many bodies, even during one short life.[13]

In conclusion, the doctrine of reincarnation implies that we and
all of Creation are part of a continuous process of spiritual growth
and transformation. Furthermore, it implies that our deeds, carried
as positive and negative karma, will influence our spiritual evolution
in successive lives. This places the responsibility for our personal
and collective destiny squarely on our own shoulders. Rejection of
this philosophy can mean an abdication of personal responsibility,
especially when an all-forgiving God, who absolves us of our sins
and even intercedes on our behalf, is substituted. If we accept the
doctrine of reincarnation, we might take better care of fellow creatures and of planet Earth, since we might expect to return to it
in future incarnations. But if it is accepted that we live only once
and animals do too, then what we do to the natural world will
have no impact on us after we are gone. Moreover, cultural narcissism and existential insecurity demand that we elevate ourselves
above "brute creation" in order to feel special and superior. The
doctrine of reincarnation implies a spiritual continuity with the Animal Kingdom and undermines this sense of human superiority and
uniqueness.

Reincarnation, Self-Realization and Animal Protection

Belief in reincarnation, in the immortality, transmigration and eventual salvation and liberation of the soul, can also spur the development of compassion toward all sentient beings. Reincarnation implies that life is a process of transformational stages. The impermanence of all forms of life is linked with the round of interdependent existence, and individuality with the unity of origin of all beings. The first cause or Father-Mother of all is manifest reality, the Pure Light of the *dharma* path or the Tao of cosmic communion, within an infolding and unfolding time-space continuum of conscious energy, wherein each entity has its own karma.

Of the myriad *jivas* or souls in this seamless web of Creation, those of the Animal Kingdom concern me especially. My concern is my choice of heart. I have no aspirations that by helping to alleviate and prevent the suffering of animals under humankind's insensitivity I will gain fame or spiritual advancement. On the contrary, my spirit bleeds for the suffering of all Creation and for the fate of a humanity that has not yet been able to liberate itself from *himsa:* acts of violence and countering evil with evil. As Leo Tolstoi observed in *My Religion* (which deeply influenced Mahatma Gandhi's philosophy), "Ninety-percent of the world's suffering is caused by our attempts to avoid the unavoidable ten-percent."[14]

When we realize the true nature of the Self, we are moved to help the souls of the Animal Kingdom realize their salvation and liberation, and to enjoy the bliss this blessed Earth offers: bee and flower and sun and grass meet and mingle as we pass among them in the pure light of *ahimsa*, seeing life giving to life, as we love life, serve life, live and let live, praise and bless.

We limit our own souls when we adopt the fatalistic view that another's suffering is its own karma and not also our concern. Likewise accepting the accelerating rate of human-caused extinction of animal species because it is the price of progress, or because their souls are immortal and so can go somewhere else, is surely wrong-minded. The journeying soul in human form eventually resolves itself and, like the dew upon the grass, gives more to life than it takes and, in passionate empathy, becomes the embodiment of *ahimsa* and an agent of compassion. In its highest expression and development, it chooses not to seek its own liberation from the world until all sentient life is freed from oppression and suffering.

Such an attitude and way of life accords with the true nature of reality for, as Thomas Berry has said, "The world is a communion of subjects and not a collection of objects." It is only when we objectify others that we harm them, and in the process of so distancing ourselves, harm ourselves. Ultimately, we find ourselves alone, alienated from any sense of kinship, belonging and communion, feeling that life has no meaning beyond the gratification of our material wants and needs. Thus we harm ourselves when we pollute the environment and let boundless violence spread. Only that which is sacred is secure; hence our security will come when we sanctify life and treat all living beings with respect and reverence.

The degradation of the human spirit continues as the suffering of all sentient life and the degradation and desecration of the Earth intensifies. This retrograde process seems to become more irreversible as it intensifies, but this need not be so. It is ultimately not an issue for government or science and technology to correct; rather, it is a question of choice, an ethical and spiritual issue over which we have control, once we realize the virtues of self-control and *ahimsa* and experience the truth of *tat-tvam-asi*, Thou art that. Such realization cannot be achieved without active involvement in animal and environmental protection causes and becoming responsible and responsive members of our own communities and religious traditions.

To live and let live and to love all and serve all are the basic elements of a humane society and of a sustainable and just global community. The Jain saint Mahavira said some 2,500 years ago, "You are that which you intend to hit, injure, insult, torment, persecute, torture, enslave or kill. Thus a wise man should not act sinfully towards animals, nor cause others to act so, nor allow others to act so. Having thus learned the nature of living beings which is in accordance with the principles of reasoning, and believing in it, a person should delight in self control. Then he or she will be delivered from all misery."[15]

Human survival and the well-being of the animal and plant kingdoms now, more urgently than ever, depend upon us all embracing the principle of *ahimsa*, living conscientiously to avoid causing harm to other living beings. As the Jain *Acaranga Sutra*, attributed to

Mahavira and dated about 550 B.C. states: "All breathing, existing, living, sentient creatures should not be slain, nor treated with violence, nor abused, nor tormented, nor driven away. This is the pure, unchangeable eternal law."(16)

This attitude of reverence is echoed in a Chinook Amerindian blessing litany, which fully expresses the necessary element of humility and gratitude toward Nature: "We call upon the land which grows our food, the nurturing soil, the fertile fields, the abundant gardens and orchards, and we ask that they teach us; and show us the way."

The modern hero is surely one who actively affirms *ahimsa* in both professional and personal realms and, rather than remaining passive or indifferent toward the myriad crimes of violence against creatures and Creation, seeks every means to expand the principle of compassionate protection of all life wherever it is needed. That humans can be the most *inhuman* of all animals is probably the reason why humanity continues to suffer. It is not a question of drawing some arbitrary line as to which creatures and to what extent we should exploit them. Rather, we should draw a circle, a boundless circle of compassion to include all creatures and Creation within the scope of our respect and reverence. By so doing, we enrich the significance of our own lives and enhance our own spiritual development.

Realizing the Sacred

When we realize that every living thing and every aspect of the natural world, including ourselves, are a sacred part of divine conception, we are moved to live in a more reverential way. This is because respect for the environment and compassion towards sentient life leads to a more intimate, empathic knowledge of the natural world, inspiring us to act in ways which cause the least harm and do the greatest good. The dawning of the sacred in each human soul cannot be separated from the realization of the coinherent and imminent, as well as omnipresent and transcendent divine quality in every natural creation, animate and inanimate, including ourselves. Moreover, as ecology reveals the instrumental interdependence of living entities and systems, so a deeper empathetic connection with the natural world provides spiritual evidence of an intelligent, self-organizing life force that is manifest in biological diversity and mirrored in our cultural and religious diversity. We are part of this life force, what Plato called the *anima mundi* or Earth-soul, and yet in our attempts to master it, to commoditize it and variously squander and desecrate it, we bring evil and suffering into the world.

When did we last have a conversation with a tree; praise the rain; help another injured or needy fellow being; celebrate the songs of birds at dawn; and thank the soil? Since we are part of this life force, part of us is immortal. The monotheistic Judeo-Christian and Islamic religions hold that only the human soul is immortal and that each soul has only one lifetime on Earth. This view is not shared by the majority of the world's peoples, especially of those of the Hindu, Jain and Buddhist traditions. Every soul—*Atman*, divine spark or *Jiva*— has its own purpose and fulfillment in countless lifetimes and in myriad forms. But even if we find it difficult to accept the notion of reincarnation or the immortality of the soul, all of us, from every religious tradition, can still be touched by the sacred, numinous dimension of all Creation, which inspires us to live gently on the Earth with respect and reverence for all life.

Animal Rights, Human Liberation and Earth First!

THE ORIGINS OF MY OWN SPIRITU-
ality and ethics are seeded in a childhood that was, thanks to my parents, linked closely with animals and Nature. A sense of wonder and
awe, as well as respect and compassion, was imbued at an early age. I
also had several experiences that laid the foundation for an attitude
of kinship and an awareness of the sacred unity, interdependence and
mutuality of origin of all life. This foundation was tested, and to some
degree enriched, by graduate training in veterinary medicine and
postgraduate research in animal psychology, ethology and ecology.
And it was later challenged when I left academia to confront the
institutionalized (and socially and religiously sanctioned and unquestioned) exploitation of animals, especially by the biomedical research
establishment, agribusiness and the commercial hunting, trapping
and "pet" industries. Yet ironically, when I joined The Humane Society of the United States (The HSUS) in 1976, there were complaints

by some members that The HSUS had "sold out" by hiring a scientist and veterinarian, and therefore a person who must be on the side of those who exploit animals!

I am not such an idealist as to believe that we should not exploit life in order to sustain our own. That we must do, and if that be the tragedy of reality, then so be it. But I cannot accept the wholesale and unquestioned exploitation of animals purely for reasons of profit, knowledge, emotional or gustatory gratification, especially when there is no reciprocal benefit to them. I find no religious basis for the chauvinistic belief that animals were created for our own use; and no scientific basis for the contention that they lack any of those qualities associated with sentience and sapience that our own species possess to varying degrees and which some claim as evidence of soulhood, potential immortality and having been created in God's image.

Self-idolatry and narcissism aside, it is a matter of historical record that the saints and avatars of the world's major religions have always emphasized our kinship with animals and the whole of Creation, and that humility, compassion, respect and reverence for all life are the key to a just, humane and sustainable society. This attitude does not preclude the exploitation of nonhuman life in order to sustain our own. Rather, it sets limits and raises questions because nonhuman life is as much a part of our moral and spiritual community of concern and responsibility as it is an integral part of the ecological community of planet Earth.

My own convictions and perceptions lead me to embrace the Creation-centered spirituality and ethics of panentheism, as distinct from primitive, superstitious pantheism and anthropocentric (and andromorphic) monotheism. I see in panentheism the antidotes to the harmful consequences that arise when materialism and industrialism are embedded either in a monotheistic, patriarchal and anthropocentric worldview, or in a purely atheistic, humanistic one. I do not see panentheism as a cultish product of New Age thinking. In actuality, it is the seed concept within the monotheistic hearts of Judaic, Islamic and Christian mysticism, as well as in the polytheistic spirit of Hinduism. For the Tibetan Buddhist, the mystical Christ-in-all is realized when there is such clarity of perception that "every being is a Buddha."

Animal Rights, Human Liberation and Earth First!

Panentheism originated, I believe, thousands of years before the advent of contemporary monotheistic religious traditions, when the human species was part of Nature as a gatherer and hunter. Anthropologists remind us that for 90 percent of our time on Earth, *Homo sapiens* have lived as gatherer-hunters. Agriculture-based civilization is only six to eight thousand years old, and industrial society a mere fraction of that.

And so, in spite of the rapid change in how we live and relate to the natural world, a panentheistic worldview lies deep in our psyches, in our collective memory, psychohistory and instinctive longing for that time when we danced with wolves and sang to the stars. Panentheism was the primal key, not back to Eden nor on to Paradise, but to living in communion. Through panentheistic sensibility, our ancestors conceived a Covenant between Creator and Creation that humankind is enjoined, spiritually and ethically, to uphold.

The Christian hermetic desert fathers tried to preserve this Covenant of consciousness and conscience. They, like St. Francis of Assisi, saw the emerging industrial age as defiling and consuming the natural world. They did not accept the new world order of the Church of Rome that placed humans above animals and Nature, men above women and God above all.

Panentheism is the essence of what I call the Old Religion of preindustrial gatherer and hunter and sustainable agrarian societies. The Hopi Indians and Australian aboriginals share the panentheistic view that God is in all. They still embrace the Old Religion—that once universal spirituality that has now become fragmented into Christianity, Judaism and Islam. (It is ironic and telling that these religious factions are still in conflict in the Middle East, where ravaged deserts littered with burning oil wells and other human carnage occupy what was once Eden, the mythic, verdant Paradise of ancestral memory.)

Panentheism is not, therefore, a New Age belief. It is as old as what is left of humanity. The panentheistic dimension of Christianity, exemplified by the statement of St. Paul: "I live, yet not I, but Christ liveth in me," is the *Parousia* of panentheistic empathy and self-realization. The perception of an omnipresent and coinherent, as well as transcendent, Creator gives rise to a worldview that is both God and Creation-centered. This panentheistic perception is clearly described in Colossians (1:16–18): "In Him all things were created . . . all things were created through Him . . . and in Him all things hold together." Many traditional peoples still practice various rituals of initiation that enable young adults to experience states of panentheistic perception and panempathic feeling. It is regrettable that the main initiations into adulthood for young members of contemporary consumer society are credit cards, shopping malls, car keys and driver's licenses and, in rural areas, guns for pubescent boys to kill wild creatures. While I have been judged by some critics as a dangerous anti-establishment cult figure, all that I have to offer is remembrance. And all that I hope for is that I can help others remember their origins, sacred connections and the inherent as well as transcendent nature of divinity. Once we can remember our origins, our ancestors, then we may yet survive ourselves and the terrible affliction that we have wrought on the Earth's Creation. Our ancient memory of Paradise, *para-desa*, the enclosed garden that sustained us all—like the memory of Eden before we ceased to feast on the fruits of a wild and untamed, but not unnamed, world—must not be lost to the hubristic enchantments of technology.

If we are not here to serve Creation, "to dress and to keep" the Garden of Eden, then what are we here for? Human life has depth of purpose and significance when it is directed to this end: to serve the greater good and follow the Golden Rule. But when our lives are not so directed, at least in part, then we continue to suffer in body and spirit as a consequence. We all have the opportunity to serve, to give to life more than we take, to heal more than we harm. Perfection of either person or planet is not the goal of compassion. Compassion is a verb, a call to action, and as history informs, it is one of the most sublime of all our callings. Benevolence to all sentient life necessitates an attitude of humility and thanksgiving toward Creation, and was a virtue embraced and promoted by the Old Religion. But in contemporary industrial society, regardless of its theisms and morality, such virtue is as rare as the scent of wild sage across an atomic desert, and as remote and abstract as renunciation and reverence.

Against this background of my own development and convictions, I offer the issues I have raised in this book for review and reflection. I am pessimistic, in the short term, about the fate of the Earth, of

Animal Rights, Human Liberation and Earth First!

humankind and of animalkind under our inhumane dominion. But in the long term I am an optimist, because I see these difficult and tragic times as a critical point of transition in the evolution of life on this planet, the continuance of which will depend primarily upon our attitude: suicide or adoration, ecocide (and deicide) or reverential respect for all Creation. I do not believe that this contention is an overstatement, since we now have power over the creative process via genetic engineering biotechnology. We have the ability to remake the world into our own image of perfection. Whether it will be an image of Eden restored or a bioindustrialized wasteland, only time will tell. Now is the time to choose.

I am involved in three movements: animal protection, nature conservation and alternative sustainable agriculture. These movements are motivated primarily by compassion and reverence for Creation, yet the industrial establishment that opposes them sees them as placing the rights and interests of animals and Nature, including the environment, over the rights and interests of people. Public opposition is increasing because of media-hyped misinformation and the public relations campaigns of those agencies and corporations who have a vested interest in maintaining a status quo that is responsible for the holocaust of the Animal Kingdom and the death of Nature.

More and more people, however, are now questioning the means and ends of an industrialism that causes much animal suffering, extinction, human injustice, and so destructively exploits the life and beauty of this planet. The significance of these contemporary social movements is linked in time, as historians will someday note, with the global environmental crisis that we face today, as evidenced by the accelerating rate of extinction of planetary life forms and indigenous peoples, and by the suffering of billions of animals exploited for questionable reasons of custom, consumption, scientific knowledge and medical progress. My own ethical sensibility arises from a spirituality that is fundamentally antithetical to the worldview and morality that sanctions such exploitation.

In some public and political circles, opposition to these movements is increasing. These people feel that eating less meat, finding alternatives to animal experimentation in the cure of human diseases, and protecting an old forest for the spotted owl are threats to the economy, to progress and to the rights and interests of the populace.

This attitude, I believe, is ultimately suicidal, for if we harm the planet, we harm the person; and if we harm other sentient beings, we harm ourselves. But to be pro-animal rights and environmental protection is, in the eyes of many, to put animals and Nature before people. Such is the ignorance and cupidity of the times.

Animal rights? "Deep" (Earth first!) ecology? The idealistic rhetoric, public demonstrations and acts of civil disobedience of the "green" tree-hugging and bleeding-heart "Bambi"-loving, radical fringe seem at first to be such a self-indulgent, anarchistic bore, and quite irrelevant to the concerns of state, business and the world community. Fanaticism, fundamentalism and ideological rigidity aside, it might further the interests of state, business and the world community to grasp the nettle of polemicizing rhetoric and consider objectively and dispassionately (but not uncompassionately) the ethos of these social movements. They will find that it is quite distinct from the simplistic rantings and fundamentalist, judgmental verbiage that are generally presented by the press as representative of these movements. "A rat is a pig is a dog is a child," and "Trees are people too," represent the kind of solipsistic rhetoric that is inflammatory, if not heretical, to establishment values and perceptions. However, it is quite wrong to conclude that animal rights and deep ecology are anti-progress, anti-science, anti-business, anti-industry, and contrary to the best interests of society. But there is a curious twist to this. I recently had a luncheon meeting with the CEO of one of the world's fastest growing agribusiness corporations, and he said, "The humane treatment of animals—farm animal welfare—isn't a moral or ethical issue." From his perspective, and for many executives in the business world, animal welfare, rights, and environmental and ecological issues are primarily of economic concern. It is to be hoped that such economic concern will be broadened by the concept of sustainability—steady-state economics rather than illimitable economic growth and development—which might in turn facilitate the recognition that animal welfare and environmental protection *are* moral and ethical concerns.

Resource Guide

I. History of the Humane Movement and the
Treatment of Animals

Anthony Brown (1974) *Who Cares for Animals? 150 Years of the RSPCA.* London: Heinemann.

Gerald Carson (1972) *Men, Beasts, and Gods: A History of Cruelty and Kindness to Animals.* New York: Charles Scribner's Sons.

Charles Magel (1981) *A Bibliography on Animal Rights and Related Matters.* Washington, DC: University Press of America.

Roswell C. McCrea (1969) *The Humane Movement.* College Park, MD: McGrath Publishing Company.

Charles D. Niven (1967) *History of the Humane Movement.* New York: Transatlantic Arts, Inc.

Henry Salt (1980 reprint) *Animals' Rights.* Clark Summit, PA: Society for Animal Rights.

M. Spiegel (1988) *The Dreaded Comparison: Human and Animal Slavery.* New York: Mirror Books.

Keith Thomas (1983) *Man and the Natural World: A History of Modern Sensibility.* New York: Pantheon.

James Turner (1980) *Reckoning with the Beast: Animals, Pain, and Humanity in the Victorian Mind.* Baltimore, MD: The Johns Hopkins University Press.

II. Ethical and Philosophical Issues

Stephen Clark (1982) *The Nature of the Beast: Are Animals Moral?* New York: Oxford University Press.

Stephen R. L. Clark (1977) *The Moral Status of Animals.* New York: Oxford University Press.

David S. Favre and Loring Murray (1983) *Animal Law.* Westport, CT: Quorum Books.

Michael W. Fox (1990) *Inhumane Society: The American Way of Exploiting Animals*. New York: St. Martin's Press.

——(1990) *Animals Have Rights Too* (A book for children). New York: Crossroads.

——(1986) *Returning to Eden: Animal Rights and Human Concerns*. Malabar, FL: Robert E. Krieger.

——(1984) *Between Animal and Man*. Malabar, FL: Robert E. Krieger.

——(1985) *One Earth, One Mind*. Malabar, FL: Robert E. Krieger.

R. Garner (1993) *Animals, Politics and Morality*. New York: Manchester University Press.

E. C. Hargrove (ed. 1992) *The Animals Rights/Environmental Ethics Debate*. Albany, NY: Albany State University of New York Press.

Andrew Linzey (1987) *Christianity and the Rights of Animals*. New York: Crossroads.

Mary Midgley (1984) *Why They Matter*. Athens, GA: University of Georgia Press.

Tom Regan (1983) *The Case for Animal Rights*. Los Angeles, CA: University of California Press.

L. G. Regenstein (1991) *Replenish the Earth: A History of Organized Religion's Treatment of Animals and Nature*. New York: Crossroads.

Bernard E. Rollin (1981) *Animal Rights and Human Morality*. Buffalo, NY: Prometheus Books.

Albert Schweitzer (1965) *The Teachings of Reverence for Life*. New York: Holt, Rinehart & Winston.

Peter Singer (1990) *Animal Liberation*. Rev. 2d ed. New York: Random House.

III. Laboratory and Farm Animals

Marian Stamp Dawkins (1980) *Animal Suffering: The Science of Animal Welfare*. London: Chapman and Hall Ltd.

Michael W. Fox (1986) *Agricide: The Hidden Crisis That Affects Us All*. New York: Schocken Books.

——(1986) *Laboratory Animal Husbandry: Ethology, Welfare and Experimental Variables*. Albany, NY: State University of New York Press.

————(1984) *Farm Animal Husbandry, Behavior, and Veterinary Practice.* Baltimore, MD: University Park Press.

————(1992) *Superpigs and Wondercorn: The Brave New World of Biotechnology and How It May Affect Us All.* New York: Lyons & Burford.

Ruth Harrison (1964) *Animal Machines.* London: Vincent Stuart Publishers Ltd.

E. A. Lawrence (1982) *Rodeo: An Anthropologist Looks at the Wild and the Tame.* Nashville, TN: University of Tennessee Press.

Jim Mason and Peter Singer (1990) *Animal Factories.* New York: Crown Publishers, Inc.

Dallas Pratt, M.D. (1982) *Alternatives to Painful Experiments on Animals.* New York: Argus Archives.

Tom Regan (ed. 1986) *Animal Sacrifices: Religious Perspectives on the Use of Animals in Science.* Philadelphia, PA: Temple University Press.

John Robbins (1987) *Diet for a New America.* Walpole, NH: Stillpoint.

Bernard Rollin (1989) *The Unheeded Cry: Animal Consciousness, Animal Pain, and Science.* New York: Oxford University Press.

Richard D. Ryder (rev. ed. 1983) *Victims of Science: The Use of Animals in Research.* London: National Anti-Vivisection Society.

Orville Schell (1984) *Modern Meat.* New York: Random House.

R. Sharpe (1988) *The Cruel Deception: The Use of Animals in Medical Research.* Wellingborough, England: Thorsons Publishers, Ltd.

IV. Animals: Wild, Captive, and Environmental Concerns

Ron Baker (1985) *The American Hunting Myth.* New York: Vantage Press.

Thomas Berry (1988) *The Dream of the Earth.* San Francisco, CA: Sierra Books.

Bill Devall and George Sessions (1985) *Deep Ecology: Living as if Nature Mattered.* Salt Lake City, UT: Gibbs M. Smith, Inc.

Jean-Yves Domalain (1977) *The Animal Connection: The Confessions of an Ex-Wild Animal Trafficker.* New York: William Morrow.

Paul Ehrlich and Anne Ehrlich (1981) *Extinction: The Causes and Consequences of the Disappearance of Species.* New York: Random House.

H. Hediger (1969) *Man and Animal in the Zoo: Zoo Biology.* New York: Delacort Press.

Aldo Leopold (1966) *A Sand County Almanac.* New York: Oxford University Press.

R.F. Nash (1989) *The Rights of Nature: A History of Environmental Ethics.* Madison, WI: University of Wisconsin Press.

V. COMPANION ANIMALS

Michael W. Fox (1990) *The Healing Touch.* New York: Newmarket Press.

———(1990) *Love is a Happy Cat.* New York: Newmarket Press.

———(1990) *The New Doctor's Answer Book.* New York: Newmarket Press.

———(1990) *Supercat: Raising the Perfect Feline Companion.* New York: Howell Books.

———(1990) *Superdog: Raising the Perfect Canine Companion.* New York: Howell Books.

———(1984) *Behavior of Wolves, Dogs and Related Canids.* Malabar, FL: Robert E. Krieger.

———(1985) *The Dog: Its Domestication and Behavior.* Malabar, FL: Robert E. Krieger.

W. J. Kay with E. Randolph (1985) *The Complete Book of Cat Health.* New York: Macmillan Publishers.

———(1985) *The Complete Book of Dog Health.* New York: Macmillan Publishers.

Konrad A. Lorenz (1952) *King Solomon's Ring: New Light on Animal Ways.* New York: Thomas Y. Crowell.

Yi-Fu Tuan (1984) *Dominance and Affection: The Making of Pets.* New Haven, CT: Yale University Press.

Notes

CHAPTER ONE / HOW AWARE ARE ANIMALS?

1. D. Griffin (1977) *The Question of Animal Awareness.* New York: Rockefeller University Press.
2. S. Walker (1983) *Animal Thought.* Boston: Routledge and Kegan Paul.
3. C. Darwin (1981) *The Descent of Man.* Princeton, NJ: Princeton University Press.
4. R. M. Rilke (1978) *The Duino Elegies.* New York: Norton.
5. P. T. Winan, et al. (1982) *Science,* 18:1332–4.
6. M. Nielsen, et al. (1978) *Brain Research,* 141:342.
7. J. Alumets, et al. (1979) *Nature,* 279:805.
8. Lord Brain (1967) Cited by W. H. Thorpe in *Report of the Technical Committee to Inquire into the Welfare of Animals Kept Under Intensive Livestock Husbandry Conditions.* London: Her Majesty's Stationery Office.
9. T. A. Sawbuck (1977) *How Animals Communicate.* Bloomington, IN: Indiana University Press.
10. M. W. Fox (1974) *Concepts in Ethology.* Minneapolis, MN: University of Minnesota Press.
11. M. W. Fox (reprint edition 1992) *The Soul of the Wolf.* New York: Lyons & Burford.
12. M. W. Fox (1986) *Laboratory Animal Husbandry.* Albany, NY: State University of New York Press.
13. M. W. Fox (1984) *Farm Animals: Husbandry, Behavior and Veterinary Practice.* Baltimore, MD: University Park Press.
14. A. Schweitzer (1965) *The Teaching of Reverence for Life.* New York: Holt, Rinehart and Winston.

CHAPTER TWO / DO ANIMALS HAVE SOULS?

1. Keith Thomas (1983) *Man and the Natural World: A History of the Modern Sensibility.* New York: Pantheon.

2. Ibid.
3. Ibid
4. Ibid.
5. Ibid.
6. In P. Edwards, ed. (1967) *The Encyclopedia of Philosophy*. New York: MacMillan.
7. Henry S. Salt (new edition 1980) *Animals' Rights: Considered in Relation to Social Progress*. Clark Summit, PA: Society for Animal Rights.
8. James E. White (1984) review of Bryan G. Norton, "Environmental Ethics and Weak Anthropocentrism," *Ethics & Animals*, V (3), 76–77.
9. In Richard Erdoes (1976) *Lame Deer, Seeker of Visions*. New York: Simon & Schuster.
10. Ibid.
11. Alice Bailey (1974) *The Soul: The Quality of Life*. New York: Lucis.
12. Ibid.
13. Hubert Benoit (1973) *Let Go! Theory and Practice of Detachment According to Zen*. New York: Samuel Weiser.
14. Ibid.
15. J. Mascaro, tr. (1962) *The Bhagavad Gita*. London: Penguin.
16. J. Hick (1972) *Biology and the Soul*. London: Cambridge University Press.
17. Michael W. Fox (1980) *The Soul of the Wolf*. Boston, MA: Little, Brown.
18. James E. Royce (1961) *Man and His Nature*. New York: McGraw-Hill.
19. Ibid.
20. Loren Eiseley (1969) *The Unexpected Universe*. New York: Harcourt Brace Jovanovich.
21. Paul Tillich (1952) *Courage to Be*. New Haven, CT: Yale University Press.
22. Matthew Fox (1979) *A Spirituality Named Compassion*. Minneapolis, MN: Winston Press.
23. Charles M. Fair (1970) *The Dying Self*. Garden City, NY: Doubleday.
24. Fox, *A Spirituality Named Compassion*.

25. Ibid.
26. Dom Ambrose Agius, O.S.B. (1973) *God's Animals.* Publisher and Distributor: The Catholic Study Circle for Animal Welfare, Flat 4, Westhill House, West Hill, Harrow on the Hill, Middlesex, England.
27. Konrad Lorenz (1980) "Tiere und Gefuhlmenschen," *Der Spiegel,* 47, from H. F. Kaplan (1991) "Do Animals Have Souls?" *Between the Species.* Summer, 138–147.

CHAPTER THREE / CHANGING CHRISTIAN AND OTHER ATTITUDES TOWARD ANIMALS

1. Keith Thomas (1983) *Man and the Natural World: A History of the Modern Sensibility.* New York: Pantheon.
2. Stephen Kellert (1980) *Knowledge, Affection and Basic Attitudes Towards Animals in American Society.* Washington, DC: U.S. Department of the Interior, Fish and Wildlife Service.
3. Ibid.
4. C. W. Hume (Second Edition 1957) *The Status of Animals in the Christian Religion.* London: The Universities Federation for Animal Welfare.
5. Ibid.
6. Ibid.
7. Ibid.
8. Ibid.
9. "Empathetic Fallacy" (1959) *American 101,* p. 567.
10. Pierre Bayle *Historical and Critical Dictionary.* Indianapolis, IN: Bobbs, Merrill, pp. 213–254, cited by Rev. Gerald E. Jones in *Deity and Death,* ed. by S. J. Palmer (1978). Provo, UT: Religious Studies Center, Brigham Young University.
11. *Deity and Death,* pp. 107–119.
12. Augustine *City of God.* 1. 20. XXII. 24.
13. Thomas Aquinas *Summa Theologica,* Part II, Question 64, Article 1.
14. Ibid., Question 25, Article 3.
15. John Calvin (1961) *On the Christian Earth.* New York: Bobbs, Merrill, pp. 131–32.

Notes

16. Martin Luther (Vol 1. 1958) *Luther's Works*. Ed. by J. Pelikan. St. Louis, MO: Concordia Publ., p. 71.
17. Ibid.
18. Ibid.
19. Peter J. Riga (Jan. 2 1986) "Animal Rights v. Human Needs." *The Houston Post*, p. 3B.
20. Andrew Linzey (1979) "Animals and Moral Theology" in D. Patterson and R. Ryder, *Animal Rights: A Symposium*. London: Centaur Press, pp. 34–42.
21. Ibid.
22. Dom Ambrose Agius, O.S.B. (1973) *God's Animals*. The Catholic Study Circle for Animal Welfare, Harrow on the Hill, Middlesex, England.
23. Ibid.
24. Ibid.
25. Ibid.
26. Ibid.
27. Matthew Fox (1989) *The Coming of the Cosmic Christ*. New York: Harper & Row.
28. Jean Guitton *Les Animaux, Nos Humbles Freres*. Paris: Le Sarment/Fayard & The Catholic Association for the Respect of the Animal Creation.
29. Agius, *God's Animals*.
30. Roger Timm (1985) *Ecospirit*, Vol. 1:3. Bethlehem, PA: Institute for Ecosophical Studies, Moravian College, p. 6.
31. Harold S. Kushner (1981) *When Bad Things Happen to Good People*. New York: Schocken.
32. K. Thomas, *Man and the Natural World*.
33. Thomas Merton (1968) *Zen and the Birds of Appetite*. New York: New Directions.
34. Thomas Berry (1982) *Teilhard in the Ecological Age*, Teilhard Studies, no. 7. Chambersburg, PA: Anima Books, pp. 20, 21.
35. René Dubos (1972) *A God Within*. New York: Scribner's.
36. United Nations General Assembly (Nov. 9, 1982) *World Charter for Nature*. New York: United Nations, A/Res/37/7.
37. Haudenosaunee (1977) *A Basic Call to Consciousness*. Geneva, Switzerland.

38. Cited in Paul Winter (1982) *Missa Gaia, Earth Mass*. Litchfield, CT: Living Music Records.
39. Stephen Budiansky (1992) *The Covenant of the Wild: Why Animals Chose Domestication*. New York: Morrow.
40. John B. Cobb, Jr. (1991) *Matter of Life and Death*. Louisville, KY: Westminster/John Knox Press.
41. Ibid.

CHAPTER FOUR / THE LIFE AND TEACHINGS OF ST. FRANCIS OF ASSISI

1. Susan Power Bratton (1991) "Sleeping with Lions," *Orion*, Summer, pp. 9–16.
2. Ibid.
3. Ibid.
4. Placid Herman (1963, translated from the Latin) *Saint Francis of Assisi* by Thomas of Celano, Chicago, IL: Franciscan Herald Press.
5. Edward A. Armstrong (1973) *Saint Francis: Nature Mystic*. Berkeley, CA: University of California Press.
6. Ibid.
7. Ibid.
8. Ibid.
9. Ibid.
10. Herman, *Saint Francis of Assisi*.
11. Ibid.
12. Armstrong, *Saint Francis*.
13. Ibid.
14. Regis J. Armstrong and Ignatius C. Brady, tr. (1982) *Francis and Clare: The Complete Works*. New York: Paulist Press.
15. E. Cousin, tr. (1978) *The Classics of Western Spirituality: Bonaventure—The Life of St. Francis* by St. Bonaventure. New York: Paulist Press.
16. Armstrong and Brady, *Francis and Clare*.
17. Herman, *Saint Francis of Assisi*.
18. Ibid.
19. Ibid.
20. Armstrong, *Saint Francis*.
21. Herman, *Saint Francis of Assisi*.

22. Ibid.
23. Ibid.
24. Xavier Schneiper (1981) *Saint Francis of Assisi*. Scala, Firenzi.
25. Ignatius Brady, tr. (1983) *The Writings of St. Francis*. Edizioni Porziuncola.
26. Armstrong and Brady, *Francis and Clare*.
27. Matthew Fox (1984) *Original Blessing: A Primer in Creation Spirituality*. Santa Fe, NM: Bear and Company, Inc.
28. Father Lanfranco Serrini (1986) "The Christian Declaration of Nature," in *The Assisi Declaration*. World Wildlife Fund, pp. 9–14.
29. H. Felder (1982) *The Ideals of St. Francis of Assisi*. Chicago: Franciscan Herald Press.
30. Herman, *Saint Francis of Assisi*.
31. Cousin, *The Classics of Western Spirituality*.
32. Paul Weigand (1984) "Escape from the Birdbath. A Reinterpretation of St. Francis as a Model for the Ecological Movement," in *Cry of the Environment*. P. N. Joranson and K. Butigan (eds.) Santa Fe, NM: Bear and Company, Inc., pp. 148–57.
33. G. K. Chesterton (1960) *St. Francis of Assisi*. New York: Doubleday Press.
34. Armstrong, *Saint Francis*. For a comprehensive collection of sources, see *St. Francis of Assisi Writings and Early Biographies*, edited by Marion A. Habig, Chicago, IL: Fransiscan Herald Press, 1972.
35. Right Reverend John Austin Baker (October 4, 1986), Anglican Bishop of Salisbury, in Salisbury Cathedral on World Prayer Day for Animals.
36. Gary Kowalski (1988) "Golden Calf or Holy Cow? Animals and the Sacred," *Between the Species* 4:263–267.
37. Thomas Berry (1988) *The Dream of the Earth*. San Francisco, CA: Sierra Books.
38. Marti Kheel (1985) "The Liberation of Life: A Circular Affair," *Environmental Ethics* 7:135–49.
39. Ibid.
40. Ibid.
41. Ibid.

42. Arthur Schopenhauer (1965) *On The Basis of Morality*. Tr. by E. F. Payne. New York: Bobbs Merrill.
43. Ibid.
44. Martin Buber (1970) *I and Thou*. Tr. by Walter Kaufman. New York: Charles Scribner & Sons.
45. J. Krishnamurti (1987) *Krishnamurti to Himself*. San Francisco, CA: Harper & Row.
46. Joseph Campbell with Bill Moyers (1988) *The Power of Myth*. New York: Doubleday.
47. Bill Neidjie (1985) *Kakadu Man*. New South Wales, Australia: Mybrood P/L. Inc. (Allen Fox & Associates).
48. Rollo May (1953) *Man's Search for Himself*. New York: W. W. Norton.
49. Jeremy Rifkin (1985) *Declaration of a Heretic*. Boston, MA: Rutledge & Kegan Paul.
50. Ibid.
51. Joseph Campbell (1986) *The Inner Reaches of Outer Space*. New York: Alfred Van Der Marck.
52. Mircea Eliade (1959) *The Sacred and the Profane: The Nature of Religion*. New York: Harcourt.
53. Campbell, *The Inner Reaches of Outer Space*.
54. Pierre Teilhard de Chardin (1964) *The Future of Man*. New York: Harper & Row.
55. Campbell, *The Inner Reaches of Outer Space*.
56. Ibid.
57. Basil Wrighton (1987) *Reason, Religion and the Animals*. London: Catholic Study Circle for Animal Welfare.

CHAPTER FIVE / PANENTHEISM: ANIMALS, NATURE AND THE GOD WITHIN

1. Chris Chapple (1993) *Nonviolence to Animals, Earth and Self in Asian Traditions*. Albany: State University of New York Press.
2. J. Haught (1986) "The Emergent Environment and the Problem of Cosmic Purpose," *Environmental Ethics* 8:139–50.
3. Buck Ghost Horse (1987) *Creation Magazine* II:3.
4. David Lorimer (1985) "Encounters of Eastern and Western Cosmologies," *Transnational Perspectives* 11:12–18.

282

5. Michael E. Zimmerman (1988) "Quantum Theory Intrinsic Value and Panentheism," *Environmental Ethics* 10:3–30.
6. B. Devall and G. Session (1985) *Deep Ecology*. Salt Lake City, UT: Peregrine Smith Books.
7. *Webster's New International Dictionary*. 2d. ed.
8. (1979) *Encyclopedia Britannica* 13:954.
9. Zimmerman, *Environmental Ethics*.
10. From an interview published by Buddhists Concerned for Animals (1984) 300 Page Street, San Francisco, CA 94101.
11. E.D. Gray (1982) *Patriarchy as a Conceptual Trap*. Wellesley, MA: Roundtable Press.
12. Thomas Berry (1988) *Dream of the Earth*. San Francisco, CA: Sierra Club Books.
13. Arnold Toynbee (1972) "The Religious Background of the Present Environmental Crisis: a Viewpoint," *International Journal of Environmental Studies* 3:141–46.
14. J.C. Niehardt (1979) *Black Elk Speaks*. Lincoln, NE: University of Nebraska Press.
15. E.A. Armstrong (1973) *Saint Francis: Nature Mystic*. Berkeley, CA: University of California Press.
16. *De Reductione Artium ad Theologiam*. Sister Emma Therese Healy, tr. (1939) New York: Bonaventure Press.
17. H. Thomas and D.L. Thomas (1941) *Living Biographies of Great Philosophers*. New York: Doubleday & Company.
18. In Richard Erdoes (1976) *Lame Deer, Seeker of Visions*. New York: Simon and Schuster.
19. John Callicott (1982) "Traditional American Indian and Western European Attitudes Toward Nature: An Overview," *Environmental Ethics* 4:293–318, Winter.
20. From H.A.R. Gibb (1962) *Mohammedism*. Oxford University Press.
21. Harold W. Wood, Jr. (1985) "Modern Pantheism as an Approach to Environmental Ethics," *Environmental Ethics* 7:151–63.
22. Francis A. Schaeffer (1970) *Pollution and the Death of Man: The Christian View of Ecology*. Wheaton, IL: Tyndale House.
23. Ibid.
24. Ibid.
25. Ibid.

26. Ibid.
27. Ernst Haeckel (1900) *The Riddle of the Universe*. Tr. by Joseph McCabe. New York: Harper & Brothers.
28. Lynn White Jr. (1967) "The Historical Roots of Our Ecological Crisis," *Science* 155:1203–7.
29. Schaeffer, *Pollution and the Death of Man*.
30. Ibid.
31. Ibid.
32. Ibid.
33. Ibid.
34. James E. Royce (1961) *Man and His Nature*. New York: McGraw Hill.
35. Matthew Fox (1979) *A Spirituality Named Compassion*. Minneapolis, MN: Winston Press.
36. Yi-Fu Tuan (1984) *Dominance and Affection: The Making of Pets*. New Haven, CT: Yale University Press.
37. John Robinson (1963) *Honest to God*. Philadelphia, PA: Westminster Press.
38. Cited by Epiphanius Adversus haereses. XXVI 3.
39. J.H. Breasted (1933) *The Dawn of Conscience*. New York: Charles Scribner & Sons.
40. Joseph Needham (1951) "Human Laws and Laws of Nature in China and the West," *Journal of History of Ideas* T:250.
41. John W. Perry (1987) *The Heart of History*. Albany, NY: State University of New York Press.
42. Lao-Tzu, *Tao Te Ching*. Gia-Fu Feng and Jane English, tr. (1974) New York: Vintage Books.
43. Henry Beston (1971) *The Outermost House*. New York: Ballantine Books.
44. C. Humphreys (1980) *The Buddhist Way of Life*. New York: J. P. Tarcher.
45. J. Mascaró (1962) *The Bhagavad Gita*. London: Penguin.
46. In Z.C. Brinkerhoff (1971) *God's Chosen People of America*. Salt Lake City, UT: Publisher's Press.
47. Jay McDaniel (1989) *Of God and Pelicans*. Philadelphia, PA: Westminster Press.
48. Ibid.
49. Ibid.

Notes

50. A. R. Peacocke (1979) *Creation and the World of Science: The Brampton Lectures.* Oxford: Clarendon Press.
51. Charles Birch, World Council of Churches, Church and Society. Flion Report, p. 68.
52. C. Hartshorne, "In God and Nature," *Anticipation* 25:58–64.
53. Matthew Fox (1988) *The Coming of the Cosmic Christ.* New York: Harper & Row.
54. J. Callicott (1982) "Traditional American Indian and Western European Attitudes Toward Nature: An Overview."
55. G. Carson (1972) *Men, Beasts and Gods.* New York: Scribner & Sons.
56. Kenneth Laidler (Oct./Nov. 1982) *Animal Kingdom.*
57. Fox, *The Coming of the Cosmic Christ.*

CHAPTER SIX / COMMUNION WITH ANIMALS, NATURE AND DIVINITY

1. Luther Standing Bear (1978) *Land of the Spotted Eagle.* Lincoln, NE: Nebraska University Press.
2. Albert Schweitzer (1965) *The Teaching of Reverence for Life.* New York: Holt, Rinehart & Winston.
3. Matthew Fox (1986) *Original Blessing: A Primer in Creation Spirituality.* Santa Fe, NM: Bear and Company.
4. Walt Whitman (1954) *Complete Poetry and Selected Prose.* J.E. Miller Jr. ed. New Haven: Yale University Press.
5. Ibid.
6. Donald St. John (1986) *Ecospirit* 2:1. Bethlehem, PA: Moravian College.
7. Ibid.
8. Haudenosaunee (1977) *A Basic Call to Consciousness.* Geneva, distributed by *Akwesasne Notes* (Mohawk Nation, P.O. Box 196, Rooseveltown, NY).
9. Standing Bear, *Land of the Spotted Eagle.*
10. Vine Deloria, Jr. (1975) *God Is Red.* New York: Dell.
11. Tarthang Tulku (1977) *Time, Space and Knowledge: A New Vision of Reality.* Berkeley, CA: Dharma Press.
12. Ibid.

13. E.A. Wodehouse (1975) "Man, Nature, Reality in the Teachings of Krishnamurti," in Luis S.R. Vas (ed.) *The Mind of J. Krishnamurti*. Bombay: Jaico, pp. 101–40.
14. Ibid.
15. Joseph Campbell (1968) *Hero With A Thousand Faces*. Princeton, NJ: Princeton University Press.
16. Paul Tillich (1952) *The Courage to Be*. New Haven, CT: Yale University Press.
17. Christmas Humphreys (1980) *The Buddhist Way of Life*. New York: J.P. Tarcher.
18. George B. Leonard (1972) *The Transformation*. New York: J.P. Tarcher.
19. W. Jackson Davis (1979) *The Seventh Year*. New York: W.W. Norton.
20. Gregory Bateson (1975) *Steps to An Ecology of Mind*. New York: Ballantine.
21. James Lovelock (1982) *Gaia, A New Look at Life on Earth*. New York: Oxford University Press.
22. J. Baird Callicott (1986) "The Metaphysical Implications of Ecology," *Environmental Ethics* 8:301–16.
23. John Seed. "Anthropocentrism," Appendix E in Bill Devall and George Sessions (1987) *Deep Ecology: Living as if Nature Mattered*. Layton, UT: Peregrine Smith, p. 243.
24. Callicott, *Environmental Ethics*.
25. Swami Vivekenanda (1986) *Practical Vedanta*. New York: Vedanta Press.
26. Cited by Rolling Thunder in Zula C. Brinkerhoff (1971) *God's Chosen People of America*. Salt Lake City, UT: Publisher's Press.
27. Jay McDaniel (1986) "Christian Spirituality as Openness to Fellow Creatures," *Environmental Ethics* 8:33–46. See also Jay McDaniel (1989) *Of God and Pelicans: A Theology of Reverence for Life*. Louisville, KY: John Knox Press.
28. Wendell Berry (1977) *The Unsettling of America: Culture and Agriculture*. New York: Avon Books, p. 31.
29. McDaniel, *Environmental Ethics* 8:33–46.
30. Rodney L. Taylor (1986) "Of Animals and Man: The Confucian Perspective," in T. Regan (ed) *Animal Sacrifices: Religious Perspec-*

tives on the Use of Animals in Research. Philadelphia, PA: Temple University Press, pp. 237–63.

31. Ibid.
32. D. Suzuki (1956) *Zen Buddhism*. New York: Doubleday.

CHAPTER SEVEN / ABORIGINAL CONSCIOUSNESS
AND THE "OLD RELIGION"

1. Bill Neidjie (1985) *Kakadu Man*. NSW Australia: Mybrood Publishing, Inc.
2. Ibid.
3. *Omni Magazine*, Summer 1987.
4. S. Arnold and G. Bicknell (1990) Unpublished, personal communication.
5. J. Corbett (1991) *Goatwalking*. New York: Viking.
6. Rainer Maria Rilke (1978) *Duino Elegies*. Tr. by David Young. New York: Norton.
7. Thomas Berry (1988) *The Dream of the Earth*. San Francisco, CA: Sierra Club Books.
8. W. Stanner and Peter Sutton (1988) *Dreaming, The Art of Aboriginal Australia*. New York: George Braziller.
9. Ibid.
10. Stanley Breeden and Belinda Wright (1989) *Kakadu, Looking After the Country: The Gagudju Way*. Australia: Simon & Schuster.
11. James Cowan (1989) *Mysteries of the Dream Time*. England: Prism Press, Bridgport Dorset.
12. Ibid.
13. Quotation from *The Edenite Creed of Life* (1979) Imlaystown, NJ: Edenite Society, p. 26.
14. Arthur Schoepenhauer (1966) *World as Will and Representation*. Tr. by E.F. Payne. Vol. 1. New York: Dover Publications, p. 155.
15. Lao-Tzu, *Tao Te Ching*. Gia-Fu Feng and Jane English, tr. (1974) New York: Vintage Books.
16. Mircea Eliade (1959) *The Sacred and the Profane: The Nature of Religion*. New York: Harcourt Brace Jovanovich.
17. Ibid.
18. Ibid.
19. Ibid.

20. Hyemeyohost Storm (1972) *Seven Arrows*. New York: Harper and Row.
21. Citations from Chang Chung-Yuan (1975) *Tao: A New Way of Thinking*. New York: Harper & Row.
22. Robert Sohl and Audrey Carr (1970) from *The Gospel According to Zen: Beyond the Death of God*. New York: New American University.
23. Chung-Yuan, *Tao: A New Way of Thinking*.
24. Gia-Fu Feng and J. English, *Lao-Tzu Tao Te Ching*.
25. Chung-Yuan, *Tao: A New Way of Thinking*.
26. Ibid.
27. Erich Fromm (1956) *Art of Loving: An Enquiry into the Nature of Love*. New York: Harper & Row.
28. Ibid.
29. Matthew Fox (1988) *The Coming of the Cosmic Christ*. New York: Harper & Row.
30. Sean McDonagh (1986) *To Care for the Earth: A Call to a New Theology*. Santa Fe, NM: Bear & Company.
31. Bruce Chatwin (1988) *The Songlines*. New York: Morrow.
32. J. Krishnamurti (1987) *Krishnamurti to Himself*. San Francisco: Harper and Row.
33. Ibid.
34. Ibid.
35. Ibid.
36. Ramachandra Gandhi (1988) "Why Should There Be Life on Earth? A Non-dualist Enquiry," *Creation*. Sept/Oct. 4:28–29.
37. Storm, *Seven Arrows*.
38. Eliade, *The Sacred and the Profane*.
39. Gandhi, *Creation*.
40. Ibid.
41. Ibid.
42. Ibid.

CHAPTER NINE / CONSERVATION AND ANIMAL RIGHTS: REVERENCE IN ACTION

1. E. F. Keller (1983) *A Feeling for the Organism: Life and Works of Barbara McClintock*. San Francisco: W.H. Freeman.

2. Lynn White, Jr. (1967) "The Historical Roots of our Ecological Crisis," *Science* 155:1205–9.
3. Ibid.
4. Robert Bly (1992) *Iron John*. New York: Vintage.
5. Luther Standing Bear (1978) *Land of the Spotted Eagle*. Lincoln, NE: University of Nebraska Press, p. 204.
6. Mircea Eliade (1967) *Myths, Dreams, and Mysteries*. New York: Harper & Row.
7. A. P. Elkin (1977) *Aboriginal Men of High Degree*, 2nd ed. Queensland, Australia: University of Queensland Press.
8. Abe Hultkrantz (1979) *The Religions of the American Indians*. Berkeley, CA: University of California Press. For further discussion, see Richard Heinberg (1995) *Memories and Visions of Paradise*. Wheaton, IL: Quest Books.
9. J. E. Brown (1987) *The Spiritual Legacy of the American Indian*. New York: Crossroads, p. 92.
10. W. T. De Bary (1960) *Sources of Chinese Tradition*, p. 573.
11. Paul Davies (1988) *God and the New Physics*. New York: Touchstone Books.
12. Kenneth Clark (1977) "Animals and Men. Love. Admiration and Outright War," *The Smithsonian*, September, p. 57.
13. Thomas Berry (1989) "Planetary Progress," *Earth Ethics*, Fall, pp. 6–8.
14. Ibid.
15. Charles Birch (1987) *In Church and Society: Report and Background Papers*. Meeting of the Working Group, Glion, Switzerland, September. Geneva: World Council of Churches, p. 75.
16. Jay McDaniel (1987) *In Church and Society: Report and Background Papers*. Meeting of the Working Group, Glion, Switzerland, September. Geneva: World Council of Churches, p. 130. See also Jay McDaniel (1990) *Earth, Sky, Gods and Mortals: Developing an Ecological Spirituality*. Mystic, CT: Twenty-third Publications.
17. James E. Royce (1961) *Man and His Nature*. New York: McGraw-Hill.
18. Ibid.
19. John MacMurray (1936) *Freedom in the Modern World*. London: Faber and Faber, p. 188.

20. John Heenan (1973) *God's Animals,* by Dom Ambrose Agius, O.S.B. London: The Catholic Study Circle for Animal Welfare.

21. Andrew Linzey (1986) "The Place of Animals in Creation: a Christian View," in T. Regan *Animal Sacrifices: Religious Perspectives on the Use in Animals in Science.* Philadelphia, PA: Temple University Press, pp. 115–48. See also Andrew Linzey (1987) *Christianity and the Rights of Animals.* New York: Crossroads.

22. Elizabeth Dodson Gray (1979) *Green Paradise Lost.* Wellesley, MA: Roundtable Press.

23. Ibid.

24. Bernard Rollin (1981) *Animal Rights and Human Morality.* New York: Prometheus.

25. B. F. Skinner (1983) *A Matter of Consequences.* New York: A. A. Knopf.

26. Ibid.

27. Ibid.

28. John Rodman (1974) "The Dolphin Papers," *The North American Review,* Spring, pp. 13–26.

29. Albert Schweitzer (1965) *The Teaching of Reverence for Life.* New York: Holt, Rinehart & Winston.

30. Vine Deloria (1975) *God is Red.* New York: Dell.

31. J. C. Niehardt (1972) *Black Elk Speaks.* New York: Simon & Schuster.

32. Loren Wilkinson, ed. (1980) *Earth Keeping: Christian Stewardship of Natural Resources.* New York: Eerdmans.

33. Ibid.

34. Ibid.

35. James Berry (1987) "The Significance of the NACCE," *The Eleventh Commandment Newsletter,* Spring, pp. 3–4.

36. *The Assisi Declarations* (1986) Geneva, Switzerland: World Wildlife Fund.

CHAPTER TEN / EDUCATIONAL AND DEVELOPMENTAL CONCERNS

1. Paul Shepherd (1978) *Thinking Animals.* New York: Viking.
2. Ibid.
3. Ibid.
4. Ibid.

5. For further discussion see Michael W. Fox (1997) *Troubled Harvest, Seeds of Hope*. Troutdale, OR: New Sage Press.

6. For details see Michael W. Fox (1992) *Superpigs and Wondercorn*. New York: Lyons and Burford.

7. Peter Kelly (1983) "Understanding Through Empathy," *Orion Nature Quarterly* 2:12–16.

8. Ibid.

9. Ibid.

10. Ibid.

11. Henry Salt (1892) *Animals' Rights, Considered in Relation to Social Progress*. Reprinted in 1980 by the Society for Animal Rights, Clarks Summit, Pennsylvania.

12. Alice Miller (1981) *Prisoners of Childhood*. New York: Basic Books.

13. Fox, *Troubled Harvest, Seeds of Hope*.

14. Martin Buber (1970) *I and Thou*. Tr. by Walter Kaufman. New York: Scribners.

15. Ibid.

16. Carol Gilligan (1983) *In a Different Voice*. Boston, MA: Harvard University Press.

17. Carlton Dallery (1978) in M. W. Fox and R. K. Morris, eds., *On the Fifth Day: Animal Rights and Humane Ethics*. Washington, DC: Acropolis Press, pp. 70–92.

18. George Orwell (1993) cited in David Ehrenfeld *Beginning Again: People and Nature in the New Millennium*. New York: Oxford University Press.

CHAPTER ELEVEN / "RAINBOW PEOPLE": RESTORING THE COVENANT

1. Michael W. Fox (1986) *Agricide: The Hidden Crisis That Affects Us All*. New York: Schocken Books. Second edition, 1995, Malabar, FL: Krieger.

2. Rudolph Bahro (1986) *Building the Green Movement*. Philadelphia, PA: New Society Publishers.

3. Thomas Berry and Brian Swimme (1994) *The Universe Story*. New York: Harper and Collins.

4. Michael W. Fox (1990) *Inhumane Society: The American Way of Exploiting Animals.* New York: St. Martin's Press.
5. Robert D. Kaplan (1994) "The Coming Anarchy," *This World.* March 13, pp. 6–10.
6. Ibid.
7. Michael W. Fox (1997) *Troubled Harvest, Seeds of Hope.* Troutdale, OR: New Sage Press, and R. Broad and J. Cavanaugh (1993) "Beyond the Myths of Rio: A New American Agenda for the Environment," *World Policy Journal.* Vol. X, pp. 65–72.
8. Paul E. Waggoner (1994) *How Much Land Can Ten Billion People Spare for Nature?* Ames, IA: Council for Agricultural Science and Technology Task Force Report No. 121.

CHAPTER TWELVE / REINCARNATION AND THE IMMORTALITY OF THE SPIRIT

1. Leo N. Tolstoi (1989) *My Religion.* London: Walter Scott.
2. Ian Stevenson (1966) *Twenty Cases Suggestive of Reincarnation.* Richmond, VA: William Byrd Press.
3. P. Teilhard de Chardin (1964) *The Future of Man.* New York: Harper and Row.
4. J. Mascaró, tr. (1962) *The Bhagavad Gita.* London: Penguin.
5. W. Y. Evans-Wentz, ed. (1957) *Tibetan Book of the Dead.* Oxford: Oxford University Press.
6. Mascaró, *The Bhagavad Gita.*
7. D. A. Dombrowski (1984) *The Philosophy of Vegetarianism.* Amherst: The University of Massachusetts Press.
8. Lao-Tzu, *Tao Te Ching.* Gia-Fu Feng and Jane English, tr. (1974) New York: Vintage Books.
9. A. Bailey (1962) *The Soul, The Quality of Life.* New York: Lucis Press.
10. Ovid (1955) *Metamorphoses.* Tr. by M. Innes. London: Penguin.
11. I. Shah (1970) *The Way of the Sufi.* New York: Dutton.
12. Walt Whitman (1959) *Complete Poetry and Prose.* New Haven: Yale University Press.
13. Bailey, *The Soul, The Quality of Life.*
14. Tolstoi, *My Religion.*

15. C. K. Chapple (1993) *Nonviolence to Animals, Earth and Self in Asian Traditions*. New York: State University of New York Press.
16. Michael Tobias (1991) *Life Force: The World of Jainism*. Fremont, CA: Asian Humanities Press.

Index

QUEST BOOKS
are published by
The Theosophical Society in America,
Wheaton, Illinois 60189-0270,
a branch of a world organization
dedicated to the promotion of the unity of
humanity and the encouragement of the study of
religion, philosophy, and science, to the end that
we may better understand ourselves and our place in
the universe. The Society stands for complete
freedom of individual search and belief.
For further information about its activities,
write or call 1-800-669-1571.

*The Theosophical Publishing House
is aided by the generous support of
THE KERN FOUNDATION,
a trust established by Herbert A. Kern
and dedicated to Theosophical education.*